OF JEAN WELZ

THE LOST ARCHITECTURE OF JEAN WELZ

Peter Wyeth

CONTENTS

The Lost Architecture of Jean Welz
By Peter Wyeth

Design: Jessica Fleischmann with Jenny Kim, Still Room
Typesetting: Carrie Paterson

ISBN: 978-1-9546000-0-3

Publisher's Cataloging-in-Publication Data
Names: Wyeth, Peter, author.
Title: The lost architecture of Jean Welz / by Peter Wyeth.
Description: Includes bibliographical references and index. | Los Angeles, CA: DoppelHouse Press, 2022.
Identifiers: LCCN: 2021952732 | ISBN: 978-1-954600-00-3 (paperback) | 978-1-954600-09-6 (ebook)
Subjects: LCSH Welz, Jean, 1900-1975. | Architecture--France. | Modern movement (Architecture) | Artists--South Africa--Biography. | BISAC BIOGRAPHY & AUTOBIOGRAPHY / Artists, Architects, Photographers | ARCHITECTURE / Criticism | HISTORY / Europe / Austria & Hungary | ARCHITECTURE / History / Modern (late 19th Century to 1945).
Classification: LCC NA680.W44 W94 2022 | DDC 724.6/092--dc23

DoppelHouse Press
Los Angeles
DoppelHouse.com

THE MYSTERY OF JEAN WELZ

IT IS PRACTICALLY UNHEARD OF these days to discover a genuinely unknown talent of the highest level in any art. With architecture, the objects loom so large and visible, so present in the world, that the idea of an unknown world-class architect is even less likely.

I came across the Maison Zilveli almost a decade ago. While it was a very unusual design, even among modern architecture, I was not sure what to make of it. Its parlous state, unmaintained and derelict, held up by a forest of sturdy but anachronistic wooden beams, with the street front leaning at a worrying angle, were all at the opposite extreme from the crisp lines of modernist architecture at its best.

However, it was sufficiently puzzling to encourage me to try to find out who built it. Over nine years have slipped by since then, a rare case that kept getting more interesting rather than the initial enthusiasm dimming, and finally I present here what I discovered about the architect, Jean Welz.

It turns out to be an extraordinary story. Welz was born in Salzburg, literally around the corner from Mozart's house. He began a course in architecture in Vienna under Josef Hoffmann, a month before the fall of the Austro-Hungarian Empire and the end of the thousand-year Habsburg regime. He went on to work for Hoffmann until he was sent to the *Art Deco* exhibition in Paris in the summer of 1925. His trip was for two months, but he decided to stay on, leaving behind a wife he had married on the rebound and a prestigious job, despite having neither work nor the ability to register as an architect in France.

At the exhibition, Welz not only sees the most avant-garde architecture but meets some of the key figures, including Robert Mallet-

Stevens and Pierre Jeanneret, the business partner and cousin of the single figure that hugely dominates modernism: Le Corbusier. Around the turn of the year, Welz is recommended to the leading Viennese modernist architect, Adolf Loos. He had heard much from his tutors about Loos, with whom they would have preferred to work, but contemporary architecture in Vienna was dominated by the extremely successful Hoffmann, whose practice was by far the main source of work for any modern-minded architect.

The younger generation, however, regarded Hoffmann as belonging to a past of artistic craftsmanship for the rich, whereas Adolf Loos was the man of the future. Welz leant towards the ideas of Loos, but Loos had little work to offer young architects. It was only in Paris that the young Viennese transplant finally met and worked with Loos, a most welcome piece of good fortune.

Loos also introduced him to a Parisian architect passionate about modernism and Loos's work, Raymond Fischer, who gave Welz the opportunity of which a young architect could only dream. Fischer had managed to obtain a commission for a modernist house, the last in a small but extremely distinguished row of three. The first, built in 1925–26, was by Mallet-Stevens; the second, the Maison Cook, built in 1926, was by Le Corbusier, and the house in which Corbusier set out his "Five Points of Modern Architecture" that would become the Commandments of young architects for generations to come. The third was to be Jean's first modern design.

Fischer also gave Welz the chance to concentrate all his energies solely on design. Fischer found the commissions, Welz focused on the architecture. The downsides were that he was neither paid a great deal, nor did the designs bear his name. Although that kept him in the shade, he was freed of the distractions involved in having your name over the door.

The exciting part of the story is what Jean Welz made of that opportunity. Put simply, from the first house, starting in late 1927, to his final one in Paris, the Maison Zilveli, built in 1933 (an independent commission), my belief is that Jean Welz set out, with a rigor unparalleled in modern architecture, to contradict Le Corbusier's Five Points with a Loosian philosophy, not just taking those ideas as inspiration, but developing them in his own highly distinctive way. Vienna at that time was arguably not the equal of Paris as an intellectual capital, but its superior.

Unlike Le Corbusier, who wrote more books than he built buildings, Welz's philosophy is really only to be seen in his designs.[1]

"Unique" and "unknown" are over-used words, but both, in my view, apply to Jean Welz, and in his case, unique in the best sense.

Welz was not one who wrote his ideas down but embodied them in the work. I see in his buildings a depth of ideas with which Vienna was able to prime him. Ideas alone are sterile, but in the case of Jean Welz they were — I argue — the seeds for a truly great imagination.

In 1936, Welz was forced by lack of work to leave his adopted country, able to afford only the cheapest passage to a new land. He had to leave his wife Inger and their son Jerry behind for a year until he could earn enough for them to join him. He carried with him his portfolio of drawings and photographs, and a slip of paper recommending him to the small group of modernist enthusiasts in South Africa, hand-written — by Le Corbusier.

This story is, in one sense, an account of why Jean Welz did not become famous. He did achieve fame as a leading painter in South Africa, but his life as an architect was a mere footnote. His painting was always a tortured struggle to achieve a poetic equivalent of his ideas, a battle that saw him destroy over half his work.

Architecture does not often afford the designer that choice and ironically, for an unknown, all his buildings in France survived. That could not be said for many famous architects, such is the rate of attrition, particularly of modern architecture.

His painting perhaps suffered from the conservatism he found in South Africa, whereas in avant-garde Paris, there were no such bounds. It was there that he was able to express the depth of his ideas, and where, in my view, they rose to the highest levels of creativity.

NOTES

1 Welz wrote but one article on architecture, ironically in praise of a Le Corbusier interior. See "Pour Vivre Heureux" (To Live Happily) in *La Libérté*, December 4, 1929.

INVISIBLE
PART I

Maison Zilveli street facade, 2013. Photo: Jean-Louis Avril.

1

JEAN WELZ DOES NOT EXIST

THE TALE BEGINS ON THE AFTERNOON of Christmas Day 2012, walking by an extraordinary avant-garde house abandoned on a Paris hillside. There was something about the occasion, perhaps Christmas cheer, that prompted me to try to find out who was behind the design. It was quite a casual commitment at the time, but would soon become anything but.

It is the dream of the curious to come upon an enigma that never runs out of steam. It rarely happens, more likely it never happens. But the most extraordinary fact about this case, by contrast, was that it never seemed exhausted, and it would renew itself just when I thought it might have finally died down. As I was finalizing the bibliography, almost two years after I felt I had finally finished this book, a key discovery came to light on the structure of Welz's Maison Zilveli, providing for the heart of the final chapter. Then just before publication, a shocking betrayal by the France he loved — the threat to raze that house by the new owner, claiming admiration only in order to destroy the last Welz masterpiece, and with full bureaucratic approval.

In the normal course of research, one would be poring over dozens of books, magazines, newspapers, photographs, biographies, letters — the usual panoply of source materials. In this case, a significant development in my investigation had been the discovery of a letter with the single handwritten word "Welz," not even by the man himself, but merely referring to him in a businesslike way. The idea of writing a full-length book on such a shadow seemed absurdly optimistic.

Welz was not just "unknown" as an architect but in effect, invisible. There was that single word, just the name, and there were a few other small clues, but that "existence," the handful of traces, were so scarce that he seemed hardly to exist, except in rare interstices of other lives.

The contrast with the ineluctable presence of buildings, houses, architecture with which he had been involved in one capacity or another, the undeniable material facts — not just a garden wall or lesser remains that could be a feast to an archaeologist, but whole houses, reinforced concrete and glass, walls and flat roofs, massive in a modest way — belied the paucity of his appearances in the historical record.

How could there be a list of buildings, that eventually numbered in the twenties, actual buildings, on the ground, before your eyes, not destroyed or erased, and hardly a word about the Welz that was involved? The massive facts versus the invisible trail was a quandary at the heart of the pursuit.

That very fact of architecture, the physical scale of a building, even of a single house, is such a large presence that it seems impossible that it can exist without a trail of papers, stories, photographs, that document who brought it into existence.

On the other hand, we are used to hearing of whole cities that have disappeared under shifting sands for millennia, so we should not be too surprised by, in this case, a ruined modernist house listed under the wrong architect.

That Christmas afternoon when I found the Maison Zilveli was, unbeknownst to me at the time, the start of what would turn out to be a very long haul.

It was a striking building but in a ruinous state, apparently on the edge of collapse. Pure lines do not age well when not looked after. Zilveli appeared to have had little attention since it was built, which I discovered was in 1933, and however daring its design had originally been, today it looked decidedly disreputable, a slum in an otherwise lovingly-maintained quarter.

The difference between 2013 and 1933 was, indeed, extraordinary. How wrong my first impression had been. It might have been a low-cost project, but it was daring and, in those pure lines, to my eyes, beautiful.[1] Even at this quick glance there was rather more to it than I had first thought. Little did I know the scale of just how much more.

The process of finding information about the house and the architect was challenging, but I soon realized that what had puzzled me initially about the design came from Vienna rather than Paris. It

Above: Maison Zilveli long facade, 2013. Photo: Jean-Louis Avril.

Below: Maison Zilveli, 1933. Women in the window not identified. The woman on the left could be Mrs. Elizabeth Kertész. The photographer is possibly André Kertész. Courtesy Welz family.

took me years to understand how that combination of influences had helped to produce Jean Welz's architecture. It was as complicated a matter as the two cities involved might suggest, but that in itself was far less interesting than eventually realizing that Welz had made a contribution of the highest quality to modern architecture, one that ought to have raised him from almost complete anonymity to an honored position. The reasons why he has remained unknown are not too mysterious but are a salutary reminder that greatness is not always, as we would like to think, bound to be discovered.

The scarcity of evidence made research a slow process, and the discovery of even a single word — or photograph — became an exciting event.

A tall figure in an innocuous winter coat, stands on a sundeck above a block of flats. It was the innocuousness that caught my eye. That man looks too tall. What is he doing there? The image is slightly surreal, the poor chap is cold when he should be hot.

There must be a purpose to the photo, perhaps at a distance they thought it would look better, more nautical with a tall chap. Perhaps he was deliberately chosen, cast almost, or maybe he just

Ginsberg & Lubetkin, 25 Ave de Versailles, Paris (1931). Courtesy RIBA Collections.

happened to be around — let's put him there, it will look better with a person in the picture, even if he is perhaps a bit too tall. Or maybe they thought tall was good, it would emphasize the heights they had carefully designed.

I was looking for material about someone Jean Welz worked with, another young architect at the time, Jean Ginsberg. There was even something odd about their names, something quite significant. The Jean part was very French, but the surnames were not. Welz sounds Germanic, while Ginsberg's father was Polish and his uncle was German. So both these architects had adopted France, as it were, with their first names. In fact, Ginsberg was born in France, but Welz was not. Even in cosmopolitan Paris it was often cultured Jews or arty foreigners who were the ones to commission modern architecture, rather than the French — who often preferred Louis XVI style to that modern stuff, called by some French architects "Boche-style." A Boche was a German, uncouth, a soldier, and any German was still not good a decade after the Great War.

The name change, in Welz's case, was symbolic of a commitment to his new home, and perhaps also a rejection of the militaristic aspect of the Austria he had left behind, another echo of the 1914–18 war. Welz changed his name to Jean shortly after he decided to stay in Paris in 1925, the year of the *Art Deco* exhibition where he was sent by his employer, the famous Austrian architect Josef Hoffmann. Hang on, you might be thinking. If this unknown chap worked for the famous Hoffmann and was sent by him to Paris, there is no way he was unknown. I did find a clue to Welz's time chez Hoffmann, I have to admit. In Vienna's Architekturzentrum archive there is a surprisingly slim record-book of the practice from 1920–1930, a workbook with every day recorded and who did what on that day, each one signed at the end of the line. Welz signed 191 times between July 1921 and June 1925 (I counted). Each task performed was hand-written, line by line. All in German, of course, and in the later days often illegible. In particular, Welz's signature at the end of each day's record was hardly recognizable. Of course, he wasn't Jean Welz then, but "Hans," so each signature had a rough approximation of "HW" in an increasingly casual scrawl. It was almost as though, by the summer of 1925, he had had enough and each mark was a record of his alienation.

In Paris, Welz discovered, as he put it, that he had a "French soul," and the name change was also partly a result of that, a vote for the freedom he declared that he had loved since he was a boy, which had been frustrated by his homeland.

The two Jeans — Welz and Ginsberg — had worked together, at one time or another, for a well-connected Parisian modern architect, Raymond Fischer, not himself a famous name, but someone who seemed to know everyone, and who mixed with the artists of Montmartre and was passionate about modernism. They were the backroom boys, the design office, and when Fischer had no work, they would go elsewhere, including to Ginsberg, who had started up on his own with the Russian emigre, Berthold Lubetkin — Lubetkin later became famous in England for his design of the penguin pool at the London zoo, with curved concrete ramps in mid-air for the penguins to carefully shuffle up and down.

Ginsberg and Lubetkin's first building together was this block of flats pictured at 25 Avenue de Versailles, commissioned by Ginsberg's father, a chemicals-industrialist. It was completed in 1931, which is when the photos were taken. After coming across this one during an internet search for Ginsberg, I immediately sent the photo five thousand miles away with the big question and barely moments later the answer came back, yes, it was the six-foot-five Jean; she — a daughter-in-law of Welz — was certain. The photo, meanwhile, had no mention of who was in the picture, what the building was, when or where, just the tall man in an overcoat who had caught my eye.

That moment was itself symbolic. There is no record of "Jean Welz" in the archives in Vienna or in Paris. It is too easy to claim the subject of a book is 'unknown'. It makes for good copy, recommends the book as some kind of detective story: but Welz *is* genuinely unknown, even to the most knowledgeable scholars and architects.

As mentioned, the biggest breakthrough on my quest was when a generous researcher sent a note saying she had come across a letter with what appeared to be the word "Welz" in it.[2] The letter was in German, in a sprawling hand that suggested it was written in a rush. It was found in an obscure part of the Sorbonne university library hidden behind the Pantheon, in a collection donated via the leading couturier of the 1920s, the very wealthy Paul Poiret. It was addressed to one of the founders of the Dada art movement, a relation of surrealism and similarly prompted by the madness of the Great War, Tristan Tzara, who, at the time, was having Adolf Loos build his house. Tzara had married well and was spending his wife's money on a striking, almost Romanesque, castle-like structure below Sacre Coeur on the hill of Montmartre.

The date was April 1926, and the content was banal, the writer apologizing that he wouldn't be able to find more builders until next week as he had only got the letter from "Welz" that night. That scrap connected Welz to the Tzara house, to Adolf Loos — note it was not to Loos that it was written, but the client, as Loos was perhaps too grand (or too absent) to deal with such matters.

The name of the author of the letter, Gabriel Guevrekian, came up again a couple of years later when I was leafing through the class records of Welz's Vienna university course. There was quite a group of famous names in his year, including the first Austrian woman architect, known for designing the "Frankfurt kitchen," Margaret Schütte-Lihotzky; Ernst Plischke; Josef Hoffmann's son, Wolfgang; and Welz's great rival on the course, Oswald Haerdtl, who shared a motorbike with Hoffmann junior. Gabriel Guevrekian, the connection from 1920 in Vienna to that one-word mention of Welz in 1926 in Paris, was among the final-year students — so it emerged how it was and in what context that he knew Jean Welz.

Back to Welz's friend, Jean Ginsberg, architect of the 25 Ave de Versailles flats in the photograph where Welz is pictured in the long coat, we find another connection. Ginsberg's father, the wealthy industrialist, had commissioned the block of flats from his son, a helpful way for a modern architect to get a start. Jean Ginsberg's uncle, whose name was Landau, was even bigger in the chemical industry, in Germany, and helped to found in Paris the international science congress center, the Maison de la Chimie.

As I ascertained from a portfolio of Welz's work, encountered later in South Africa, in the same year that 25 Ave de Versailles was finished and photographed, Welz got his first independent commission, a small house just outside Paris on a very modest budget, but with an interesting internal layout. The client's name was Landau; I know nothing about this Landau, whether it was the same man who was the client, or a son or daughter.

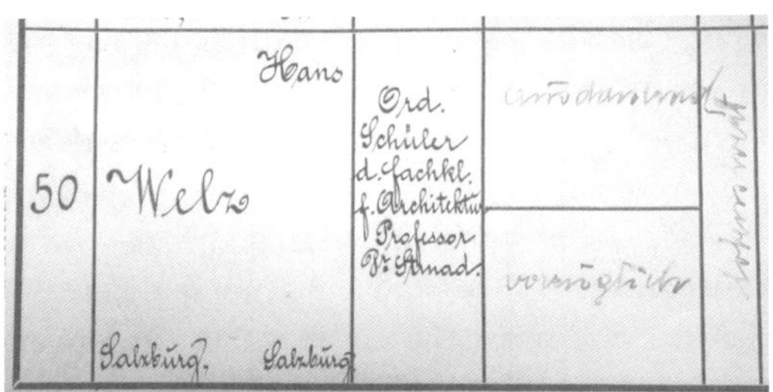
50 Hans Welz
Ord. Schüler d. Fachkl. f. Architektur Professor Dr. Strnad
Salzburg Salzburg

Course record from 1919 with Professor Strnad. Courtesy of the Technical University of Vienna.

My resulting inquiry into more of Welz's work was complicated by the absence of the usual corroborative evidence and meant that I was forced to really look at everything visual I could find of the designs, the buildings, the photographs. They were, after all, primary evidence, but often that gets lost in the words, the documentation, the letters, the articles and books, the memories of associates, which duty-bound are studied as scholarship. None of those were available in this case. The architecture is the real resource, and here, thankfully in some ways, there was little option but to investigate it as closely as possible. It sounds obvious but, like crowds at an exhibition, most people stand reading text on a wall rather than looking at the pictures. Pictures are both easier and more difficult to look at than buildings. How many people stand before a painting and feel they don't really know what they are looking for? With plans, photographs and drawings we don't even have a painting before our eyes, but only various ways of representing space.

Reading plans is difficult and mostly a bore. Translating plans into the reality of a building is a transformation most of us find hard if not impossible.

The fascination for me lay in the story behind the plans, one that only gradually emerged through forming some kind of understanding of Welz's ideas. I was forced, in a way, towards unearthing the conflicts between ideas, cultures, cities, and the famous architects who wielded their names in their various causes. The information opened up like secret messages for which I was only gradually able to work out the code, and in so doing offering up clues as to what Welz was for and what he was against. They were not just plans now, but vital arguments in graphic form that were the pen and ink battle-ground of twentieth-century architecture.

Among the obstacles to this challenging but exciting quest was the fact that most of the designs Welz worked on were credited to his boss, Raymond Fischer. That is not so unusual, the name over the door often takes the credit, but at a distance of ninety years, with all the principle players dead, it made poring over the evidence in order to work out who did what more complicated. Welz also worked "on the black" in Paris — not registered as an architect — which meant that even the abandoned Zilveli house that set me off was listed in the Town Hall as by his boss. There was nothing underhand in that, quite the opposite, in that his boss Fischer was probably kindly lending his name as a registered architect in order to get official building permission for the house, from which he did not profit, as it was an independent commission for Welz. However, as I found out that Welz had only two commissions actually in his own name, I had to question first: To what degree was Welz responsible for the designs he produced for Fischer?

Again, the absence of corroboration meant that I had to try to deduce from the sparse clues potentially available in plans and photographs, and a few words from interviews with Fischer, what was the truth. Much of the evidence was circumstantial and interpretation inevitably involved a degree of speculation. That sounds too risky, in terms of writing an architectural history, but as I learned more about Welz's background in Vienna and pieced together the elements of his time in Paris, the circumstantial became rather well-supported by context, and the process felt more like justifiable extrapolation than unfounded speculation.

It was only in the last stages of research that I finally saw a clear pattern emerge, although most of the elements of that pattern had been present from early on. Sometimes, one needs a step back to see what in retrospect should have been clear, and in this case I was allowed that permission by the very factor of time.

Upon first seeing the 1931 Maison Landau image, I had the sense that Welz had set himself against the dominant architect in Paris, Le Corbusier (see Chapter 17, "Maison Landau"); I speculated that he had done this through other architectural work and his unbuilt designs

Jean Welz, Maison Landau (1931). Courtesy Welz family.

(and not at all in words) — an absolutely unique effort which could only have come from a quite extraordinary determination and confidence. I began to see that Welz's designs were his personal response to Le Corbusier — a kind of silent dialogue that pitched a contrasting and conflicting set of ideas against a huge dominance, one that few, if any young architects would dare to stand against. And it seemed to me that Jean Welz had done so profoundly.

In the period Welz was active in Paris, there were loud voices raised against Le Corbusier, but mainly from the conservative Beaux Arts tradition. A famous debate in 1931 had ended in uproar, with hundreds of his opponents, who had not been able to get into the hall, shouting and demonstrating in the street outside. At the same time, there were arguably no effective critiques of Le Corbusier from any side — modern or traditional. His achievement was dazzling — he's still widely regarded as the greatest architect of the twentieth century — and although he was terribly depressed by those who sought to constantly tear him down, one may fairly say that intellectually and aesthetically he had no real challengers.

But I discovered that the *unknown* Jean Welz constituted that challenger, although invisible, confined to the backroom, and with many of his achievements quietly credited to his employer.

There were two elements to this opposition he mounted anonymously. The first was true to his background and training in Vienna, but seemed to me very likely indeed to have been considerably influenced and strengthened by his personal contact with perhaps the one figure who could provide the intellectual backing for an alternative and conflicting approach, namely Adolf Loos. Welz claimed a close friendship with Loos, an association that began early in 1926 and went on until at least September 1931. Loos, according to Jean, often stayed with the Welz family in their tiny basement flat when he visited Paris, after Loos had returned to live in Vienna in 1928.

From Welz's first major design, upon which he began work in December 1927, until his last built design in France, of 1933, I gradually developed the strong feeling that there was a consistent and highly sophisticated opposition to the ideas of Le Corbusier's manifesto, the Five Points of Modern Architecture. He effectively contradicted those five commandments in the way of building a modernist building; for example, retaining solid load-bearing walls instead of creating the "curtain" wall of the Corbusian manifesto. None of this was, as far as I know, written down anywhere by Welz, but his methods strongly reflected the deeper ideas of Adolf Loos and "Second Wave" Viennese Modernism. Loos had developed a philosophy that was arguably at least equal to that of the Parisian avant-garde, and in fact could be seen as more solidly founded. Loos's close circle included Wittgenstein, regarded as the greatest philosopher of the twentieth century; Schoenberg, of twelve-tone music fame; Oskar Kokoschka, painter and expressionist playwright; and writer Karl Kraus, the least known in the English-speaking world, but by some way the most famous in the Vienna of the time, which all together suggest Loos's intellectual standard and standing.

The second, and for this tale, more important element of what I will call Welz's critique, was that Welz showed himself, through the close visual examination of his designs which I was to eventually undertake, to be a particularly strong creative force in his own right. In other words, he was not only working with several sets of ideas, but bringing something personal to them that put him on a level approaching that of his strongest two examples or 'mentors', Le Corbusier and Adolf Loos, each recognized as the most important architect of the twentieth century within their own cultural spheres.

That a complete unknown should even be approaching their status would be a remarkable find, in fact, almost incredible. Be that as it may, I have come around to the view that with Welz's last two houses, of 1932 and 1933, he achieved two masterpieces — and of quite different character. While the latter house goes out, almost literally, on a limb that puts Welz arguably beyond the most avant-garde architects anywhere at the time, on the other hand I regard the former as perhaps his greatest design, and the best modern house that I know. In that house, Welz has gone past, as it were, both Le Corbusier and Loos, ironically by returning to an even bigger name in the history of architecture — Andrea Palladio. Le Corbusier told a foreign modernist that his houses of the 1920s were an attempt to recreate the "spirit" of Palladio, and Welz's take is both a contrast and a way forward for modern architecture when the heroic era of the 1920s had to some extent run out of steam. But it is much more than that, in being an exquisite design that both respects Palladio whilst transforming him for the modern age with a creative power and strong judgment.

Even that anecdote has a final kick in the tail, in that the foreign modernist talking to Le Corbusier about Palladio was a South African who later worked alongside Welz at the University of the Witwatersrand

(Wits), Rex Martienssen. In 1938, he was designing a modern house that, in a number of important particulars, bears a strong resemblance to Welz's 1933 masterpiece. Martienssen wrote an article on his sources for that house that numbered over two dozen pages, but without acknowledgment of his colleague Jean Welz. In more than one sense, and on more than one continent, the architecture of Jean Welz has (been) disappeared.

Soon after his move to South Africa, Jean Welz was forced to give up his profession, his passion, his life so far, due to tuberculosis, and was left with just his drawing skills and his intellect to eke out a living for his wife and children. Somehow he survived and prospered when the odds were on his death as the outcome. When he actually died, more than thirty years later, he had five boys and an outstanding reputation as a painter. But Jean Welz's achievement as an architect was no mere aside.

NOTES

1 "As attractive as a gorgon's head" is how many view modern architecture — Summerson's memorable phrase from *The Classical Language of Architecture*, London: Thames & Hudson, 1980, p. 10.

2 Cecile Poulot, researching Adolf Loos in Paris.

2

LE CHÂTEAU MOCHE — PARIS, CHRISTMAS DAY, 2012

I COULD HARDLY HAVE BEEN MORE WRONG — I like to think I have an eye for design, but my Christmas postprandial saw me walk past the sorely-declined modernist concoction with two reactions.

The first was the patronizing sense that whoever had designed this house was only semi-skilled. I thought the person to be untutored, a bit ham-fisted and clumsy. It could be a worthy attempt by an amateur fan of modernism that aped Le Corbusier but didn't quite get it. The windows on the street facade looked as though holes had been cut in the blank wall and crude metal frames inserted, without any practical concern for dispersing rainwater from above or providing a ledge below. Holes in the wall. Below, a squarish pillar was at angle and cracked, suggesting a serious lean to the side away from its neighbors.

The side elevation was even worse; the pillars showed rust marks from the reinforcement-bars which had suffered from water-penetration into the concrete, which in turn had expanded and burst the concrete, leading to the pillars failing. There were messy washes of faded paint all over the walls and most of all a stunning balcony was gone, leaving an incongruous hole in the wall ten meters in the air with what was left of the door poorly wedged into the opening.

That whole side was visible from the street, as it was next to a small community park that always seemed to be closed, accessible only to residents and tumbling down the hillside, with a few vines and distant views across Paris. The far end of the house hovered precariously over the steep hill, in mid-air, pointing in the same direction towards Sacre Coeur cathedral above Montmartre.

A long period of neglect was obvious, and the "temporary" inserted wooden framework under the raised floor made it look as though the whole thing would collapse, were it taken away.

It was a bit Miss Havisham, the wooden forest below the raised floor, the broken door in the aerial wall, the cracked window-glass and dirty curtains on the street front, the twisted metal window frames and the angled pillar. The Butte Bergeyre had only been opened for housing — the tape cut by Josephine Baker — in 1927. And the house must have been a low-cost commission.

To my eye it seemed to be an ugly building and in very poor condition, but it was also unusual, daring even, and if it was in danger of collapse, perhaps that again suggested an amateur architect who had aspired further than his skills would carry him.

In retrospect, one irony was that I first saw the blank street facade as elementary. I mistook something I later came to value at the top of the scale, for a mistake. The plainness was not an absence but a resolute presence. It was no mistake. It was the opposite of a mistake. It is has been said that the top of the scale in art is when anything extraneous has been removed, leaving only the pure essence. The unnecessary, the superfluous has been eliminated. But don't let that point go too easily. It is extremely hard work to achieve. It requires a recognition that something is not required and can be dispensed with. Not only will that not make it weaker, but it will make it stronger. Colin Chapman, the racing car-designer's chief principle, was "adding lightness." At one hundred and twenty miles per hour, Stirling Moss lost a wheel off one of Chapman's cars as a result, and so did not entirely trust Chapman's credo. Welz added air underneath the Maison Zilveli and eighty years on, the house had dropped by sixty-five centimeters. Add to that the fact that clean modernist lines lose a lot when they are no longer sharp or straight.

My initial reservations about the design — the shocking plainness of the street facade and the apparent clumsiness of the raised floor — were both failures on my part. On the other hand, I think it might have been the combination of daring and decay that attracted me. I definitely wanted to know more about the daring, and wondered about the decay. If the architect was well-known surely the house would have been better maintained. If he was not well-known, then who was he, and where had he found the daring to design what I would come to regard as such an extraordinary house?

The elderly neighbor opposite, who leaned out of her window and nodded towards the house, contemptuously dubbed it "Le Château" and declared it *moche* (ugly). She may have lived there long enough to see it go from bad to worse, but she may also have disliked it at its best. After all, the surrounding houses were mainly in smart red brick and even back in 1933, Le Château Moche must have stood out,[1] but more than that, it was perhaps also intentionally something of a slap in the face for its more conventional neighbors.

What sent me off on this long and winding crusade was something to do with the optimism of that plain facade. The nerve to put holes in the wall for windows without the slightest ornament. I didn't realize at the time that behind this gesture was an immensely sophisticated cultural context, far from Paris, namely Vienna, and in particular the ideas of Adolf Loos — the banishing of ornament. Yet in the Maison Zilveli, Jean Welz had been more radical, in virtually every direction, than his mentor and friend. This 'aerial' house was more than adventurous, more than avant-garde; it was an extraordinary conception.

NOTES

1 Henriette Zilveli, originally from Normandy, was the client for the house. Her husband, Athanase, born in Turkey of Greek origin and educated in Zurich, was a chemical engineer and accountant who worked in the 1930s on color film for Kodak, bought the land and had the house built for his wife as a birthday present. He gave chess and piano lessons and was friends with an eminent Greek sculptor who designed a massive, fitted dining table for the house. This information comes from Laurence Nguyen (née Zilveli), granddaughter, who lived in the house.

3

THE TRADOUW PASS — 1940

A MAN OF SIX-FOOT-FIVE LIES PROSTRATE, coughing his lungs out. He languishes in an isolated rustic house on a mountain pass accessible only by rough vertiginous tracks, two hundred and fifty kilometers from Cape Town, South Africa. The plain whitewashed cottage is dominated on all sides by lowering mountain peaks, often cut off from view by heavy mist that descends within a matter of seconds. The feeling is one of desolate foreboding, entirely cut off from civilization. That was my own feeling, when I visited, very kindly taken there by Jean's eldest son, Jerry, who had lived in the remote cottage himself as a small boy.

Flashback to a few weeks before this scene from the sickbed: just outside Johannesburg, a large black American sedan bounces to a halt on its soft suspension, creating a dust cloud as it slowly makes its way down the earth track to a small cottage. Out steps a smartly suited businessman and knocks at the door. Somehow, he has heard of the plight of the tall man who lives there, and has come with a proposition. He has built a house for a woman, not his wife, in a spot that might suit Mr. Welz, his wife, their toddler and ten-year-old, first-born son. The businessman's wife discovered his project, which as a result has had to be redirected. The gentleman, a sharp fellow but not without redeeming features, proposes the Welzs move in as caretakers for a small monthly wage, and perhaps, as they are foreign, and in his mind this is what foreigners do, set up a teahouse to supplement their income. The air is healthy, the house is new if simple, and the wage is just about survivable.

Lying on that bed in the Tradouw Pass, it is the second time

Above: Jean Welz, Tradouw Pass pastel, 1940. Courtesy Welz family.

Below: The Welz cottage at the Tradouw Pass. Photos courtesy of the author.

Jean Welz, apartment conversion in Paris off Avenue Foch for a businessman, perhaps Harry Oppenheimer, from the extremely wealthy family, owners of De Beers diamonds, circa 1930s. (See note 2, opposite page.) Notice the yacht picture in the upper photo. Courtesy Welz family.

tuberculosis has struck the tall man down in the two years since he arrived at Cape Town. The first was bad enough, but this recurrence is both life-threatening and has effectively finished off his erstwhile career. His doctors told his wife that this time he has to give up architecture. In 1940, there was no known cure for tuberculosis, and his only hope was clean mountain air.

However, for some, this move to the mountains is a cause for suspicion. It is 1940, and there are murmurs asking why this Austrian has taken up residence in a remote spot — what is he up to? Two men arrive from Cape Town to investigate, and the threat of internment as an enemy alien adds to the small family's woes.

Few brave the rough road through the mountains, but those that do are either adventurers or the wealthy in expensive motorcars, some of whom are attracted by the cut-out metal sign of a teapot Jean has painted and hung outside the cottage. One day Jerry, the boy of ten, sees a big Packard draw up with steam hissing from its radiator. Out of it steps a distinguished man, used to giving orders, and asks the young lad to fill up the steaming radiator with cold water. Jerry, a practical boy, obliges and watches as his father comes out of the house to greet the visitor. He is surprised to see the men walk up to each other and shake hands with enthusiasm. Jean later told Jerry that the wealthy traveler had known him in Paris in the 1930s, where he had converted two adjoining flats into one apartment for him on the Avenue Foch, and his name was Oppenheimer.[1]

That era feels like the distant past for Jean. Now forty, he has no money, no income, a wife, a two-year-old and Jerry, and at best a fifty-fifty chance of surviving tuberculosis. In a remote part of a country, where he arrived understanding neither English nor Afrikaans, the future looks as bleak as the mountains looming over the lone cottage. "My husband seems to care so little whether we live or die, but being an artist, and not in good health, I think one must forgive him."[2]

NOTES

1 This story came from Jerry Welz, the small boy at the time, but is otherwise unconfirmed.

2 Inger Welz correspondence, September 24, 1941.

VIENNA

PART II

4

FINIS AUSTRIAE — VIENNA, OCTOBER 1918

JOHANN FRIEDRICH WELZ ARRIVES IN VIENNA to begin his architecture course on October 1, 1918. "Hans," as he is known, is eighteen and enrolls at the School of Arts and Crafts.[1]

He could not have arrived in the capital at a more momentous time. It is the most extraordinary moment in the history of Vienna for virtually a millennium. In a few weeks, the Great War will finally grind to a halt with Austria badly defeated. The Habsburg monarchy, with its near thousand-year history, will fall, never to return, and with it the Austro-Hungarian Empire. A Republic will be declared and the brief flowering of Red Vienna begin. Austria is reduced from a Great Power to a rump of seven million people, a quarter of whom live in the capital.

The preceding generations of a desperately-maintained surface stability have masked the long decline that came to a head with the humiliating defeat to Prussia in 1866. The Habsburgs had, for centuries, regarded their mission as uniting the German speaking peoples, but the rise of Prussia destroyed that raison d'être, and left them in a perilous state, which the creation of the Austro-Hungarian Empire in 1867 did little to ameliorate. In fact, it was the increasing tensions among the many nationalities within the Empire that led to the Great War, via the assassination of Crown Prince Franz Ferdinand, whose unfortunate wife, it seems, was related to the Welzs.[2] Ironically, Ferdinand was the best friend Serbia had among the elite, yet was killed by a Serbian anarchist. He was also said to be by far the most intelligent of the Habsburgs, who seem to have made a pretty poor show on that score. It was said of the Emperor, Franz Joseph, on the throne since 1848, "Never before in the history of the world had such a nonentity stamped his mark on everything."[3]

Welz's course began on schedule, but even on something as distant from the great upheaval as marking-sheets, I noticed that the ubiquitous "K&K" (King and Kaiser/Emperor) heading had been crossed out as the Empire fell.

Hans comes to Vienna from Salzburg, then a sleepy provincial city right on the Western border of Austria with Germany. It would be 1920 before the Salzburg Festival was founded, which becomes a big boost for the City, but its musical past has long been intimately tied to Mozart, born in a house around the corner from where Hans himself was born. Like all his family, he is very keen on music, he and his siblings had to sing when visiting family and friends, and he seriously considered a career as an opera singer before deciding upon architecture. He plays the violin and the guitar but is also talented in drawing and painting — witnessed by an "architectural" drawing at the age of twelve (see following page), and a portrait of a boy painted when he was eighteen — perhaps before leaving Salzburg for Vienna.[4]

Hans was born March 4, 1900, one of five children, three girls and a younger brother, Friedrich, who dramatically appears later in this story. He was much closer to his neurotic, sensitive Czech mother than to his conservative father, also named Friedrich, who had set up a picture-framing and guilding business, the third generation in the metier. His mother was very proud of Hans, who achieved brilliant results at the Realschule in Salzburg, and was helpful and affectionate to her, a pleasant personality at home. The emphasis of family life was on art, music and the discussion of contemporary aesthetic arguments.[5] That last might sound strange, but it was both a typical and highly significant combination in the Austria of that time, representing the common turning away from politics and instead investing great energy in artistic issues — from living in a rigid, hierarchical and conservative society.[6] His father had in fact been exiled to Salzburg from the family home in Vienna, regarded in Austria as the equivalent of the English being "sent to Coventry." He was not by inclination a businessman, and lived a Belle Epoque life, sitting at the same table every day at the Tomaselli coffee-house, reading his paper.

On the other hand, his father's brother, Max (b.1876), was energetically entrepreneurial and had turned their father's picture-framing shop in Vienna, which he took over at age nineteen when their father died, into an important manufacturing enterprise, making it his concern to become friends with the leading-lights in the Vienna

MAX WELZ

„Grand Prix“
auf den Weltausstellungen:
Paris 1925 · Barcelona 1929
Brüssel 1935 · Paris 1937
Brüssel 1958, Goldmedaille

Fabrik für Rahmen, Leisten, Karniesen, Möbel und Innenausstattung
→ Wien VII. Schottenfeldgasse 45, Telephon 93 37 23, 44 16 80
Filiale: Wien V. Reinprechtsdorfer Straße 17, Tel. 43 52 698

Top two: Max Welz company advertisement, 1913, and business card with address.
Center row: Max Welz picture frame designs from the late 1920s.
Below: Jean Welz mirror frame for Max Welz's company.

Photos: Patrick Kovacs, Vienna.

Werkstätte, particularly the architect Josef Hoffmann. Max made frames for the Werkstätte artists, and had some of them design for him, including Hoffmann, for whom he later also made furniture after the Werkstätte closed down.[7]

It was Max, trained by a sculptor and a gilder, who early on had spotted Hans's creative gifts and intelligence, and influenced him to study architecture under Hoffmann, perhaps actively paving the way, as the architecture course Hans started at the Applied Arts university was headed by Hoffmann.

Uncle Max seems to have been fond of Hans, and introduced him to Viennese artistic circles as well as taking him to museums, galleries and concerts, encouraging him to investigate progressive ideas and contemporary trends in the arts at the Academy for Applied Arts where he studied, plus introducing him to friends of his who owned Impressionist paintings. Max also had Hans design picture-frames for the business, from the time he was a student in Vienna, and introduced him to his Werkstätte clients.

Jean's eldest son, Jerry,[8] told me a nice tale of Hans attending a black-tie event in Vienna, invited by Max, when Stefan Zweig, author of *Letter from an Unknown Woman*, turned up in lederhosen and a feathered-hat, a decided faux pas against the formal manners of Vienna. Jerry and his wife Cora had extremely kindly taken me on a tour of his childhood locations from the early years of Jean being in South Africa when I visited in July 2014. We had stopped for a couple of days at a hot spring, Warumwatersberg, and it was the last morning

Hans Welz, age twelve, pen and ink on paper. Courtesy Welz family.

when Jerry had told me everything he could remember about those days long-ago, more than seventy years earlier.

As we three had breakfast together, he noticed I had a book by Zweig, the sad memoir he had written just before the suicide pact with his wife, in exile in Brazil. It was just that chance that sparked Jerry's memory of the tale.[9]

All along a journey such as this, in this case both literal and metaphorical, how many chances escape you, for one reason or another? Do the gods arrange matters so pearls drop on your head at appropriate intervals, or do you miss nine-hundred-ninety-nine out of every thousand, because that is just the way it is? It's a constant anxiety, if you allow it to be so. I felt on balance the gods had worked pretty hard on my behalf, and at some point you have to stop worrying.

NOTES

1 Welz's university records show that until he started that course he had been at school in Salzburg. Although surrounded by momentous events from the first day of his course, it would appear that he was neither involved in the Great War, nor affected by it and "never spoke of WW1" — note by Elza Miles in her book on Jean Welz the painter, *The World of Jean Welz* (Fernwood Press, Vlaeberg, South Africa, for the Rembrandt Van Rijn Art Foundation, Stellenbosch, South Africa, 1997).

2 A grandmother was the illegitimate daughter of a Countess, from an eminent family with a famous baroque palace that still carries their name in Vienna. She was first-cousin to the Countess Sophie Chotek, killed by the first bullet from Gavrilo Principe, the anarchist whose second bullet killed Franz Ferdinand at Sarajevo, precipitating the declaration of war in August 1914.

3 Frank Field, *Kraus's Vienna*, 1976, p. 98.

4 Miles, *The World of Jean Welz.*

5 From family records consulted by Jalka, daughter of Jean's sister Erna. Details emailed to me April 2017.

6 See *The Austrian Mind*, William M. Johnston, UCLA Press, 1972.

7 The Welz family's artisanal skills can be traced back to at least the 1700s, as celebrated clock-makers in Swabia, their clocks highly-prized by collectors. The master-clockmaker Johann Welz, from Bruggen in the Allgäu, died in St. Pölten in 1797. His works are in the Viennese Clock Museum and still in the office of the mayor of St. Pölten. This information was kindly researched by the late Dr. Peter Prokop.

8 Jerome Welz (1930–2017), an inventive engineer, was something of a Huckleberry Finn character as a boy and kept a baboon he named Rachel in his bedroom.

9 Many years after the Zweig event, when Max Welz had emigrated to the United States with his American-Jewish wife, he thoughtfully sent his evening suit and patent-leather dancing shoes to Jean, aware that money was still tight for his talented nephew. This story comes from Jalka, daughter of Jean's sister Erna, in conversation, Vienna, February 8, 2017.

5

JOSEF HOFFMANN AND THE FIRST WAVE

AMONG HANS WELZ'S CHOICE OF OPTIONS in his first year, was art-education for children, taught by a renowned educationalist Franz Cižek.[1] In fact, he had no interest in being an art teacher, but he signed up for the course because in it there was a beautiful Italian fashion student, Carmela Prati, with whom he had fallen in love.

Hans was described by his tutor Oskar Strnad, an important architect who plays a part in the later story, as "Very talented at drawing, very punctilious, very able at structure, very serious and knowledgeable, with very good taste."[2] His family heard that he was one of the top two students on the course, with Oswald Haerdtl, who he saw as a much more competitive type and who also vied for Carmela's affections.[3] Hans was, by his own account, not much concerned with academic marks, and gained a reputation as a bohemian, playing the guitar and wearing a denim suit, which was made for him by Carmela. To his family, he was a student who loved philosophy, literature and hiking (but was strongly against alcohol and smoking).

While Haerdtl's academic ambition propelled him to graduate top of the class, Hans came second. Both were given jobs by Hoffmann. In 1922, Haerdtl was at the art school as teaching assistant in the master class of Josef Hoffmann. Haerdtl and Welz did not get on, it would appear. Hans's view was that Haerdtl was better at sucking-up to Hoffmann than as an architect,[4] and may have been jealous of Hans's relationship with Carmela.

Haerdtl went on to a successful career in Austria, becoming Hoffmann's assistant by 1928, and with a section in the Austrian architects' archive dedicated to him. A book on his work was issued by his old university in 1957, and another more comprehensive one published in 1990 in Salzburg.[5]

Unsurprisingly, perhaps, Welz is not mentioned.

Starting in 1903, Josef Hoffmann (1870–1956) had taken the Professorship of the course Hans was to attend, bringing Hoffmann considerable influence in the critical debate about architecture. He was one of the most renowned architects of his day, designer of the luxurious Palais Stoclet in Brussels (1905–11), a founder of the Vienna Secession in 1897 and co-founder of the Vienna Werkstätte in 1903, which was dedicated to raising standards in the arts and crafts, and inspired by, among others, William Morris and Charles Rennie Mackintosh. Hoffmann held a position of great power in Vienna, and when Welz met him, he was considered *the* modern architect, the leading figure in the first wave of modern architecture. To some extent, Hoffmann took up where the older Otto Wagner had left off as father of a modern approach that emphasized a stripped-back design with the emphasis on the function of the building — best represented by his Post Office building of 1904–1906.

Wagner died in the April of 1918, only a few months before the Austria he knew disappeared.

However, in one way Hoffmann could also be seen as representing the past. He saw the architect as an artist whose task was to infuse every aspect of a building, from the doorhandles to the exterior, with his signature. His aim was to stamp his artistic personality on everything, to create a total artwork in the tradition of composer Richard Wagner's Gesamtkunstwerk.

This Romantic conception of the artist had its roots deep in the nineteenth century, but in the twentieth century it came increasingly under challenge from new realities and a belated recognition of some old ones — namely that there had been an Industrial Revolution that had largely swept the artisan away for everyday objects that were designed and then produced in factories in their thousands and even millions. For some, these objects were anonymous and the result of alienating the creative process from the producing process — the opposite of their view of a healthy approach to making things.

For an artist like Josef Hoffmann, highly skilled at drawing and painting, designing furniture and glass as well as houses and exhibition halls, it was predictably how he saw the creative process.

When the Emperor decided on a limited modernization of Vienna, in the 1880s, he had the remains of the city walls demolished and allowed the Ringstrasse to be built — with grand mansions and public

Above: Otto Wagner, Vienna Post Office (1904–1906). Source: arth.upenn.edu/spr01/282/w3c3i29.htm. Photographer unknown.

Center: Josef Hoffmann, Palais Stoclet, Brussels (1905–11). Source: Woka.com/en/lexicon/palais-stoclet.html. Photographer unknown.

Below, left: Gottlieb Th. Kempf-Hartenkampf, Portrait of Otto Wagner, 1896. © 2022 Artists Rights Society (ARS), New York / Bildrecht, Vienna. Photo: Wien Museum. Below, right: Josef Hoffmann, 1902. Public domain. Photographer unknown.

KUNSTGEWERBE-SCHULE

DES · ÖSTERREICHISCHEN · MUSEUMS · FÜR · KUNST · UND · INDUSTRIE

WIEN · I · STUBENRING · NR · 3

SCHULJAHR · 1920 – 1921		ORD · SCH · – ~~HOSP · SCH~~
ICH · HEISSE MIT · MEINEM	Hans VORNAMEN	Welz FAMILIENNAMEN
MEINE · GEBURTSDATEN SIND	TAG 4. MONAT März	JAHR 1900
	ORT Salzburg	LAND Salzburg
ICH · BIN · ZUSTÄNDIG	NACH "	IN "
MEINE · VOLKSZUGEHÖRIGKEIT · IST	[illegible]	MEINE · RELIGION · IST [illegible]
ALS · LEBENSBERUF · STREBE · ICH · AN	Architekt	
MEINE · VORBILDUNG · VOR EINTRITT · IN · DIE · KUNSTGEWERBESCHULE · IST	Realschule (Matura)	
MEINE · PRAXIS · VOR EINTRITT · IST	—	
DAS · DATUM · MEINES · EINTRITTES · IST	TAG 1. MONAT Oktober	JAHR 1918.
ICH · HABE · BISHER · AN · DER · KUNSTGEWERBESCHULE · FOLGENDE · ABTEILUNGEN · BESUCHT	ALLGEMEINE ABTEILUNG · VON 1918 BIS 1919	~~ORD · SCH~~ HOSP · SCH
	FACHKLASSE DES PROF. Strnad · VON 1919 BIS 1920	ORD · SCH ~~HOSP · SCH~~
ICH · BEZOG · IM · LETZTEN SCHULJAHR · AN · DER KUNSTGEWERBESCHULE NEBENSTEHEND · VERZEICHNETES · STIPENDIUM	NAME · DES · STIPENDIUMS [illegible]	
	ICH · BEZOG · ES · SEIT Oktober 1919	
	IM · JÄHRLICHEN BETRAGE · VON 000 KRONEN — HELLER	
MEIN · JETZIGES · MILITÄRVERHÄLTNIS · IST	—	EINTRETENDE VERÄNDERUNGEN WERDE ICH · SOFORT · IN DER · DIREKTIONSKANZLEI MELDEN
MEINE · ADRESSE IN · WIEN · IST	VII [illegible] 5	
NAME · UND · STAND · MEINES · VATERS · ~~VORMUNDES~~ IST	Friedrich Welz [illegible]	
DESSEN · ADRESSE · IST	Salzburg [illegible] 6	
WIEN · AM	29. September 1920	

ORNAMENT		STILGESCHICHTE		ANATOMIE		BAUKONSTRUKTION	/	KERAMIK	
SCHRIFT		CHEMIE		KUNSTGESCHICHTE	/	LICHT · UND FARBENLEHRE		CHEMIE · DER KERAMIK	
TECHNISCHES ZEICHNEN 1		TECHNISCHES ZEICHNEN 2		TECHNISCHES ZEICHNEN 3		GESCHÄFTSAUFSÄTZE · RECHNEN U · BUCHFÜHRUNG		METALLPLASTIK	
DEUTSCH 1		DEUTSCH 2		DEUTSCH 3				EMAILARBEIT	
LITURGIK		BÜRGERKUNDE		ABENDAKT				TEXTILARBEIT	

VISUM · DER DIREKTION Roller — UNTERSCHRIFT · DES ABTEILUNGSLEITERS Strnad

LEHRGEGENSTÄNDE

DIE · DER · SCHÜLER · AUSSER · DEN · HAUPTFÄCHERN · ZU · BESUCHEN VERPFLICHTET · WAR

GEGENSTAND	VERWENDUNG	FORTGANG	UNTERSCHRIFT
AUFSATZLEHRE · RECHNEN · UND · BUCHFÜHRUNG	ausdauernd	vorzüglich	Merth m. p.
BÜRGERKUNDE	befriedigend	lobenswert	Dr. Friedrich m. p.
PROJEKTIONSLEHRE · SCHATTENLEHRE · UND · PERSPEKTIVE	befriedigend	lobenswert	[illegible] Roller m. p.
SCHRIFT, HERALDIK	ausdauernd	lobenswert	Larisch m. p.
ORNAMENTALE · FORMENLEHRE	ausdauernd	befriedigend	Cizek m. p.
STILGESCHICHTE	ausdauernd	vorzüglich	Kenner m. p.
GEWERBLICHE · CHEMIE	ausdauernd	lobenswert	Dr. Schloh m. p.
~~KULTUR- UND~~ KUNSTGESCHICHTE	ausdauernd	vorzüglich	Dr. [illegible] m. p.
ANATOMISCHES · ZEICHNEN · U · MODELLIEREN	—	—	—
ALLGEMEINES · AKTZEICHNEN	—	—	—
Kunstgewerbl. Liturgik	ausdauernd	vorzüglich	Dr. Cauker m. p.
Deutsch I	nach Enthebungsprüfung befreit		für Prof. Dr. Alfred Roller m. p. [illegible]
Deutsch II	nach Enthebungsprüfung befreit		für Prof. Dr. Alfred Roller m. p. [illegible]
Technisches Zeichnen I	ausdauernd	vorzüglich	Dr. Strnad m. p.
Technisches Zeichnen II	ausdauernd	vorzüglich	Dr. Strnad m. p.
Baukonstruktionslehre	ausdauernd	vorzüglich	Dr. Frank m. p.

DAS · VERHALTEN · DES · SCHÜLERS · WAR lobenswert.

Hans Welz, 1918–21 course record. Welz's professors, including Oskar Strnad and Josef Frank, named in the last column. Courtesy Vienna Technical University.

buildings that aped aristocratic values, in taking their style from the Baroque or Neo-Classical, adorned with elaborate ornamentation. This concession to the rich bourgeoisie permitted modest change in order, as it were, that everything would otherwise remain the same.

To Hoffmann this was anathema — he wanted modern Vienna to develop its own aesthetic, to encourage its own artists and artisans of the day to create a modern style that was distinctively Austrian. In that sense, Hoffmann was a modernizer, and the establishment of the Werkstätte, with its own highly stylized building, marked the push for modernism. But however beautiful the objects the Werkstätte produced, they were expensive, individual and handmade.

This kind of modernism essentially looked back, like William Morris, to a fabled past in which artists and artisans worked together in harmony to create beautiful houses filled with beautiful objects. Hoffmann's modernism reacted against the excessive Viennese liking for ornamentation, favoring simpler, more abstract decoration, whether on buildings or objects. But his approach was more an updating than a revolution, a reflection of a modern age but in a gilded mirror.

The Palais Stoclet, his most famous building, "bore a formal and remarkable resemblance"[6] to Charles Rennie Mackintosh's "House for an Art Lover," designed in 1901 for a competition (on which Hoffmann was one of the judges).[7] Mackintosh was in some ways the most advanced architect of his time, and feted by Hoffmann and the Vienna Secession, but Hoffmann's borrowing of Mackintosh elements was only partial, suggesting he had not quite comprehended the more radical aspect of Mackintosh, "omitting Scottish austerity in favor of Viennese glitz... the very antithesis of the simplicity inherent in the Mackintosh original."[8]

On the other hand, Hoffmann had a large practice with many wealthy clients and the Professorship, and when Hans Welz started his course he was undoubtedly the force to be reckoned with — the preeminent Viennese architect.

Even though Hoffmann was head of the course, it seems likely that Hans had little contact with him. Another student, an American interior-designer of Austrian extraction[9] who had fallen in love with Hoffmann's decorative work and enrolled in his school in 1922, aged only fourteen, found Hoffmann a remote presence, and the nearest he got to teaching was wordlessly to turn a drawing face down if it didn't show sufficient promise. His instructions were passed down through his assistant (Hans's classmate and competitor Oswald Haerdtl, who became an assistant to Hoffmann in 1922).[10]

Remote he might have been to students, but Hoffmann did represent the first wave of Viennese modernism. In contrast, from the second year of the course, Hans was much more closely in contact with the "second wave," a modernism that opposed much of what Hoffmann stood for, and this through his own personal tutors, who happened to be prominent proponents of the next generation.

NOTES

1 Jean Welz admired him and still followed his methods in South Africa in the 1950s.

2 Quoted from the Kunstgewerbe school course records, inspected February 2017.

3 Elza Miles, *The World of Jean Welz*, p. 15.

4 As told by Jean to his son Martin.

5 See Chapter 19, "Oswald Haerdtl — 1932" for more on him.

6 In Andrew MacMillan, "Houses for Art Lovers and the Modern Movement," in *House for an Art Lover* 2nd Edition, Glasgow, 2004, p. 37.

7 The Mackintosh house was finally built nearly eighty years after his death, near Glasgow, between 1989 and 1996.

8 MacMillan, p. 37.

9 Also a friend and admirer of Carmela Prati/Haerdtl.

10 Lillian Langseth-Christensen, *A Design for Living*, New York: Viking, 1987, p. 98. (Dedicated to Carmela Prati-Haerdtl).

6

ADOLF LOOS AND THE SECOND WAVE

I KNEW FROM HIS FAMILY that Welz had retained a strong affection for one of his Professors, Oskar Strnad (1879–1935),[1] who had taught him about the genius of Roman lettering; that the Romans understood exactly how to create weight and power by the way in which they carved letters into stone. I learned this from his eldest son Jerry, who realized that his father had remembered that lesson as late as the 1960s, when he was commissioned to design a monument in South Africa, which Jerry took me to see.

It also showed in one of his simplest and most beautiful designs, a headstone in the Père Lachaise cemetery for Marx's daughter,[2] an important if small element in Welz's career, to which we will return.

As I was getting towards the end of the long period of research, a sudden and unexpected light flared in the dark. An important new book by Christopher Long[3] not only mentioned Strnad, otherwise little-known, but put him right at the center of a revolution in Viennese architecture.

Strnad, along with Josef Frank (1885–1967), were the key allies of that major figure for Welz, Adolf Loos (1870–1933), and the three of them were the dominant figures in the Second Wave of Viennese modernism.[4] They developed what Long has termed The New Space, representing a quite different (Austrian) strand from the dominance of Le Corbusier's brand of modernism, or from the Bauhaus and "International Style."

The matter of their break from the first generation of Viennese modernists was more complicated than simple adherence to new principles, as both were also professional associates of Hoffmann;

Strnad worked with him from time to time, and Frank was considered a protege of Hoffmann's, while the two younger men also had a joint practice from 1913. Strnad created an interior feature for the *Art Deco* exhibition in Paris in 1925, where Hoffmann was commissioned to design the Austrian Pavilion. Frank designed a "Café Viennois" at the *Art Deco* exhibition site, and was later also the only Austrian to attend the famous first international meeting of modernist architects at La Sarraz in Switzerland in 1928, along with Corbusier and Rietveld, and lesser-known names like Guevrekian.

Although Hoffmann and Loos were the same age, they represented different generations of modern architecture. Hoffmann finally completed the Palais Stoclet in 1910, and the same year Adolf Loos built the Steiner Villa in Vienna. As MacMillan put it, "The Steiner Villa took up the baton for progress while the Palais Stoclet was the dying flourish of Art Nouveau: the last of the artistic houses, the end of the era of the 'handmade, unrepeatable object.'"[5]

Loos had long been a critic of Hoffmann, going back as far as 1898, which coincided with Hoffmann rejecting Loos as a participant in the decor of the Secession building of 1897. But while Loos tended to keep his distance from other Viennese architects, he was on good terms with Strnad, and Frank often attended Loos's discussions in the Café Museum, Loos's first substantial design, of 1899. Those discussions were part of Loos's informal Bauschule ('Building school') from 1915–23.[6] The two younger Professors were quite a bit closer in their ideas to Loos than to Hoffmann.

Loos's architectural philosophy could be said to have three major strands — his ideas on external ornament, how internal space can be organized, and the question of what constitutes 'good building' as opposed to the false worship of novelty.

Loos was notorious for his rejection of external ornamentation, expounded upon in various lectures and in his controversial essay "Ornament and Crime." His first large commission, 1909–10, was the gentleman's outfitters store Goldman & Salatsch, which became known as the Looshaus and was located in Michaelerplatz by the main entrance to the Imperial palace. In this very exposed corner location, Loos intended to replace the ornate decoration of Viennese building with a facade of plain plaster. In that context, such a plain exterior was seen as quite outrageous.

Today that building seems an extremely mild version of "modern," with classical pillars and marble on the facade (features said to have been added under Habsburg pressure). The objection to its almost total lack of ornament — around the window-frames for example — led to it becoming locally christened as "the building without eyebrows." The probably apocryphal story is that the Emperor Franz Josef loathed the building so much he avoided using the facing exit from the Hofburg Palace.

In this era of a decaying empire, Loos's critique of ornament made him a rabid revolutionary, added to which, his personal antipathy towards his arch-enemy, Hoffmann, only increased as time went on.

Strnad and Frank's relationship to Hoffmann and Loos was complicated. Frank was the only architect to compose a tribute to both Hoffmann and Loos on their sixtieth birthdays (in 1930), and Strnad continued to work with Hoffmann in the 1920s and 1930s. The fact was that the respective situations of Hoffmann and Loos were very different. Hoffmann was the most powerful figure in Viennese architecture, and as well as appointing Strnad and Frank as Professors in 1919 (when Welz began courses with Strnad and Frank), Hoffmann had considerable patronage to bestow upon other architects — as with Strnad's commission for the 1925 *Art Deco* exhibition.

In contrast, no matter how much his ideas attracted a younger generation, Loos was an outsider with no practice, no permanent staff, and little in the way of patronage. He was a great supporter of others when he was able, as with his promotion of the painter Oskar Kokoschka, but his power and influence were nowhere near that of Hoffmann's.

Adolf Loos, Goldman & Salatsch Building ("Looshaus") (1909–11). Michaelerplaz, Vienna. Source: designculture.it. Photographer possibly Martin Gerlach.

Strnad, Frank and another Professor, Max Fellerer, under whom Welz would work as a graduate, all found work with Hoffmann rather than for Loos — despite the sympathies of all three with Loos's more radical ideas.

In the case of Strnad and Frank in particular, questions of architectural philosophy went well beyond an attitude to external ornament, and were in sync with Loos's radical ideas about the second pillar of his philosophy, the design of internal space.

"My architecture is not conceived in plans, but in volumes. I do not design floor plans, facades, sections. I design spaces. For me, there is no ground floor, first floor, etc... For me, there are only contiguous, continual spaces, rooms, anterooms, terraces, etc. Stories merge and spaces relate to each other."[7]

Loos was not a systematic writer of his ideas in the way that Le Corbusier was. The above is, however, a concise statement of the essence of his approach: "I design spaces...contiguous, continual spaces" — this is the heart of the matter.

Loos conceived the house as a set of cubes, later christened the Raumplan. Each room could be moved up or down within the larger cubic area of the external walls according to its function, and would have different dimensions including ceiling height, according to need. The side wall of a 'library' could be opened out to overlook a larger 'hall' or 'drawing room' situated at a lower level. The house did not merely have two or three levels, but six or more linked by multiple short stairways. In theory, a house based on the Raumplan could contain more rooms in less space, and with a greater variety of accommodation.

With a two-year exposure to Strnad and Frank as an undergraduate, it would make sense that their ideas together with those of Loos (who influenced them) had an influence on Welz, first as a student and then as a young architect; they were certainly to show up strongly in his Paris designs from the very first house.[8]

Although influenced by Loos's ideas about the organization of internal space, Strnad and Frank both independently, and in parallel, developed sophisticated views of The New Space, what Welz's boss in Paris, Raymond Fischer described as Le Chemin Aérien/The Aerial Way.[9] Essentially, this comprised the route through a house that a visitor would take, the dramatic sense of progression from the street entrance to the top floor, and the intention of making that route as varied as possible. The ideal version possessed something of the character of a maze, so that the route, and what was being presented along the way, was a puzzle to the visitor, rather than being instantly clear upon entering the house.[10]

It was not an entirely new idea. The 1904 publication of "The English House" by Muthesius in Germany had highlighted similar themes in the more avant-garde English architects such as Baillie-Scott, Norman Shaw and Voysey. The interest in the English 'country' house was one shared by Loos and Le Corbusier, and arose from the notion that English houses, unlike the Viennese mansions of the Ringstrasse, for example, were not creatures of vulgar fashion, but evolved from a simple concern with unpretentious comfort, arrived at over generations of practical evolution.

A similar theme was taken up by Loos in regard to English tailoring, both phenomena being seen as essentially functional rather than fashionable, about suitability for purpose rather than pretension, and in that regarded as a vital lesson for the future direction that a genuine architecture should take. This was in opposition to the 'false' development of new fashions and ornamentation of the haute-bourgeoisie, which was seen by some as, in effect, Hoffmann's legacy.

Architectural debates, as any others, owe their dynamic to their times and the personalities involved, and that is certainly the case with the Hoffmann-Loos opposition. However, behind the individuals, and the overheated atmosphere of Viennese culture, there lay a profound opposition between facing backwards to find comfort in an ideal of the past and, on the other hand, embracing the realities of twentieth-century society — that is to say, industrial production on a massive scale. It would not be surprising that those tempted towards comfort would hardly be encouraged to embrace that particular reality in the wake of the industrial-scale killing that occurred in the Great War.

The third element of Loos's philosophy is summed up in his provocative claim that "only tradition counts for me." He admired classical architecture on the one hand, and on the other often featured inglenook seating and a fireplace in his interiors, the epitome of the traditional English 'country house' values of comfort and the cozy — in both cases another angle on rejecting the fashion of the new for its own sake.

The consistency of Loos's philosophy is evident in that he both rejected new ornament in Hoffmann, but also new materials and methods in Corbusier, seeing both as fundamentally irrelevant to the questions that occupied him — good building — building "like the Romans."

Above all, he disliked the modern 'industrial' aesthetic of

concrete, metal and glass. Loos built fairly conventionally, with load-bearing walls, marble, stucco and plaster — rather than the reinforced concrete pillars in Le Corbusier's Dom-Ino structure of 1914 (see below). Set back from the floor edge, the pillars bring the 'curtain wall' into the domestic sphere, which Loos had always fiercely protected from such public display.

Furthermore, Loos had no essential interest in the use of new materials and techniques, which was to him a kind of fetish, a formalism that arbitrarily linked modern ideas with steel, concrete and glass — elements which had no necessary connection to him. For Loos, that was fashion, not architecture; superficial and superfluous. This profound view set Loos apart from other "modernist" architects, and will be crucial to understanding Jean Welz.

When Corbusier chose a bentwood Thonet chair for his interiors, Loos mocked that he had chosen the wrong model — putting formal shape ahead of comfort. While Corbusier viewed architecture as an art, Loos had a more functional conception, reserving the status of art only for monuments and graves.

The relatively recent discovery of Loos in the English-speaking world has highlighted that there was another path to modernism, and one in conflict with the dominance of Le Corbusier.

The great challenge for Welz — in Paris — would be how he could find his own way in the context of the conflicting cultural philosophies behind these two rather different post-Hoffmann modernist philosophies.

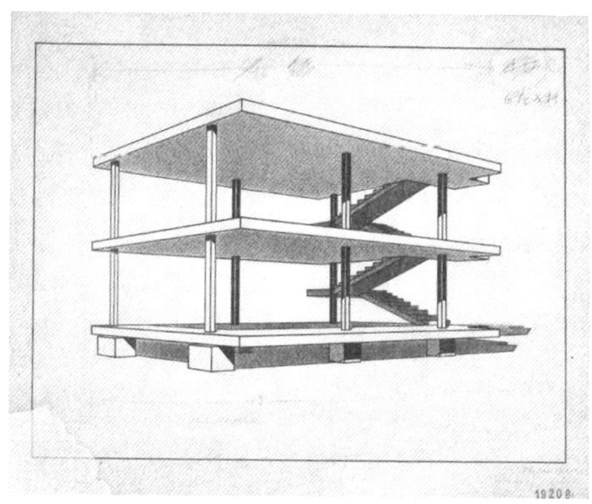

Charles-Édouard Jeanneret (Le Corbusier), Maison Dom-Ino (1914–15).

NOTES

1 Martin Welz relayed this to me in 2014.

2 It was also dedicated to two other revolutionary socialists. See Chapter 26, "A Tale of Three Monuments," for the gravestone.

3 Christopher Long, *The New Space: Movement and Experience in Viennese Modern Architecture*, New Haven: Yale, 2016. Professor Long very generously made a pre-publication version of the text available to me, just one of many kindnesses.

4 When I visited the University of Vienna archives a year later, I saw that Welz's two key professors (in his second and third years) were the same Strnad and Frank (see page 42). Another member of that group worked with Frank, Ernst Plischke, whose name I found alongside Welz's in the university class-lists as fellow-student.

5 MacMillan, p. 38.

6 Also attended on two occasions by Jean Welz's employer in Paris, Raymond Fischer, in 1920 and 1922.

7 Karel Lhota, "Architekt A. Loos," *Architekt* SIA 32 (1933).

8 Welz copied a side-facade window from Frank's Beer house of 1931 — possibly via Carmela Prati, who wrote an article on the house that year. See Chapter18 "Villa Darmstadter — 1932."

9 Raymond Fischer's use of the highly visual phrase Le Chemin Aérien/The Aerial Way for Loos's interior ideas may have come from attending Loos's Bauschule. However, Loos was not fluent in French so it is possible it came from Jean Welz, related to his work for Fischer on the Maison Dubin of 1928, or indeed from Fischer himself. See Chapter 12, "Le Chemin Aérien."

10 Long, *The New Space*. Long's research brilliantly manages to reconstruct what had largely been hitherto a lost history of these ideas.

Above: Max Fellerer, exhibition catalogue cover (Ausstellung der Österreichischen Gesellschaft fur Architektur, Wien), 1967.

Below: Max Fellerer, 1950. Source: CC BY-NC-ND 4.0 from MA 8 - Wiener Stadt- und Landesarchiv, Fotos des Presse- und Informationsdienstes, FC1: 50137/3.

7

HANS WELZ
ARCHITECT

FOLLOWING HIS GRADUATION, HANS WELZ had to learn his trade. He went to work for Josef Hoffmann under the supervision of Max Fellerer, Hoffmann's Chief Architect, who effectively became Welz's boss. On a visit to a Vienna architecture archive in February 2017, as mentioned, I counted one hundred and ninety-one signed entries in Hoffmann's office records by Welz dating from July 9, 1921, which must have been very shortly after finishing his degree, to June 27, 1925, on everything from door handles to the front elevation of a traditional country house for a Kurt Graumann, a wealthy client of Hoffmann, the house a wedding-present from Graumann to his son.

Although Fellerer was said by a longtime associate to have "appreciated Josef Hoffmann for his ingenuity and 'Noblesse', and Otto Wagner for structural clarity, [he] rejected the Decorative in both architects and felt more akin to Adolf Loos."[1] Fellerer is further described by E. Hofmann (no relation) in 1934: "One of the most important architects of the so-called 'second Viennese Modernism' in the interwar period, [Fellerer's] work was generally characterized by simplicity and technically and formally meticulously-formed details. He renounced decorative elements, lending the buildings instead precisely thought-out functional construction and impressive aesthetic appearances […] clarity, transparency, strength, but also elegance and grace […] combined."[2]

If we add Fellerer's supervision of Welz over those five years to that of Strand and Frank during the previous two, that period constitutes a long and potentially decisive seven years' influence from close adherents of Adolf Loos.

Above, left: Carmela Prati (Haerdtl), at a boat racing in Vienna, 1932. Above, right: Carmela, 1937. Source: Adolf Stiller/Architekturzentrum Wien, *Oswald Haerdtl, Architekt und Designer*, Salzburg: Verlag Anton Pustet (2000), p. 34. Archive Adolph Stiller, Vienna. Photographers unknown.

Below: Oswald Haerdtl (right) and Max Fellerer (left), Welz's boss from 1921–25, in the room Haerdtl designed for the 1925 *Art Deco* exhibition in Paris. Source: *Oswald Haerdtl, Architekt und Designer*, p. 28. Archive Adolph Stiller, Vienna. Photo (signed) Henri Manuel, Paris.

Meanwhile, Hans Welz's relationship with Carmela Prati, which began at the start of his course, seems to have carried on until nearly two years after his graduation. However, when news of this attachment eventually got through to her parents in Italy, her father, a high-court judge, hastily traveled to Vienna to put a stop to it, ordering her home for a while. It would seem that a view of Hans as a bohemian had alarmed her father sufficiently for this dramatic intervention. As a dutiful daughter, Carmela had little choice in the matter, but when Martin Welz (born 1945) visited her almost sixty years later, in 1979 in Vienna as a widow, she held fond memories of Hans, and he took away the impression that if it hadn't been for her father she would have stayed with him.

Letters from Welz's rival Oswald Haerdtl to Carmela appear to begin in June 1923,[3] so Hans must have been outcast some time before that, but the relationship between Hans and Carmela had lasted from October 1918 to perhaps as long as early 1923. Her father looked more favorably upon Oswald as a more reliable, professional type, and sanctioned the relationship; a few years later the couple were married.

Apparently on the rebound,[4] Welz married Eva Ottilie Augusta Wagner, described as an exceptionally beautiful and sophisticated model, and half-Jewish (not insignificant in the context of Austrian anti-Semitism). I could find no record of Eva, despite her splendid name and even more splendid description.

However, a coincidence was uncovered on my behalf by the generous Dr. Peter Prokop. He found out that there was a leading Viennese couturier, founded in the second half of the nineteenth century, by one Ottilie Wagner. It had remained active until at least the 1920s, and the enticing possibility opened up that Welz's short-lived wife had perhaps acted as a 'house model' in the couturier founded by what may have been her grandmother.

The closeness of the names was highly encouraging, but when Prokop tried to find out more, he drew a blank. The couturier's records had disappeared and with them any chance of being able to confirm this theory.

Prokop kindly offered to do more research on my behalf. It was through his assiduous work in the Viennese city archive that I could hazard a guess that the marriage must have taken place around August 1924, as that is when the Vienna records show they moved in together. However, Jean left for Paris in July 1925, which would mean that they were together for only ten months, and what is more, subsequent events lead me to believe that the break was a final one.

All of these dates would suggest that Welz's last year or two in Vienna were, to put it mildly, emotionally complicated.

Whether his marriage was actually over before he left for Paris is not clear, but when he departed there may well have been reasons, both personal and professional, that would have encouraged him towards thoughts of a new start.

On the professional front, Hoffmann had been appointed to design the Austrian Pavilion for the 1925 Paris *Art Deco* exhibition, and ran a small competition in the practice for his staff to design a room interior for the pavilion. Welz entered but was judged runner-up to Oswald Haerdtl, who won with what Welz rather pejoratively described as an "insufficiently modern"[5] and "conventional"[6] design.

Although there is no record of Welz's design surviving, there is a photograph of Haerdtl's room as built at the *Art Deco* exhibition, within Hoffmann's Austrian pavilion.

Even though there may have understandably been a subjective element in his view, Welz's idea that Haerdtl's design was not modern enough would echo the contrast between Hoffmann and the Second-Wave Viennese Modernists (Strnad, Frank, Loos and Fellerer).

The polite room Haerdtl designed is not in itself a bad design — the screen on the left has echoes of Japanese screens, the rear frames appear to open onto artful foliage — but the carpet and furniture we can see, while not exactly old-fashioned, were by no means avant-garde. There is a sense here that what might have gained the approval of Hoffmann would have been seen by Welz as far too conservative.

Imagine him working over several years, under Fellerer, on the traditional country-house for a wealthy client's son. When he finally has a chance to submit his own design, it loses to the very man who is also deemed a more appropriate, because conservative, partner for the woman he has loved for five years, and whom he sees as better at cultivating Hoffmann than at architecture.

No doubt this is again subjective, but such sentiments would be understandable in a "bohemian" young architect with avant-garde sympathies.

For Welz, with seemingly little chance of achieving more modern work under Hoffmann, and having taken a personal gamble on marriage, he may, at twenty-five years old, have felt that living a "double life" like Strnad, Frank and Fellerer — working for Hoffmann while sympathizing with Loos — was not a situation he wished to repeat. Welz was probably already firmly on the side of the Second Wave, seeing Hoffmann as the old-guard, a block to really modern ideas.

Nevertheless, as runner-up to the *Art Deco* competition, Welz was sent to Paris — to help supervise the construction of the Haerdtl room.[7] That must have felt for Welz like having his nose rubbed in it, and at best, it cannot have been an unalloyed delight to be alongside the doubly victorious Haerdtl; yet a trip to Paris, home of the avant-garde, may not have been perceived by him as all bad.

Austrian conservatism and prejudice was etched into Welz's mind even sixty years later in South Africa. His family recalled his story of being told-off as a child by a neighbor for playing with Jewish children, a poignant reminder of perhaps why he left his native land.[8]

NOTES

1 Comments from Eugen Worle, Fellerer's longtime employee, quoted in Iris Meder, "Fragmente zu Leben und Werk des Architekten Otto Bauer: "Ihr Platz ist in der Welt," (Fragments on the life and work of architect Otto Bauer: "Your place is in the world") DAVID: Jüdische Kulturzeitschrift, no date. http://david.juden.at/2008/76/15_meder.htm

2 E. Hofmann, 1934, quoted in Meder.

3 Adolf Stiller/Architekturzentrum Wien, *Oswald Haerdtl, Architekt und Designer*, Salzburg: Verlag Anton Pustet, 2000, p. 20.

4 Via Martin Welz, April 2017.

5 Via Martin Welz, April 2017.

6 The word quoted in Miles, p.17.

7 Information from a South African obituary of Welz, presumably supplied by his wife, Inger.

8 Via Martin Welz, July 2017.

PARIS
PART III

8

ART DECO
— PARIS, 1925

HANS WELZ ARRIVED IN PARIS IN JULY 1925. His work on the Hoffmann Austrian Pavilion at the *Exposition internationale des Arts décoratifs et industriels modernes*, later known as the *Art Deco* exhibition, was only for two months.

Though the *Art Deco* assignment must have had overtones of humiliation in the light of the defeat to Haerdtl, there were a number of positive aspects for Welz to working on the exhibition site.

The fact that Welz's uncle Max had asked him to design a stand for the framing business, which actually won a Gold Medal and reviews in French newspapers, perhaps gave him confidence. On the *Art Deco* site, he met Pierre Jeanneret, Le Corbusier's cousin and business-partner, as construction of the avant-garde Esprit Nouveau building was progressing, and later through him met Le Corbusier. He also met Robert Mallet-Stevens, at the time a better-known modernist architect than Le Corbusier, with a number of important commissions under his belt, and a reputation as dapper and highly professional. Mallet-Stevens was a great fan of Hoffmann, and his drawing-style was heavily influenced by him.

Mallet-Stevens's first experience in architecture was working on the Palais Stoclet, Hoffmann's masterpiece. Stoclet was, in fact, Mallet-Stevens's uncle, hence his getting the job. Because he deeply admired Hoffmann, the fact that Welz had been both a student under Hoffmann and had worked for him for four years, and was still working for him on the Paris site, must have carried some influence.

However, Mallet-Stevens's admiration did not extend to the Viennese habit of staying up very late at cafes discussing art and politics, and then showing up late for work. After three months of that behavior, Mallet-Stevens had had enough, although whether Welz jumped or was pushed is not clear. Nevertheless, the dates suggest that if Welz worked on the exhibition site for a couple of months and then had three months with Mallet-Stevens, that brings us to the end of the year, when Welz got his first big break in Paris.

The precise circumstances leading to how Welz met Mallet-Stevens I have not been able to find out, but another architect present at the *Art Deco* exhibition was Welz's classmate in Vienna, Gabriel Guevrekian, who, at the time, was working for Mallet-Stevens. These experiences of the avant-garde, which would also have included the extraordinary Melnikov pavilion for the Soviet Union, may well have made a considerable impact on the young Welz. He would have been able to compare the "insufficiently modern" design of Haerdtl with the international avant-gardes, and quite possibly noted how his former classmate, Guevrekian, had both the freedom to design a "cubist" garden, and had also achieved a certain fame in Paris from creating it.

After four years of grind on a traditional country-house under Hoffmann, banned as a "bohemian" by the father of the woman he

Robert Mallet-Stevens, Tourism Pavilion, *Exposition internationale des Arts décoratifs et industriels modernes*, Paris, 1925. CC BY-SA 4.0 by SiefkinDR / Desaturated from the original photograph of the color drawing and tinted.

had loved for five years, losing her and then the Hoffmann *Art Deco* competition to Haerdtl and his conservative design, added to the failure of his ten-month marriage, it would not have been surprising had Welz concluded upon his first time seeing the international avant-gardes that he had little future in Vienna.

The Austro-Hungarian crowd frequented the Dôme Café in Montparnasse, where Jean got to know another recent arrival, André Kertész. According to Welz, they became good friends. It seems that around the same time that year both made the decision to change their first names to the French equivalent.

Changing your first name was no small matter, and to change your Christian name was a serious commitment, in this case, to Paris and to France. Likely this important decision was made after Welz, at least, had made the decision to remain in the city, and give up both his prestigious job at Hoffmann's and potentially the family business that as the eldest son he would have inherited in Salzburg. Welz often repeated in his later years that he had been attracted as a young man to the motto Liberté, Égalité and Fraternité, and most of all to liberty, to freedom. It seems he recognized that freedom, not in Vienna, but in Paris.

André Kertész, photo of the Dôme Café, circa 1925, with the "Hungarian" table in the foreground — the standing man is the architect Ernö Goldfinger.
Courtesy Ministry of Culture in France: Donation Kertész Collection at Médiathèque de l'architecture et du patrimoine.

On one occasion, according to Welz family lore, he was at the Dôme with a circle of friends when he spotted a tramp-like figure shuffling past the cafe. He pointed out the man in a shabby winter coat to his friends, remarking something like "There goes Kerensky. A lesson to us all." Kerensky was the Russian leader deposed in the 1917 Revolution, now in exile, poverty and apparently alone in Paris. As a young man of twenty-five years old, with his hopes before him, the irony may not have occurred to Jean Welz that poverty and anonymity was the norm in the intensely-competitive Paris avant-garde, a lesson that would soon come closer to home.

Once the decision was made to stay in Paris, however, Welz was not one to look back. His family had often remarked on his absolute determination to keep his face firmly set to the future, especially in what would become the most difficult of circumstances.[1]

Reflecting on his overall situation as the *Art Deco* exhibition closed in the Autumn of 1925, Welz had made extremely useful contacts, felt that the French avant-garde chimed with his own "French soul," as he saw it; but nonetheless, he had arrived, carrying in his baggage as it were, the extraordinarily strong inheritance that was Viennese culture, one that would, perhaps unbeknownst to him at that moment, play a decisive role in the future awaiting him.

NOTES

1 His son Martin said that Jean always refused to look back, only forwards, including speaking German. He had heard it a mere handful of times, usually when the children were not supposed to know what was being said.

Letter from Gabriel Guevrekian to Tristan Tzara regarding Tzara's house designed by Adolf Loos, featuring the word "Welz," dated April 1926. Found in the Bibliothèque littéraire Jean-Doucet, Paris, November 2016. Used with the permission of Marie Thérèse Tzara. Photos courtesy of the author.

9

THE GUEVREKIAN LETTER

WITH JEAN WELZ VIRTUALLY UNKNOWN as an architect, there are only the most fragmentary clues to his existence in Paris. His story is an intriguing case of reading between, not even lines, which would be a luxury in this context, but sometimes around a single word — and that, just his name.

Pictured here is one of the very few instances of it on record in correspondence. If you look for the fourth line down on the right, the first three letters are clear, and the "z" looks quickly scribbled.

Deciphering this handwritten letter, preserved in a Paris library, it did occur to me whether we will be able to get even such sparse information in the future, with hand-written letters almost disappeared. The value of this example lies not in the fact of the word itself but in the web of unexpected connections it reveals. The white shine on either side betrays the fact that this letter is kept in a clear plastic sleeve, preserved and valued by an institution.

The Bibliothèque littéraire Jean-Doucet, gifted via the famous couturier in 1929,[1] is a branch of the Sorbonne university library based in an anonymously handsome building behind the Pantheon, which was once a church, converted after the Revolution as a memorial to the heroes of France. To gain entrance to the library there is another anonymous building along the street to go to first. The doorbell goes unanswered, but a friendly man having a cigarette and a chat in the freezing January wind lets me in and kindly shows me up the rather lovely creaking circular wooden staircase typical of many older Parisian buildings. On the first floor, a fast-talking woman-colleague of his explains that I will have to go upstairs to register for a pass — a laissez-passer. Emails had been efficiently exchanged the week before, but there is nevertheless paperwork involved, handwritten still. Upstairs to the second floor, to the man who had let me in, and three pages to fill in, for which I was kindly lent a pen as I had limited myself to my phone if any notes and photos were to be involved. Expecting to return downstairs, I am told that no, the document I seek is in another building altogether, and complicated instructions follow, not just to the building, two hundred meters away, but once inside it, to the many left and right turns involved.

In that much-larger building the woman at the desk hardly looks up, suggesting her importance and my lack of same, an attitude typical in Republican France. A similar series of turns is imparted as instructions, and I find myself in a fair-sized reading room where a friendlier woman asks if I have been there before and takes me to an open doorway barred by a thick rope with a mysterious darker corridor ahead, lined with bookcases. At the end of the corridor a smaller reading-room awaits, with a very stiff official behind a single desk, raised on a podium and more-than-faintly Dickensian. As I wait before him he eventually deigns to looks up, I show my pass, and he dismissively waves towards a visitor-book behind me, which also has to be filled in. I return to his desk and he points to a row of desks, one of which has a large open file like a book. I am mystified until I

Congrès Internationaux d'Architecture Moderne's La Sarraz Declaration, 1928. Gabriel Guevrekian is standing front center-left; Le Corbusier is between two women at the back, wearing his classic specs. CC BY-SA 4.0 by Perpetualtoday.

realize the file is open at the page of the letter I have come to see. I was frankly expecting to wait while it was retrieved from miles of shelving somewhere underground, but no, the charade seems designed to make amends for the unfortunate fact that my letter was ready and waiting.

The plastic-encased letter is only one page. It is in German, and I have a hard time trying to make out the individual words, which appear as though they were written in a hurry. I speak no German but later, a German friend-of-a-friend translates it over the phone into French, a slightly surreal experience.

Even the biting cold couldn't dim my good mood as I left the library. Walking along characterful seventeenth-century streets past cozy, dignified restaurants in the winter sun, I felt very fortunate indeed. Back home an email from the library awaited, telling me I had left my passport behind. I was fortunate. I was booked on an early train to London the next morning but had time to retrace my steps and tell myself that fate sometimes has to remind you of its fickleness.

As I turned over the French translation in my head, the meaning fell into place, a significant connection between Welz and Gabriel Guevrekian, the author of the letter. Guevrekian, lesser known among his peers, appears prominently in the photograph of the famous first international meeting of modern architects at La Sarraz in Switzerland.

He is at the front of the group in a smart suit with a shaved head and in fact was one of the La Sarraz organizers. As he appears in the photo, he is the only one there who would not look out of place in a Chicago gangster story (ironically, he ended up in Chicago years later). Thanks to Cecile Poulot, a Loos researcher in Paris, the final piece came together in November 2016 — Guevrekian, and by association, Jean Welz, had been working for Tristan Tzara, the artist, founder of Dada, for whom Adolf Loos designed the only house he was to build in Paris.

The Welz family story turned out to be the same — Jean worked on the Tzara house, which is how he finally met Adolf Loos. The letter is dated April 1926, only a few months into the *chantier*, the building-work for the house. Jean was said by the family to have been employed as a building-supervisor, and the letter ties in with that. It would seem that perhaps via Tzara, Jean Welz had asked Guevrekian for more workers on the job. In the letter, Guevrekian is apologizing to his client that he only got Welz's letter the night before and it will not be possible to find more workers immediately, but perhaps the following week.

It may well be that it was Guevrekian who recommended Welz

to Adolf Loos. Guevrekian had met Loos in Vienna in 1921, shortly before he himself left for Paris, and it seems they kept in regular touch. Loos went to Paris in 1922 and was lionized by the avant-garde as the author of the infamous essay "Ornament and Crime" (Le Corbusier published the article in the first edition of his journal *L'Esprit Nouveau*), and Loos returned from Vienna to live in Paris in 1924, beginning the designs for the Tzara house around August 1925.[2]

The family story continues that Welz was recommended by "one of the people he knew," as he was doing the rounds of the few modern architecture practices in Paris in order to find work. This person had said to Loos that Welz was "another Austrian obsessed with detail," as Loos was displeased with what he saw as the slack approach of his French construction managers. As the construction only began in 1926 and the letter is dated April, this was perhaps towards the beginning of Welz's work on the house, when Loos came to realize that there were not enough quality builders being employed to get the job done.

As Welz had worked at Mallet-Stevens's, headed up by Gabriel Guevrekian as chef d'agence (manager), it seems reasonably likely that it was in fact Guevrekian who put forward Welz's name to Loos.

Guevrekian was of Armenian origin and seems a bit mysterious — even his date of birth is uncertain, in some accounts it is given as November 1891 and in others as 1900, which would have made him the same age as Welz. Born in Istanbul, he was brought up in Tehran and then went to live in Vienna with an architect uncle, Caloustian,

Gabriel Guevrekian, Perspective of a Project, Paris, 1923. image 005.jpg from the University of Illinois at Urbana-Champaign Archives.

who influenced him away from a career as a musician, his first love (similar to Welz), to one in architecture. He attended the same course as Welz, with Strnad and Frank, under Hoffmann, but started in 1915, only ending in 1919 and actually graduating in 1921. Guevrekian also shared with Welz having worked in Hoffmann's office for a year — so there were many connections.

In 1922, Guevrekian moved to Paris, working with Le Corbusier (with whom he said he regularly played football) and André Lurçat, but mainly with Mallet-Stevens, until 1926. His celebrated "Garden of Water and Light" for the *Art Deco* exhibition of 1925 gave him some notoriety, and from 1926 he worked independently until 1933, when he was summoned back to Iran.[3] His early drawing style, interestingly like that of Mallet-Stevens, is also reminiscent of Hoffmann.

Mallet-Stevens seems to have played a role in connecting Guevrekian with clients from the world of fashion. There was a natural shared interest in the new among leading fashion designers, artists and modern architects. Guevrekian himself married the daughter of a well-established Paris fashion house that originated in England in 1760, Creed, still going today as a top-drawer parfumier, and Guevrekian's own major house design in Paris was for another fashion designer, Jacques Heim.

It's worth noting by way of sympathies among colleagues that Welz was also connected with the world of fashion — remember, he had fallen in love with a fashion student, and on the rebound, briefly married an "exceptionally beautiful" fashion model, possibly the granddaughter of the founder of one of the leading Vienna fashion houses.

The two major clients that Guevrekian connected with via Mallet-Stevens were Paul Poiret, whose big (1922–24) house was left unfinished — and amazingly has only recently been completed, almost a century later; and Jacques Doucet — another house unfinished by Mallet-Stevens — who had collected one hundred thousand books, which were donated to set up the library.

The letter in the Jacques Doucet library that, for once, puts the name of Welz in Paris in early 1926, thus connects Doucet to Mallet-Stevens, Guevrekian, Jean Welz, Tristan Tzara, and finally, Adolf Loos.

Loos had no office in Paris, nor in fact in Vienna. He was something of an itinerant, traveling around hotels and cafes in the capitals of Europe, bringing in students to effect drawings for him — so that it would be no surprise that Guevrekian was acting as a kind of project-manager for the Tzara house in his 'spare' time, as it were, from his running Mallet-Stevens's and then his own architectural office.

By way of an example of Loos's utilization of those he had informally trained through lecture and apprenticeship, Loos had one of his most talented former students, Zlatko Neumann, as assistant for the Tzara house in Paris. It seems he started in August 1926 which is possibly when Welz either stopped work there, or worked under Neumann.

At the same time as the Tzara house, Loos was building the Moller house in Vienna with Jacques Groag, who had informally attended Loos's Bauschule before becoming Loos's engineer and collaborator, and was passing back and forth between the two capitals. Both houses were on the go in 1926, and when Guevrekian came to build his own major house in Paris, the Villa Heim at Neuilly, the very next year, the design seems to have owed much to Loos and the Moller house. The Villa Heim (1927) makes an interesting comparison point for Jean Welz's adoption of similar concepts in 1927–28 on the Maison Dubin, which we will soon examine.

Another fragment of evidence, that I spotted by chance, came to light while searching for plans of the Tzara house, and finding one of the Piano Nobile.

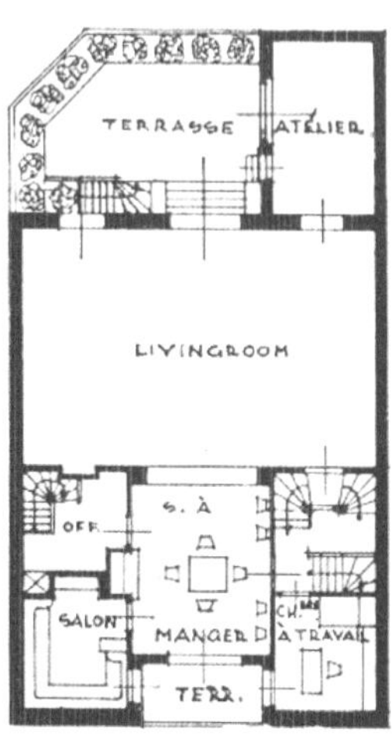

Adolf Loos, Tristan Tzara House (1926), plan of the Main Floor (Piano Nobile) with distinctive "R" presumed to be in Jean Welz's handwriting. Right: Tzara house facade, photo possibly by André Kertész. Source: fr.wikiarquitectura.com.

What immediately struck me was that the hand-drawn lettering was familiar in style from later plans known to be from Welz's hand. The element that struck me was the rather distinctive "R," which has a low stroke beneath the rounded top part of the letter. The plan appears to be from a late stage in the work, possibly after completion.[4] Could the plan be a drawing by Welz?

As it seems to be of the finished house, that would suggest Welz carried on in some capacity, for Loos, after his assistant Neumann took over in August 1926. That would also square with the relationship Welz developed with Loos from that time on.

There is a further connection. The photographs of the house, including later stages of the work, are by André Kertész. By his own account, Kertész met Tristan Tzara and Adolf Loos at the Dôme Café, and they invited him to take a look at the house, and then to photograph it. Loos and Tzara had known each other since 1917, meeting in Zurich.

As Welz and Kertész were together regulars at the Dôme, it could be, circumstantially, that Jean was the intermediary, although it has to be admitted that Kertész does not mention him in any interviews or correspondence.

While Welz's wife, for example, obviously knew that Kertész was a good friend in Paris, (Kertész took photos of their first-born as a baby), I can find no mention in Kertész of Welz. The photographer was, however, known to compartmentalize his life; for example, his longtime fiancée in Budapest knew nothing of Kertész's marriage in Paris before he was divorced and summoned his prior fiancée there from the Hungarian capital.

Left: Jan Sliwinski. Right: Zlatko Neumann with Adolf Loos in the latter's Paris apartment. Both photos: André Kertész, dates unknown. Courtesy Ministry of Culture in France: Donation Kertész Collection at Médiathèque de l'architecture et du patrimoine.

Whatever the actual connection was in reality, the Austro-Hungarians certainly assembled at the Dôme, which became their headquarters, their cafe, as though they were back in Vienna or Budapest. The Dôme is in Montparnasse, the opposite side of Paris from the Tzara house at Montmartre, so hardly around the corner.

Kertész got the job, he was part of the Austro-Hungarian circle, and reputedly already knew Tzara as one of the "Austrian" group around the gallery/music shop Au Sacre du Printemps, run by the Viennese-born Jan Sliwinski.

At the gallery, we find a connection to Welz and to Guevrekian. The shop facade and interiors of the Sacre du Printemps was the first design job for Guevrekian (1923/1925) and the gallery was the location for the first solo exhibition of a photographer in the world, that of André Kertész, in 1927. The Paris avant-garde of the 1920s was relatively small in number, and was composed of a series of overlapping groups. For example, around Loos there were three groups — a French one including Georges Besson, the first publisher anywhere of "Ornament and Crime"; a modern-architecture group, as early as 1913, that included Le Corbusier, Mallet-Stevens, Guevrekian and Raymond Fischer; and the Sacre du Printemps crowd, which included Tzara, Kertész, and Man Ray along with other artists and photographers. As with many such circles, the latter lasted comparatively few years, from 1925 to 1929, but in its time was a

Gabriel Guevrekian's first design, Au Sacre du Printemps, Paris, 1923. image 001.jpg from the University of Illinois at Urbana-Champaign Archives.

magnet for the Austro-Hungarians and Poles (Sliwinski was of Polish extraction).

Guevrekian was involved in two of the three circles around Loos, and from the letter to Tzara it would appear he was responsible for providing building-trades for the job.[5]

It is interesting that the Guevrekian letter is not to Loos, the architect, but Tzara, the client, which suggests Tzara had a more active role in the build than the average client. The fact the letter is in German also shows the tenor of the circle around Loos — staying with their own culture rather than switching to French — whereas Jean Welz was determined to learn French and realize his "French soul."

The moment he connected with Loos could hardly be more significant for Welz, twenty-six years old a month before the date of the Guevrekian letter. To understand just how important, we need to return to the Vienna Welz had left less than a year ago, where he had first studied and then practiced architecture.

"Jean" had adopted that name in France, and it would have been exciting to meet and work with an architect feted by the Paris avant-garde, but as one born and bred in Austria in the particular way that Welz was, the reverberations surrounding finally meeting the legendary Adolf Loos would have been so much greater.

NOTES

1 Cecile Poulot kindly informed me it was Doucet's son who was the actual donor.

2 Information kindly supplied by Cecile Poulot — the first drawing of the Tzara house dates from August 1925.

3 1937–40 he worked in London with Connell, Ward & Lucas, an eminent modernist practice, before returning to Paris in 1940, avoiding working with Vichy and the Nazis, and went to America post-war. He was a professor in Chicago from 1947–69, at which time he retired to Antibes, where he died in 1970. http://www.architektenlexikon.at/de/193.htm

4 From https://fr.wikiarquitectura.com/index.php?title=Maison_Tristan_Tzara

5 That connection was not something I had otherwise come across in relation to Guevrekian, and there is no mention of anything similar in the French book on his work. However, I later confirmed the connection in an article by the late Iris Meder, a German art-historian who worked in Vienna. See Meder, "Fragmente zu Leben und Werk des Architekten Otto Bauer: 'Ihr Platz ist in der Welt.'"

Above: André Kertész, *Auto-Portrait* exhibition at Le Sacre du Printemps, 1927. One of Kertész's displayed portraits may be of Jean Welz, the bottom-left portrait is Sliwinski. Courtesy Ministry of Culture in France: Donation Kertész Collection at Médiathèque de l'architecture et du patrimoine.

Below, left: Jean Welz, circa 1930s, attributed to Kertész. See Plates, Figure 7 for the color version. Below, right: Jean Welz in Corb specs, circa 1930s, possibly by Kertész. Both courtesy Welz family.

10

THE THIRD MAN
MALLET-STEVENS / LE CORBUSIER / JEAN WELZ

JEAN WELZ HAD COME INTO CONTACT with the Paris avant-garde on the *Art Deco* exhibition site, and subsequently had worked for Mallet-Stevens and Adolf Loos, but on the surface he seemed no closer to the opportunity that every architect lives for — to build. The Tzara house was built in 1926, and in the following year, 1927, Jean's "good friend" André had his remarkable breakthrough — the first ever solo exhibition of a photographer.

The exhibition was not a fancy affair; the Sacre du Printemps gallery was modest in scale if not ambition.[1]

At the end of the same year, Welz finally got his own big break.

The self-proclaimed biggest fan of Loos in France was another Parisian architect passionate about modernism — Raymond Fischer. He knew everyone in the avant-garde: painters, filmmakers, architects, and, in an interesting coincidence, as a young man, he and his father were involved in the premier of the actual Sacre du Printemps. When the new avant-garde magazine *L'Architecture d'Aujourd'hui* was founded in 1930, he was invited to be on the "patrons" board alongside Le Corbusier.

Loos had sent brilliant Viennese students of his to Fischer before, and the latter had come to rely upon his "nègres viennois," emigres without work-papers looking for congenial work. Fischer had recently obtained a major commission and was on the look-out for another talent, and it seems likely that Loos recommended Welz to Fischer after Jean had worked on the Tzara house.[2] Jean was offered by Fischer the post of chef de cabinet, chief architect, and before 1927

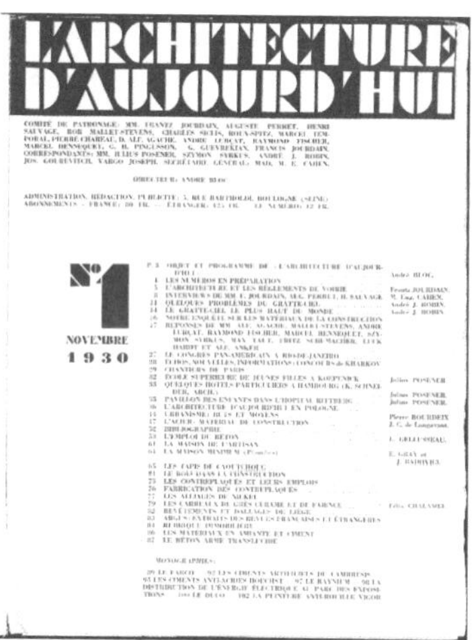

L'ARCHITECTURE D'AUJOURD'HUI

N°1

NOVEMBRE 1930

Above: Raymond Fischer, circa 1925. Source: *L'Architecture d'Aujourd'hui* no. 1, November 1930, p. 21, via portaildocumentaire.citedelarchitecture.fr. Public domain.

Below: *L'Architecture d'Aujourd'hui* no. 1, November 1930.

was out, Welz began work on his first modernist project. Moreover, this was not just any modernist project, but one which could hardly have been a greater or more exciting challenge.

Welz's situation at the end of 1927 must have seemed as though the gamble to leave Vienna was about to pay off handsomely — and to work among the most elevated company imaginable.

The design is the third of three houses in a small terrace, today a stone's throw from the Boulevard Périphérique in the suburb of Boulogne-Billancourt, where many artists settled in the early twentieth century. The first house, built in 1925–26, is by Robert Mallet-Stevens, arguably the pioneering modernist. The second is by Le Corbusier, built in 1926. Le Corbusier's first modernist house dates from 1923, but this house, the Maison Cook, has a particular significance as it is the house through which Le Corbusier articulated his Five Points of Modern Architecture, which would become an enormously influential credo for young architects for generations to come.

Le Corbusier's five principles were:

First, Pilotis: The house should be raised above the ground on concrete pillars to allow air to flow underneath the building.

Second, Free Facade: The use of reinforced concrete to support each floor meant that for the first time, the external walls were freed from their task of being structural and were transformed into 'curtains' whose function was to protect the rooms within from the elements.

That gave rise to the third point, Fenêtres en Longueur/Ossature Indépendent (the long or free window): Traditionally, windows were limited by having to have structural support above, but without that literal pressure, windows could extend as long and high as desired, even the entire length of a facade, and around the corner to boot.

The fourth point is Open Plan: the use of concrete pillars set back from the edges meant that the rest of each floor had no need of internal structural walls, and could assume an openness hitherto not possible.

The fifth point is the Roof Garden: The complement of the pillars on the ground floor was that the flat roof allowed a roof garden and/or solarium to be installed on top of the building, bringing fresh air and sunbathing to every such house.

Le Corbusier had elaborated some of the basic principles with the 'Dom-Ino' concept of 1914–15[3] (see Chapter 6, "Adolf Loos and the Second Wave"). However, the Maison Cook realized this five-point program in every detail, and the manifesto-incarnate was about to have Jean Welz's first design, at the age of twenty-seven, literally joined onto it through a shared-wall.

It is hard to imagine a greater dream for a young architect enthused by modernism, who had admired the Esprit Nouveau pavilion of 1925 at the *Art Deco* exhibition[4] but who was already armed with a sophisticated contrasting philosophy to the Five Points, one originating with the New Space architects and specifically, Adolf Loos.

In addition, Welz had landed as Chief Architect for the one person in Paris who was not only sympathetic to Loos's ideas, but the biggest proponent of them. When in Paris, Loos often took a corner in friends' offices to work on drawings — for the Tzara house he did that in Fischer's office,[5] as well as with Mallet-Stevens.

Such a situation could have been very tricky if Raymond Fischer turned out to be the competitive or insecure type, who insisted on stamping his signature on everything he touched whatever his contribution, and had to feel that he alone understood Loos's ideas — after all, Fischer had attended Loos's Bauschule in Vienna on two occasions.

However, Welz was doubly lucky with his employer, as Raymond Fischer generously acknowledged, even many years later, how much he had learned from him, including the relationship between architecture and music, and he had even actively encouraged Welz to work on independent commissions from his office.

It was with all of this in the background that Welz went to see Le Corbusier, whom he probably already knew through meeting his cousin and business partner, Pierre Jeanneret, at the *Art Deco* exhibition in his first days in Paris. He politely wanted to ask if he should follow the roofline Le Corbusier had set with the Villa Cook. The Master generously told him that it was his house and he could do as he wished.[6]

With Fischer's support and a free hand from Le Corbusier, Welz embarked on his first design, alongside the houses of the two most famous Parisian names in modern architecture.

NOTES

1 As an expat avant-garde center, the gallery was named in tribute to Stravinsky's *Rite of Spring*, a pivotal modernist composition that had caused a riot when it premiered in 1913 at the Thêatre du Champs Élysées.

2 Miles, p. 18: "Loos … approached Welz to work with him." There are two

Fischer versions; in one, Loos introduced him to Welz, the second was the other way around, he introduced Welz to Loos. By April 1926, Welz was working on the Tzara house for Loos, which would mean Welz would have had to meet Fischer before then. That could make sense if Jean was doing the rounds of Parisian modernists to find work after his decision to stay in Paris. However, Fischer also stated in 1987–88 that Welz came to Paris on the advice of Loos in 1930, so his memory may not have been altogether reliable by then (Pascal Zeller, *Raymond Fischer 1898–1988 Le Chemin Aérien*, Dissertation. Lyon: Ecole d'Architecture de Lyon, July 2, 1992, p. 61). It seems on balance more likely that Fischer met Welz via Loos.

3 Although the Dom-Ino is the best-known image, the curtain-wall idea with recessed pillars to support a concrete deck was used by Walter Gropius and Adolf Mayer in 1911 in the Fagus factory office, enabling the famous corner windows going around the corner without apparent support. (I have written in *The Modernist* on that building.)

4 According to Miles, *The World of Jean Welz,* he saw the Esprit Nouveau pavilion on the *Art Deco* site where it had been put in a corner by the organizers to minimize the controversy of its avant-garde design.

5 Fischer's account in Zeller. As Welz seems to have done at least one post-completion drawing of the Maison Tzara, it may be the case he met Fischer through using the Loos "corner" of his office, which would have probably been in 1926.

6 Welz's own account from a talk in 1972 at the National Gallery in Cape Town. A cassette-recording exists, with the sound quality kindly cleaned-up by his grandson, Konrad Welz.

11

RAYMOND FISCHER

RAYMOND FISCHER WAS AN ARTIST, a lifelong radical socialist and politician, and an architect who built in a total of thirty-five towns and cities in France. Appointed architect for the Defense of Paris in 1940, he lost eighty percent of his archive in fleeing the Nazis for the Vercors, where he became right-hand man to Resistance leader Henri Frenay and a Resistance hero described by General Maurice Chevance-Bertin as totally fearless when he was sent on many dangerous missions, and "un vrai" (a true hero).[1]

As architectural work became scarce in the wake of the 1929 crash, from the mid 1930s he developed a career as a politician that lasted for over forty years, including a stint as a Mayor for almost twenty years at Hirson in northeast France. In his eighties, his architectural work was rediscovered by a new generation, prompting an interview book and three student theses. His involvement with modernism, as mentioned, can be traced back to Stravinsky's Rite of Spring in 1913, often quoted as the birth of modernism, the staging of which he worked on, aged fifteen, with his father, as enthusiastic volunteers.

Born Louis Raymond Robert Fischer in 1898, a couple of years older than Jean Welz, he dropped his first name as a mark of rebellion against his Beaux Arts architectural education, and threw in his lot with the avant-garde.

He passionately embraced pacifism in reaction to the Great War and the nationalism it exacerbated, and in 1916 joined the socialist party. His family was Jewish, from East Prussia, and had emigrated to France in the mid-nineteenth century to settle in Lyon. His father, a surgeon, had moved to Paris and was a Freemason, pacifist and internationalist influence, an amateur of modern literature and theatre who wrote plays, poetry and literary essays.

Growing up in this particularly cultured family, the young Louis discovered the contemporary arts alongside political and artistic activism. One of his father's patients was an architectural student, Michel Roux-Spitz, later an eminent modern architect, and he enthused Louis to study architecture at the Beaux Arts. Louis did so in 1917 only to be called-up, serving on the front line in 1918. He survived the war and entered the Beaux Arts in 1920. On Roux-Spitz's advice he also joined the practice of Georges Redon, architect brother of the artist Odilon Redon.

Fischer soon rebelled against the academic Beaux Arts approach, which conflicted with his ideas of contemporary architecture, and adopted the architects of the modern movement as his inspiration. Reading the architectural manifesto by Adolf Loos, "Ornament and Crime," published in the first edition of Le Corbusier's *L'Esprit Nouveau* journal in 1920, inspired him to visit Loos's Bauschule in Vienna, where he helped out at his lectures in 1920 and again in 1922. Fischer took Loos as his master, adopting his critique of ornament, his ideas of a "rational" architecture, and his dynamic three-dimensional conception of interior space, translated by Fischer as the Chemin Aérien, or Aerial Way.[2]

On Loos's advice, Fischer visited Walter Gropius, founder of the Bauhaus, where he returned several times between 1920 and 1921, and took two trips to the United States between 1921 and 1923, visiting Frank Lloyd Wright and working in Chicago for three months. In America he was struck by the efficiency of practices that had both salespeople out front and design offices in the back. He visited Loos again in 1922, and when his father died in the same year, he felt free to leave his Beaux Arts course.

Loos left Vienna in 1924 and settled in Paris, where he received a hero's welcome, and lived full-time from 1924–28. How much Fischer had to do with Loos's decision is not clear, but his only house commission in Paris came from Fischer's friend, Tristan Tzara, whom Loos had also met some years before.

Between trips, Fischer frequented the cosmopolitan and artistic world of Montparnasse and, among others, knew Juan Gris, Jacques Lipchitz, André Breton, André Masson, Robert Delaunay and Marc Chagall, many of whom he met via Loos, as Fischer put it: "*Il connaissait énormément de monde a Paris.*"[3] (He [Loos] knew an enormous number of people in Paris.) He learned his trade in architecture by working in the practices of the pioneer of reinforced concrete, François Hennebique, the entrepreneurs and architects Gustave and Auguste Perret, and the architects Raoul Brandon, Louis-Hippolyte Boileau, Hervé Tauzin, Hector Guimard (designer of the Paris metro entrances), Michel Roux-Spitz, Henri Sauvage and Robert Mallet-Stevens. These experiences reinforced his desire to defend modern architecture and strengthened his aversion to what he saw as the out-of-date teaching of the Beaux-Arts.

At the same time, he was active politically, a delegate for the socialist party in 1920, and joined the anti-Communist SFIO (French section of the International Workers' party), in which he was to be active for over fifty years.

In 1923, Fischer set up as an architect in Paris, using the promotional techniques he had seen in America to help him get his first commissions. Like his father, he was a Freemason, which may have also helped him obtain clients. His early clients insisted upon conventional Louis XV- and XVI-style houses, but enabled him to build a customer-base which he hoped to convert bit-by-bit to more contemporary designs. He entered a modern design for the *Art Deco* exhibition of 1925, which was rejected, but as consolation he was offered a place on the selection panel.

From 1924–26 he built a block of flats in a modestly modern style in Paris, with a Robert Delaunay painting of the Eiffel Tower in the entrance lobby. The rather classical design featured bow windows in the style of Roux-Spitz.

With house-remodeling for the painter and animal-sculptor Jacques Nam and then the Maison Dury (1925–28) (see Chapter 13, "Un Nègre Viennois"), he began to be recognized as a modern architect.

Only then did he create his real practice in Paris, employing architects like Francois Heep and Bruno Elkouken, but "above all Jean Welz [...] who would be his principal collaborator and chief-designer between 1927 and 1935."[4]

Fischer was a genuinely passionate campaigner for modernism. Such was his attachment to the ideas of Adolf Loos that, after his speech (defending Le Corbusier) was shouted down at the infamous Salle Pleyel debate of December 14, 1931, organized by *L'Architecture d'Aujourd'hui*, for which 3000 Beaux-Arts conservative students and teachers filled the hall with hundreds more in the street, the editor of the magazine, Andre Bloc, denounced Fischer's "excesses [...] in the struggle against ornament."[5]

Fischer was increasingly against a sole concern with artistic form rather than equal attention being paid to social issues, warning colleagues like Mallet-Stevens and Perret against formalism. This matter led to a final break with *L'AA* and his setting up *L'Architecture Rationnelle* in 1933 with the art-historian Élie Faure, which produced three issues dedicated to a "rational" architecture.

For Fischer, architecture was always a social matter as well as aesthetic, and his view of Le Corbusier's Five Points[6] was more concerned with the potential for mass-housing in ideas like the open-plan and the roof-garden, whereas, in effect, both Corbusier's clients and Fischer's own for individual houses were wealthy individuals interested in art, rather than activists interested in housing to benefit ordinary people. There is evidence from Fischer's late interviews, where he mentions Welz, of Fischer's opposition to the Open Plan (see page 174), but Fischer supported Welz's use of Loos's ideas.

Fischer's blocks of flats in the Rue de Charonne (1930–32), seemed to enthuse him more than his modernist houses, as they presaged a "rational" modern architecture, in the sense of one that brought benefits to ordinary people.

He lectured in Moscow for *L'AA* on the same theme; in the circumstances creating an unfortunate echo of the criticism of "formalism" in the Soviet Union from Stalin, and in favor of the "Socialist Realism" that was a complete retreat from modernism.

Left: Raymond Fischer, circa late-1970s or early-1980s. Courtesy Madame de la Croix via Jean-Louis Avril. Photographer unknown.

Right: Raymond Fischer, remodeled house for Jacques Nam (1925–27). Photo: Chevojon. Source: Raymond Fischer, *Villas et Petits Hôtels*, Paris: Charles Massin (1930).

Raymond Fischer with collaborator Jean Welz, Rue de Charonne flats (1932), from the Welz portfolio.
Photo courtesy Jean-Louis Avril and the Welz family.

After his lecture, Fischer had a visit from the Soviet Police. He had not expected that, and it gave him a thorough fright as they relentlessly queried his views, suspecting him of being in reality against true socialism. Fischer was up to the moment, though, and managed to bravely fob them off with the idea that he was in fact protecting real socialism from bourgeois ideas by his espousal of workers' housing rather than modernism in a vacuum. As a passionate modernist himself, the subtleties of his being for modernism and against "formalism" did not make sense to the Soviet Police, even if it went down well in certain Parisian circles.

On the Rue de Charonne blocks of flats, Jean Welz was credited by Fischer as Collaborator. The element of his contribution most valued by Fischer may have been to make the most of modest spaces, using up every bit of space as rationally and creatively as possible, so that even a small flat could be a high-standard design: the "minimum flat" idea, to benefit as many people as possible through cheap and efficient housing.

Fischer gave Welz collaborator credit on two other projects, one where Welz's ideas were central (Maison Dubin, see Chapter 12, "Le Chemin Aérien") and another where he was probably the sole designer (Montauban, see Chapter 16, "Inondation"). Although a rather different situation, it is possible that the Charonne flats may be, in reality, a Welz design throughout: the facades as well as the layout, as the elements are necessarily integral to each other, and the depth of planning as well as the rigorous facades, as we shall see, all speak of Welz.

Fischer also complimented Welz in *L'AA* for his first independent house, the Maison Landau (1931), (see Chapter 17, "Maison Landau") as a contribution to the "maison minimum": along with the minimum flat the "minimum house" was a concern for modernist architects who wished to create mass housing of a high-standard at modest cost, rather than just villas for the rich.

On the aesthetic rather than social side, Raymond Fischer's main Modernist ideas were summed up[7] as first, the use of "regulating lines" to achieve good proportions outside and in. These are lines traced over the drawing of a facade, to try to give the design a quasi-mathematical rationale or "regulation."

Two, the "Open Plan," offering a variety of internal and sometimes unexpected perspectives. That is a different emphasis from Le Corbusier, and seems to have more of a connection to Loos's and the New Space idea of a journey through a house that can yield surprising and pleasingly, unexpected internal views as the visitor ascends from street to roof.

Three, the layout of surfaces and volumes has a sense of composition, which is a more or less formalist and painterly approach.

Four, a reasoned use of color on the smooth surfaces of walls.[8] The latter can be seen in the Villa Darmstadter (Chapter 18) where the large open-plan area on the ground floor has one color part of the way up the wall and a contrasting one from there to the ceiling. The notion of "reasoned" here again tries not to be arbitrary, as an artist-painter might follow her or his instinct. Whether the reasoning is genuinely "scientific" or, in effect, a nod in that direction would need further investigation.

The first, the use of regulating lines, is familiar from Corbusier, seen by Fischer as a rediscovery of principles going back to the Egyptians and invoking geometry and the Golden Section to regulate proportions. Fischer used the idea for the floor plan as well as the facade — which was Corbusier's main focus.

The second, the Open Plan, is also from Corbusier, but influenced by Loos's multiple floor-levels creating a variety of internal views (later known as the Raumplan).

The third, the layout of surfaces and volumes, relates to Loos's interiors in the idea of volumes moved up and down within the four external walls as well as to Corbusier's manipulation of the external facade, but also to Fischer's view of Loos and other Viennese as architectural Cubists — seen most clearly in Fischer's "cubist" Villa at Marnes-la-Coquette for a M. St. Leger.[9]

The fourth, the reasoned use of color, again has echoes of both Corbusier — his published color palettes — and Loos, via Fischer's idea (popular in Vienna) that the ornament rejected by Loos could be replaced by the use of color in the modernist house. This last seems to be an abiding passion of Fischer's, featured in all his modernist villas, although post-dating Corbusier's use of color to similar effect in the Maison La Roche (1923–25).

The basic idea seems to be to use color as a kind of substitute for ornament, so the changes of color break up a wall without, for example, the use of a picture rail to divide one color from another.

One important conclusion about Fischer's passion for modernist ideas,[10] was that he was less an innovator than a proselytizer for the ideas of others: "Raymond Fischer gives the impression of being a very active supporter, a militant who defends the ideas of modernity already expressed, rather than a creator of his own ideas.[11] Raymond

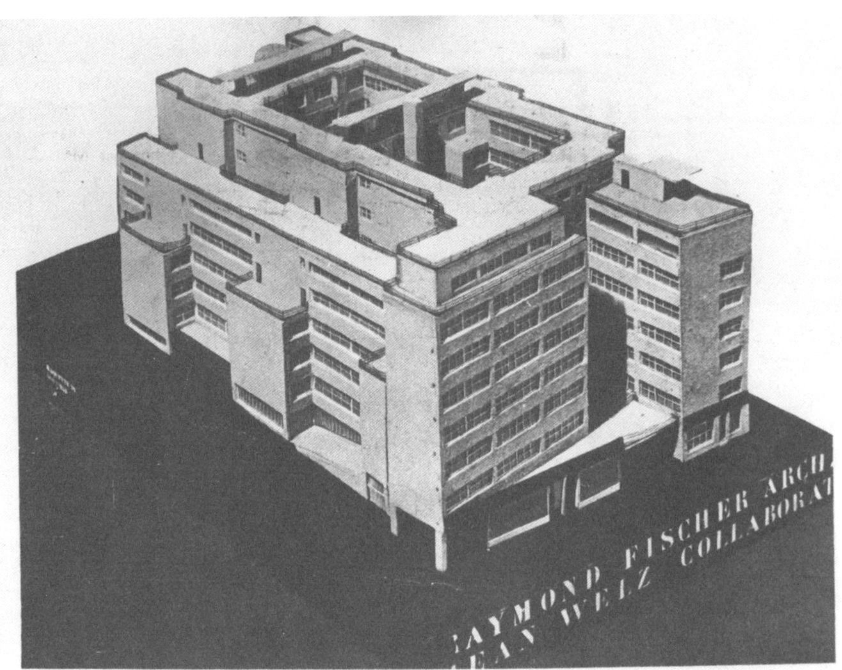

MM. Raymond Fischer et Jean Welz. — Maquette d'immeuble a Paris

Rue de Charonne flats (1930–32). Collaborator credit given to Welz on maquette front edge. Source: "L'Architecture et le Mobilier au Salon d'Automne," *L'Architecture,* 1930, Vol XLIII, no 12, p. 440, via portaildocumentaire. citedelarchitecture.fr.

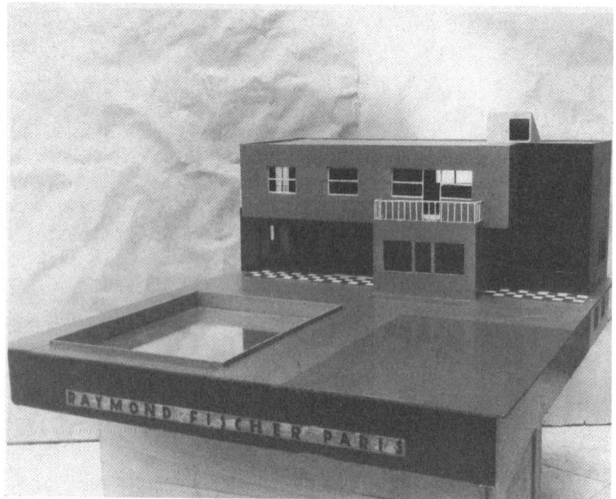

Above: St. Leger Villa at Marnes-la-Coquette (1928). Photo: M. Gravot. Source: *Villas et Petits Hôtels*, Paris: Charles Massin (1930).

Below: Thérèse Bonney photograph, SIL-SIL-Bonney-ADF014-A, France, c.1926. Maquette for concrete villa at Marne-la-Coquette near Paris. Balcony with iron-tubing railing. Swimming pool. Bonney notes that this model is headed for autumn exhibition at Marshall Field's store in Chicago. Louis Raymond Fischer (1898–1988) architect, obtained from Smithsonian Libraries and Archives.

Fischer explains ideas, speaks at conferences, participates in debates. He's a representative, that's his real contribution. To be modern in an epoch where not to be is normal."[12]

The significance of that view comes into sharper focus when trying to assess the relative contributions of Fischer and Welz, especially where Fischer does not give Collaborator credit to him — the Villa Darmstadter being the key case here.

A key point in relation to Jean Welz was Fischer's admiration for Loos combined with a sometimes-critical view of Corbusier; for example, siding with Perret in favor of the vertical window, rather than with Corbusier and the long horizontal window.

The context could hardly have been more favorable for Welz, working for an admirer of Loos who admired Corbusier, but was not overwhelmed by him in the way that many architects seemed to be.

That Fischer is considered to be a publicist rather than an innovator in modernism is significant in terms of their professional relationship, as he himself states, "*Welz m'avait appris à faire des colonnes légères et m'avait aidé à définir ce que j'appelais le plan libre à (trois) dimensions [...] comme Jean Welz connaissait mieux ce système de trace dans l'air, la valeur du vide, il m'avait bien aidé dans l'emboitement des pièces.*" (Welz taught me to make the columns light and helped me to understand what I call the free-plan in three dimensions [...] as Jean Welz better understood the system of moving through space, the value of open space, he helped me a lot in the interconnection of rooms.) Fischer admitted, "*Une des difficultés lorsque l'on avait écouté Loos, était de transmettre dans la réalité ce principe.*" (One of the difficulties when I listened to Loos was how to turn this principle into reality.)

That is a generous acknowledgment both of his own shortcomings and of Jean's abilities — but he went still further in describing Welz: "*Il avait l'état d'esprit de Vienne; c'est à dire de ces gens subtils qui étaient tout le contraire des solides germaniques de l'Allemagne du nord. Il avait le même état d'esprit que Loos, lorsque ce dernier avait construit à Prague la maison Muller.*" (He had the spirit of Vienna, that is to say of those subtle people who were completely opposite to the solid Germans of Northern Germany. He had the same spirit as Loos did when he had constructed the Müller house in Prague.)[13]

The Müller house (1930) is regarded as Loos's masterpiece, his ultimate development of the Raumplan, so that is no small tribute.

Fischer did utter one critical remark about Welz in the December 1987 interviews, to the effect that if Welz had his way, the use of the

Open Plan would have gone much further, while Fischer preferred rooms with doors. That aside, apparently out of nowhere, assumes considerable significance in the later discussion of the Villa Darmstadter (see Chapter 18, "Villa Darmstadter").

When Welz's son, Martin, visited Fischer in 1979, he was a charming host and complimentary about Martin's father as "extremely talented" with the caveat "...but undisciplined."

That comment will be considered in detail later, but a highly significant point that Martin made clear to me was that Welz was always the artist, always his own man, never one to be dominated by others and always had his own ideas, never ever relying on the ideas of others.

Later known as a painter, Welz never gave thought to time; he was never willing to compromise, always obsessed with his work — a degree of commitment that may not always sit easily with the proprietor of an architectural office trying to obtain commissions to keep his staff employed. In such a context, an artist's obsessive passion may well present itself to his employer as indiscipline if not a liability.

As late as 1972,[14] Jean Welz said that giving up architecture had not been so hard for him, as he would never have made a "good" architect. In one way that is a surprising declaration, in another way fairly predictable. What did he mean by a "good" architect? Given his passion and commitment from 1918 to 1939, does it mean he had lost confidence in his artistic abilities as an architect? It would seem to me more likely that he was merely being realistic about his strengths and weaknesses.

It might suggest he was well-aware that he was either not equipped or not prepared to run a practice business-wise, as "the name over the door," tied down to constant compromise with clients in order to be able to pay weekly wages. He probably experienced that during his time with Raymond Fischer, the best part of a decade, including the 1929 crash which made things so much more difficult for everyone, let alone architects trying to convince conservative clients to go modernist.

In that light it could be seen that Welz showed a realistic self-knowledge. He knew that his metier was to stay in the backroom, thinking only of the design. He would not be prepared to expend his time and energies on all the other aspects required to be a good manager of the business side of architecture. He would have seen time and again Raymond Fischer using his energies and social skills to try to keep the atelier afloat, and it would be predictable that after exposure to that side of the business, he decided it was not for him.

However, after two and a half years in Paris at the end of 1927, Jean Welz was now Chief Architect, that is to say chief designer, for the most sympathetic employer he could have dreamt of finding. Up against Le Corbusier, "the greatest architect of the twentieth century," and with his very first design, how would he fare?

NOTES

1 From the biographical dictionary entry by Pierre-Yves Brest, "Raymond Fischer (1898–1988), Architekt" in *Allgemeines Künstlerlexikon (Thieme & Becher)* Leipzig: Saur, 2004, p. 40.

2 "Way" as the sense of connection between various points.

3. Zeller interviews, December 1987.

4 Pierre-Yves Brest.

5 Le Corbusier was also there and shouted down by the Beaux-Arts students. The evening was organized to show films, including Chenal's film *L'Architecture d'Aujourd'hui* about Le Corbusier's buildings. This story courtesy Tim Benton.

6 The Five Points were published in Germany in 1927 and in Paris in *L'Architecture Vivante* autumn-winter edition 1927. Versions of the Five Points are present in earlier lectures, but the formulation dates from 1927 and was a formalist response to the functionalism of other architects at the Weissenhof Siedlung in 1927. This information courtesy Tim Benton.

7 Pierre-Yves Brest.

8 LR Cobos, June 1998, *The Concept of the Raumplan and the Architecture of Raymond Fischer*, Dissertation, Ecole d'Architecture de Paris Belleville, p. 60.

9 Of 1928; see Chapter 11, "Raymond Fischer.

10 LR Cobos dissertation.

11 My translation from the French.

12 LR Cobos dissertation.

13 From Zeller, p. 62. The phrase "Free Plan in Three Dimensions" (the actual quote says Two Dimensions but it seems likely he meant Three) is an interesting one, as he doesn't use the phrase Chemin Aérien here. See the following chapter's discussion about the phrase and its origin and significance.

14 In a talk he gave at the Cape Town National Gallery provided to me by his grandson, Konrad Welz.

Maison Dubin (1928). Photo: M. Gravot. "*En souvenirs de la collaboration de J Welz à mon agence [signed] Raymond Fischer*" (In memory of Jean Welz's collaboration at my practice). Courtesy Welz family.

12

LE CHEMIN AÉRIEN (THE AERIAL WAY)

THE MOST FORTUNATE CIRCUMSTANCES for Welz on the Maison Dubin were that Fischer was not just the leading fan of Loos's ideas, but also prepared to freely admit that he did not know how to turn them into practice, that Welz understood them better than he did, and furthermore, fully encouraged the young architect to put those complex ideas to work.

Many other bosses in Raymond Fischer's position could have treated Welz as an inexperienced assistant and taken full credit for the ideas produced in his office, however brilliant Welz appeared to be. Fischer was not like that, and in the end gave joint credit to Welz, writing his thanks to Jean for his collaboration on the project on a signed postcard of the finished house.

In this sympathetic and unusual context, Welz found himself with the perfect challenge. Raymond Fischer seems to have given Welz a relatively free rein.

Though taking a lead from the horizontal emphases in Corbusier's Maison Cook next door so that the three houses have some continuity, Welz nevertheless varied it in several important ways.

The first was the tiny cubic balcony on the facade (see the signed photograph opposite). Welz told his son Martin that it was intended to announce the theme of the cube in the way that a theme starts a piece of music, then is subject to repetition and variation later in the piece.

The second was the use of full-height windows in contrast to the long horizontal windows favored by Corbusier and detailed in his Five Points of Modern Architecture.

Raymond Fischer was an advocate of full-height windows, and as mentioned, took the side of Perret against Corbusier in the pages of *L'Architecture d'Aujourd'hui* in 1931,[1] and it is quite possible that Welz was here following his instructions in including them. They would also have aided bringing more light into the interior simply through the volume of glazing and letting light in at different angles of the sun, which was the claim that Welz made to Fischer for his successively modified internal design:[2] "*Regardez, on arrive à une meilleure luminosité.*" (Look, I have worked out better light.)

The distinctive box window on the front facade is an idea that Fischer claimed he had brought back from Vienna;[3] indeed, it has a striking similarity to Loos's Moller house, also of 1928. The particular design, and its later use on Fischer's houses, however, was probably from Welz (see Maison Kolpa, in Chapter 15, "House for an Artist").

The emphasis on the "gothic" use of light to bring out the emotional impact of empty high spaces that Fischer had particularly recalled from his time with Loos in Vienna[4] also relates to Welz's formation under Strnad and Frank, together with Loos, the pioneers of the New Space identified by Christopher Long.[5]

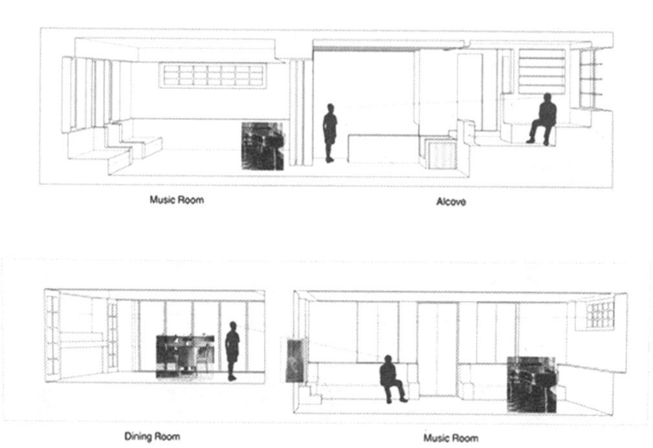

Adolf Loos, Villa Moller (1927–28). Drawing by Yuang Feng, 2013.
Sourced from http://www.behance.net/gallery/13323793/.

In contrast to Corbusier's Open Plan, the second wave of Viennese modernism wanted internal space "to reflect the modern way of life while also offering respite from it."[6] The penetration of light through the common areas, and the use of full-height windows offered a solution to the first part of the formulation, while the room volumes offered privacy that fulfilled the demands of the second part (see Zeller drawing next page).

Where Corbusier had the "living" floors as open as possible, the Loosian approach was keeping the rooms themselves as semi-closed volumes or, for example with a library area overlooking a lower-level hallway, cutting away a wall above waist level to allow overlooking downwards while still closed-off to a degree, plus linking the common spaces at different levels with short flights of stairs.

Fischer also brought back from his sojourns with Loos the term Le Chemin Aérien, or "The Aerial Way." The phrase is said to be Fischer's translation of Loos's own words,[7] but it is not clear if it is a term that Loos used (which is otherwise unrecorded), or Fischer's interpretation and translation from the German. Whatever the origin of the term, it is a particularly useful one that summons up a visual image of Loos's three-dimensional approach to design — perhaps the most distinctive and dynamic conception that he contributed to modern architecture.

While Corbusier's conception of floors was essentially horizontal, supported by reinforced concrete pillars and joined by full flights of stairs,[8] Loos's conception brings to mind an orchestra-conductor tracing rising patterns in the air with his baton, a complex route from ground-level to roof-level.

Welz worked night and day to solve the tricky problem of turning Loos's abstract ideas into concrete form for the Maison Dubin project. He produced a model (maquette) and kept modifying it, time and time again, until he achieved a 'eureka moment,' and only then presented it to Fischer.

Cubes/rooms, which moved up and down within the overall volume of the house frame, were not easy to combine with another Loos theme that Fischer had picked up at Loos's architecture school, which was to have light coming down through the building as in a gothic cathedral, creating voids penetrated by light that would illuminate the stairways from the top to the bottom of the house.

With typically intense focus, Jean ingeniously solved the quandary, and as a result that is how the Maison Dubin was constructed.

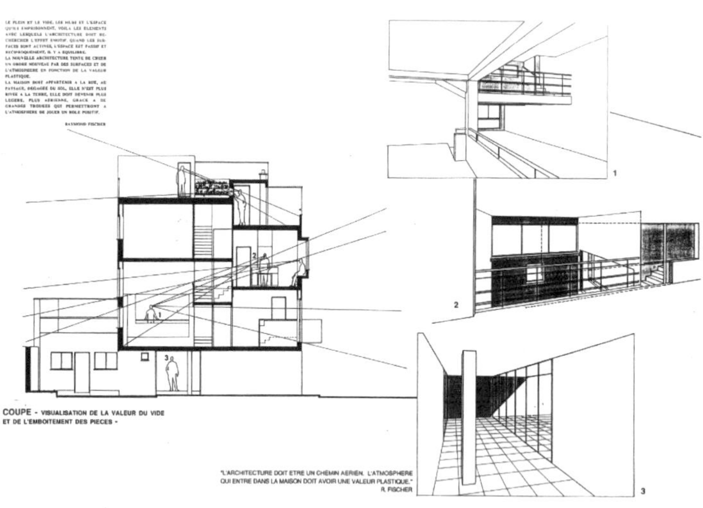

1
2
3
COUPE - VISUALISATION DE LA VALEUR DU VIDE
ET DE L'EMBOITEMENT DES PIECES -
"L'ARCHITECTURE DOIT ETRE UN CHEMIN AERIEN. L'ATMOSPHERE
QUI ENTRE DANS LA MAISON DOIT AVOIR UNE VALEUR PLASTIQUE."
R. FISCHER

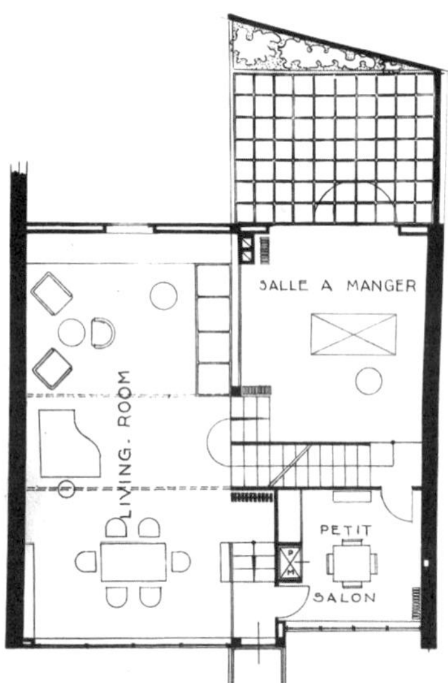

Above: Pascal Zeller, drawing of Raymond Fischer's Maison Dubin, for which Welz was the chief architect. Courtesy of Pascal Zeller. Source: Zeller's Master's thesis *Raymond Fischer 1898–1988 Le Chemin Aérien*, University of Lyon, 1989.

Below: Maison Dubin, first floor plan. Note the small cubic balcony projection, which had the street view. Source: *La Construction Moderne*, September 22, 1929, pp. 645–48, via portaildocumentaire.citedelarchitecture.fr. Public domain.

Architect Pascal Zeller's sectional drawing of Welz's unique solution reveals the Chemin Aérien over the course of six different levels on the top three floors,[9] and also the variety of viewpoints created through the house.

This is arguably the first time that the Aerial Way received such a thorough treatment in a house in France,[10] and it is interesting to compare it with the latest ideas Loos himself was working on at the same time for the Moller house.

When Loos received the Moller commission in 1927, he was living full-time in Paris, and the Moller design drawings were done there. Besides Welz's link to Loos from the Tzara house, remember that Loos, according to Fischer, had a corner in his office and Mallet-Stevens's, so it is quite possible that Welz and Loos had discussions there. The Moller Villa was built in 1928, the same year as the Maison Dubin. In both houses the first floor has multiple levels: three for the Moller house and three for Dubin. Moller has a dining room a few steps higher than the living-room and a cantilevered balcony with a window seat at a little higher level.

Meanwhile, Dubin's first floor is divided into two halves, the right side is four[11] steps higher than the left. On the left side, featuring full-height glazing and a view of the front garden, is a dining/seating area with four steps up in the center to a platform with the small "cubic" balcony ahead, projecting from the front elevation. On the front right is a small card room; a door at the back of it leads to a platform over the stairs below, and then into a large formal dining area ("salle a manger") that opens onto a terrace at the rear of the house; a low wall to its left with a semi-open railing overlooks the living room with a piano (shown centrally on the plan) and sofa and easy chairs towards the rear courtyard and garden view.

Above the music area with piano is a gallery (denoted by the dotted lines and seen in the photograph, next page) allowing views into the double-height living area.

In effect, the whole of the left side and the rear half of the right side are open, with the two raised areas to the small balcony at the front and the large room right rear further expanded by the left rear double-height volume. The use of space in three dimensions is striking on this floor, as not only are there two rooms at half-levels higher, as with the Moller house, here achieved by a broadly left/right division of the floor area (easier and cheaper to build than three separate floor levels as in Moller), but also a double-height space overlooked by a gallery.

4e Année — 1928-29. LA CONSTRUCTION MODERNE Pl. 219.

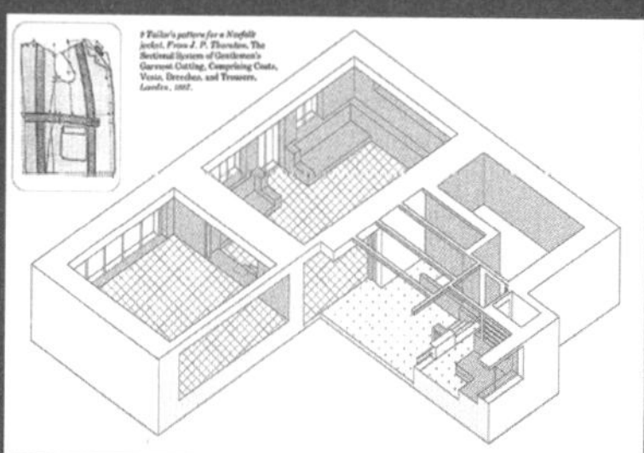

Above: Photographs of first floor views of the Dubin house toward the garden. Source: *La Construction Moderne*, op. cit.

Below: Renderings of the Moller House interior. Yuan Feng, 2013. Source: op. cit.

Looking at the second floor (with the rear garden view at the top of the plan), we see that the gallery (shown in the photo opposite) is also at a lower level than the front bedroom, again with four (the plan shows three) steps off the main staircase (see arrow on the staircase) up to the second bedroom on that half-floor.

The result is that both bedrooms and the bathroom (ensuite to the double bedroom at the front, and accessed off the hall to the single bedroom to the rear) are at the higher level than the gallery.

Loos's Moller House plans from August 1927 were conceived in Paris. The first state of the Dubin plans are precisely dated March 29, 1928.[12] The Moller House, "the end-point of Loos's long intellectual journey,"[13] was the culmination, along with the Villa Müller in Prague (1930), of his conception of the Raumplan. Although the headline version of the Raumplan emphasizes different floor levels (the "three steps up, three steps down" of Loos's own words),[14] there are only three major changes of level at the Moller House, all on the first floor.

At the Maison Dubin, by contrast, there are eight changes of level, from the ground floor to the fourth, the roof level. While the number of levels is not the be-all and end-all for any house, the achievement of such an intensive Raumplan arrangement — or Chemin Aérien, as Fischer would call it — is at the least a confirmation of Fischer's sense that Welz thoroughly understood Loos's ideas and was very

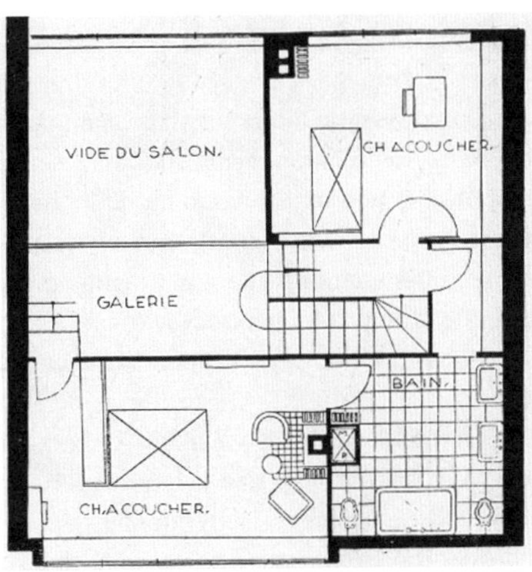

The second floor of the Maison Dubin with the front of the house at the bottom of the plan. The gallery is a few steps lower than the front bedroom, on the same level as the bathroom and the rear bedroom across the stairs.
Source: *La Construction Moderne*, op. cit.

much able to translate them into practice. Welz also created differences in room height on the same floor level, most obviously on the first floor, the piano nobile living area, but also on the top floor (see Zeller drawing) where the heights of the rooms vary throughout.

Additionally, the amount and variety of accommodation Welz managed to pack into Dubin, along with the "gothic" light penetration through the house he was able to achieve from the arrangement of stairs and floors, is a remarkable achievement for anyone, let alone a neophyte.

One should properly hesitate in assessing the first modernist project of a twenty-seven-year-old architect against a master thirty years older, but it was perhaps Welz that Loos included when he suggested architects in the future may take his spatial ideas further.

It is worth pointing out again that Welz would not have learned Loos's ideas from magazines or books, but most likely from face-to-face conversations resulting from their "close friendship."[15] The opportunity to spend hours discussing architecture, and possibly the detailed plans of Moller and Dubin, would have been invaluable for the young Jean Welz, an opportunity available to perhaps only Zlatko Neumann, Heinrich Kulka[16] and at most a handful of other young architects during Loos's Paris period. It would seem likely that Welz already started on Dubin well-versed in Loos's methods and ideas, having known him in a working context for about two years, when Fischer took him on.

The Maison Dubin was on a much tighter site than the Moller House, and presumably on a much lower budget, precluding the luxury materials of marble and exotic wood found in the Loos house.

The facade has a projecting balcony, but a very restricted one on Dubin, in this case the announcement of the idea of the cube rather than a usable balcony, and inspired by the musical strategy of theme and variation, hence the "cube" appearing in various guises within the interior.

The balcony on the Moller House is a first for Loos, as it projects outward, whereas the Tzara house had a recessed balcony inset around a projecting "bow" window, both effectively serving as a protecting porch over the front door. The second phase plans for Dubin added a box window to the front facade, a feature reminiscent of Loos's Moller House (and repeated by Welz on the Villa Kolpa the following year.)[17] In Dubin it is a box-window to the second-floor main bedroom, as a window seat, the same kind of seating as in Moller (said to be so that someone could read with the light at their back), but it is also a discrete architectural feature that appears later with Welz, specifically for his 1937 entry for the Paris Exhibition's Austrian Pavilion (see Chapter 21, "Mont d'Or and Pavillon d'Autriche"). When Welz takes the additional step of including a tiny balcony to set the theme — arguably a youthful excess, as it is not particularly useful — and also a box window as a feature for the main bedroom, he shows an ability to take ideas and reassemble them to meet his own aims, a similar attitude of confidence, even on his first modernist design, to how he will respond to Le Corbusier.

Dubin shows a complex use of space in three dimensions, but it is also part of achieving a lot of varied living space on the plot — especially when compared to the Maison Cook next door. Le Corbusier's Cook has no accommodation on the ground floor, with the bedrooms on the first floor. The living room and dining-area are on the second floor with a large double-height to the living-room (on the left of the plan). It is possible that Madame Dubin wanted more rooms than the Cooks, which could have been part of the brief.

The point here is how elegantly that was achieved by Welz, both in terms of the three-dimensional use of space bringing variety of perspectives in the living rooms, but also throughout the building, as Zeller's drawing shows so well: the small cubic balcony on the front facade of Dubin is the 'theme' taken up in the rooms behind it, creating five volumes of different sizes.

What Fischer called the Chemin Aérien has certain similarities to what Corbusier called the Promenade Architecturale, the route from the street through the building from ground to roof, but the differences are more marked at Dubin, the profusion of levels in particular.

Loos, but also Welz's tutors Oskar Strnad and Josef Frank, aimed to make the route unpredictable and complex in order to provide as much variety and surprise as possible.

With Corbusier's Maison Cook the route is fairly clear — the only entrance can be via the curved structure on the ground floor, approached directly from the front garden (see floor plans, next spread).

With Dubin, by contrast, there is glass double-door to enter on the left (see ground floor plan, page 104) — as with Cook (see the following spread), the area on the left is open (the Dubin garage in the center may have been a client-specification). But then, a right turn is followed by another to access the stairs on the opposite side from the entrance passage via two steps up a level.

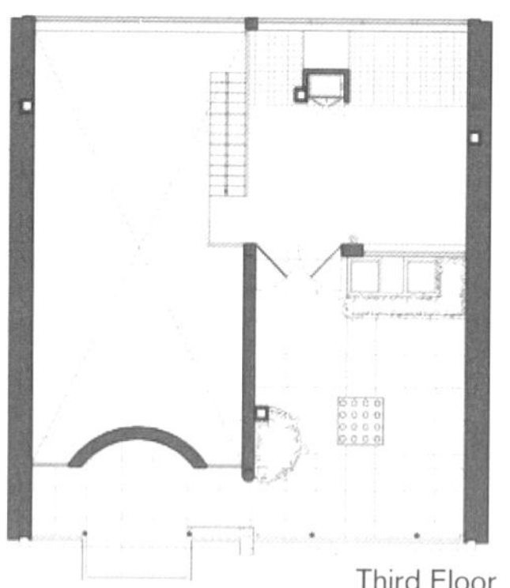

Third Floor

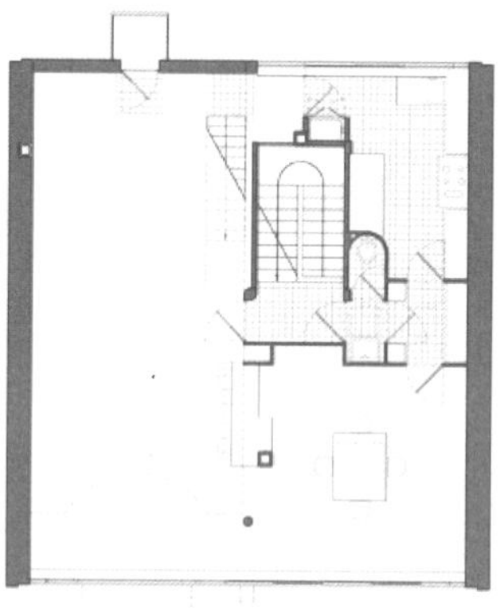

Second Floor

Le Corbusier, Maison Cook (1926), floor plans.

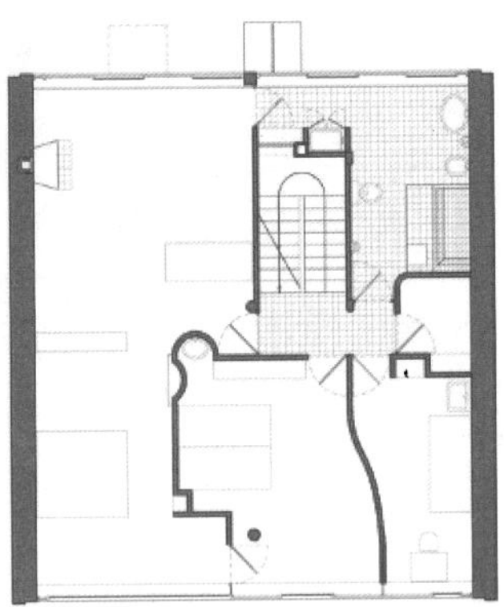

First Floor

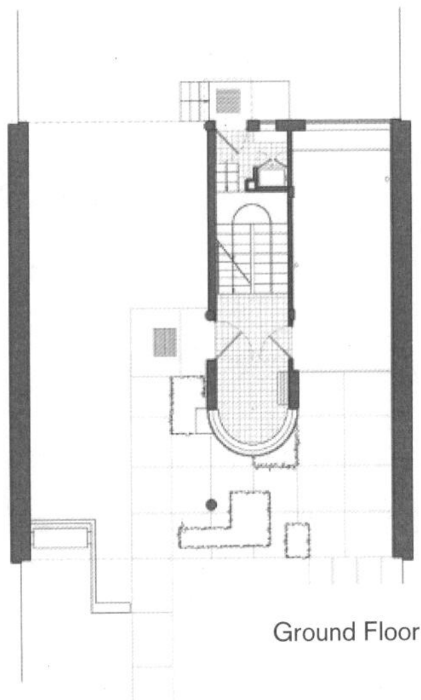

Ground Floor

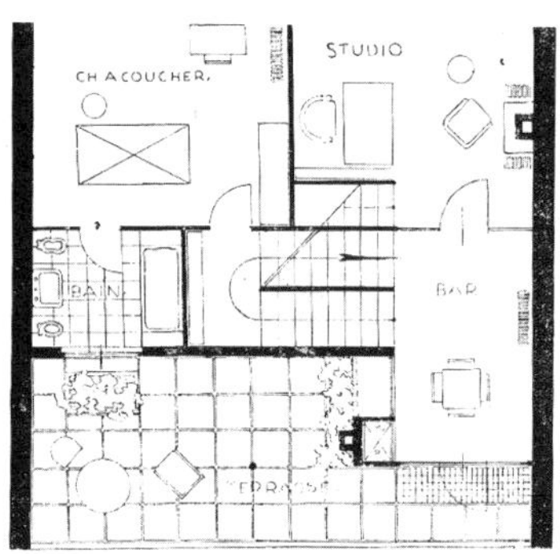

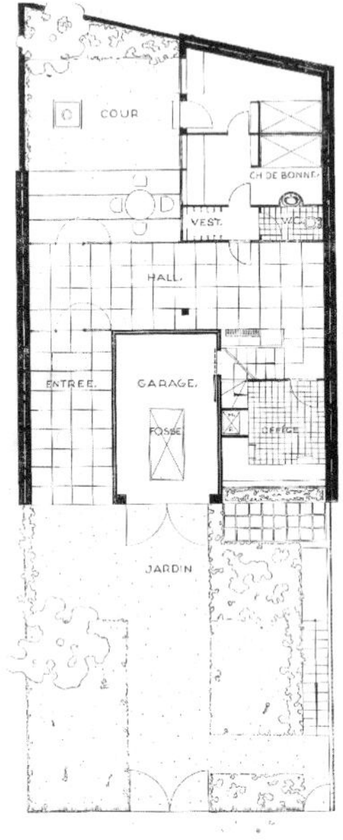

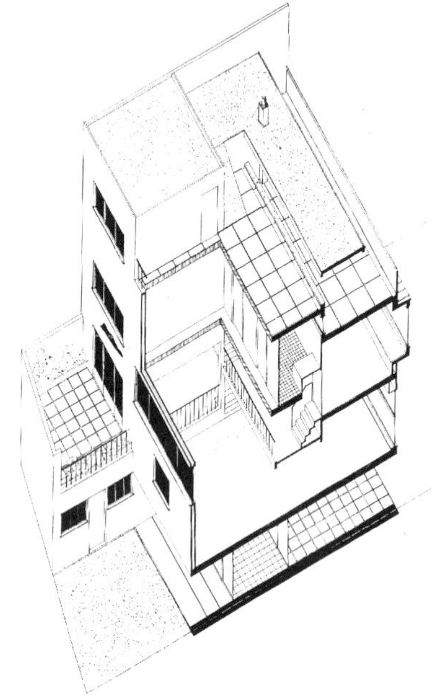

Above: Maison Dubin top floor plan
Left: Maison Dubin ground floor plan

Right: Maison Dubin axonometric viewed from the Maison Cook side with the front facade to the right. Note the door to the rear terrace from the "studio" below is shown opening onto the paving of the terrace. The sloping roof above the main staircase was later made into steps onto the roof area over the front terrace, adding another level.

Source for all: *La Construction Moderne*, op. cit.

The stairway in Dubin is at a right angle to the access door and then ascends directly to the first floor — three ninety-degree turns later.

Four more right turns and one change of level are required before ascending the flight of stairs to the next — gallery level — from which a small flight of four stairs in either case ascends to one or other of the bedrooms.

The top floor plan is also on two levels, up one half-flight of stairs to a bedroom with ensuite bathroom and up a further half-flight directly to an open "bar" and enclosed "studio," which also has another half-flight of stairs up to an extensive rear terrace (over the rear bedroom and bathroom), whose paving is partly visible in the axonometric view.

The half-level rise between the front terrace and rear terrace can be seen in the axonometric drawing as well as in the photograph: the low wall to the rear with the metal bar across the aperture gives an idea of the height difference between the pictured upper terrace and the preceding one. Note that on the plan, the doorway to the terrace is onto the front, whereas in the photo the front is all window at full height and the door put around the side.

Contributing to the penetration of light throughout the house is the single bar across the aperture on the left where the rear terrace is located, and the circular glass bricks in the floor to the right of the photo in front of the glazed full-height window. All of these features will reappear in our next discussion of Welz's architectural contributions: the double bar under Maison Zilveli in the garden area; the glazed bricks in the Villa Kolpa and the earlier Maison Dury roof terrace.

Maison Dubin. Front elevation roof terrace. Source: *La Construction Moderne*, op. cit.

What should be clear by now is the sheer complexity of the ascending route from the street — the Chemin Aérien — and what an achievement it is within the narrow confines of the site. Carrying on the building line from the Mallet-Stevens and Corbusier houses gives over half the site to the front garden (see ground floor plan, previous page).

The addition of maid-accommodation on the ground floor to the rear — which is also used to provide another terrace on the roof of the one-story extension — removes much of the sense in providing a rear garden, but the paved area giving access to the rear maid's room is used creatively with the addition of a sculptural water-feature, readily visible through the glass wall of the entry as well as from the first-floor terrace and the window of the living room area.

This elegant water-feature in the "cour" (courtyard), accessed through a door in the glazed wall to the rear of the hall area is one of several minor changes between the plans and the finished house, and it is striking in its final result. Note in the photo opposite the elegant shadow-gap below the fountain's front low enclosing wall seen both on the interior and exterior, the varied flagstones, and what appear to be four different colors of mosaic.

The compact nature of the plan achieved an extensive amount and variety of accommodation: fifteen rooms (including the garage and raised room adjacent to the main living-room) plus the large ground-floor hallway and open gallery, and including the front-to-back dining/music/living room with the last at double-height, and three terraces, the tiny cubic balcony and the courtyard with fountain, a washroom, maid's room, office, and two bathrooms. Maison Cook, though more spacious, has six rooms, one bathroom, one washroom and one terrace, across four floor-levels — Dubin has nine levels.

The Maison Dubin has received littlc, if any, attention, whereas the Corbusier house has had endless coverage. That is only to be expected, given Corbusier's eminence and the importance of the Five Points of Modern Architecture in his ideas of the 1920s, but the other factor is the relative anonymity of Adolf Loos's ideas, which have only become more familiar, in the English-speaking world, at least, around seventy years after the house was built.

At the time, there was little discussion of Loos's three-dimensional approach to the use of space, and even today one of the most discriminating guides in English to the architecture of Paris, despite a mention of Loos and the Raumplan,[18] dismisses the layout of the Maison Dubin with one word, "contorted."

Above: View from the roof terrace, Maison Dubin rear terrace and garden with sculptural water feature. Note the top of the water feature at the bottom of the photo, with what appear to be four different mosaic varieties, and the designed layout of the garden flagstones.

Below: Maison Dubin water feature on the rear terrace and garden.

Source for both: *La Construction Moderne*, op. cit.

To have managed to fit so much accommodation and in particular the subdivision of spaces for reception and leisure (card room, separate dining room, etc.)[19] into the relatively confined plot, at least speaks of skill in the use of space. To have combined that with a complex Chemin Aérien that provides a whole series of twists and turns, views and surprises from street to roof, along with the "gothic" penetration of light down the building, is a quite remarkable achievement. It is no wonder Fischer was well-pleased with the young Welz's contribution.

Number of rooms is no criterion for architectural excellence, even in a modest space, and the obverse criticism would be one of squeezing too much into one's first efforts, from an excess of enthusiasm. However, the program for the Maison Dubin shows a noteworthy complexity and subtlety.

There is undoubtedly more to be said about the design, and the fountain in the yard alone is worth more consideration and brings a classical dignity to a very tight garden space,[20] but in relation to its two closest "neighbors," the literal one next door and the metaphorical one of Loos's Moller house, it is at the very least a worthy companion, an auspicious debut for Jean Welz.

Yet in Welz's plan there are still references to Corbusier: while Moller goes from a confined entrance and stairway to an open and multi-level first floor, Dubin's entrance is much more open, akin to the Maison Cook, but using the open hallway, glazed full-height front and back, with a view on the yard and its fountain, as a more ambiguous start to the Aerial Way that ascends all the way to the third terrace to the rear of the top level.

It could be argued that Welz's interpretation of that directed route is, if anything, a more extreme version of the Raumplan than in the Moller house, which concentrates the varied levels on the first floor only, and even in Loos's later Müller house of 1930, regarded as the ultimate realization of Loos's ideas.[21] In also fulfilling the task of creating the "gothic" through-lighting that Raymond Fischer took from Loos's Bauschule, the Maison Dubin becomes a remarkable realization and synthesis of the Loosian spirit.

In relation to Corbusier's Five Points, the Maison Dubin, strictly speaking, has none of them. There are no circular pillars holding up the house, but the plan is opened out with a through view from the front garden entrance on the left of the facade and threshold of the open hallway via two full-height glazed walls to the sculptural fountain in the back courtyard.

With structural walls versus pilotis, the open ground-floor theme is inflected towards the New Space of the second-wave Viennese modernists, rather than as an observance of the Corbusian mantra.

On the floors above, there is no "long window" in a "free facade" curtain-wall, and where there is a large open-plan area, its character follows Loos, with the floor split into two multiple overlooking levels; although in also managing to create a double-height void on that first-floor level there is an echo of the Maison Cook next door, it is one that adds to the Loosian schema.

Likewise, although there is a roof terrace, in fact there are three distinct ones: a terrace at the front and a larger one at the rear at a half-level above, and from that, steps up to one on the roof at the front of the lower terrace — again an intense working-through of Loosian ideas that, in a way, upstages Corbusier by getting more into a similar envelope.

It would also be fair to say that the Maison Dubin is not subjugated to the New Space of the Loos/Strnad/Frank program, either.

The achievement of Dubin is to work with both sets of ideas but in such a way as to probe their validity and then tailor solutions suited to the particular nature of the site and the client brief. To demonstrate that level of discrimination and confidence rather confirms the view that Jean Welz was always "his own man" with his own ideas, and not beholden to anyone, however eminent, even at the age of twenty-seven.

It is not hard to understand how the Chemin Aérien that Welz created with the full support of Raymond Fischer should, as late as 2003, appear merely "contorted" in a context where Le Corbusier's Open Plan is highly familiar and Adolf Loos's architecture and ideas are less known, less appreciated and understood (as even Fischer admitted), and all the more so in 1928. Even today, despite the Loos revival of the last twenty or thirty years, his ideas are so different from what might be called mainstream modernism, and so difficult to read on plan, they can be quite difficult to grasp.

That a thorough application and development of them by an unknown young architect in an almost unremarked house next to Maison Cook, launchpad for the Five Points, has not been recognized should perhaps be no surprise.

What is surprising is that Jean Welz achieved — on his first opportunity —such an intensive and thorough program that is both a tribute to Adolf Loos and an implied critique of Le Corbusier, whilst at the same time adding his own distinctive contribution.

NOTES

1 In the third issue, January 1931.

2 From Zeller interviews.

3 In Zeller, p. 28: "*Les bow windows en surépaisseur que j'utilisais fréquemment me venaient de ce que j'avais vu en Autriche. Les autrichiens essayaient d'avoir des volumes creuses et des éleménts en saillie. C'est à travers Loos que j'ai été influencé par le mouvement cubiste.*" (The projecting bow windows that I used frequently came to me from what I had seen in Austria. The Austrians tried to have recessed volumes and projecting elements. It is from Loos that I have been influenced by the Cubist movement.) This influence can be seen most clearly in the M. St. Leger house at Marnes-la-Coquette) (1928).

4 Zeller, p. 37: "*Loos nous explique que c'était la grande difference qui existait entre l'architecture romane, où l'effet émotif était donné par le mur de pierre, et l'architecture gothique oú le volume du vide donnait l'effet de religiosité.*" (Loos explained to us the great difference that existed between romanesque architecture, where the emotional effect was achieved by the stone walls, and gothic architecture where the volume of the void gave an effect of religiosity.)

5 Christopher Long, *The New Space: Movement and Experience in Viennese Modern Architecture*. New Haven: Yale, 2016.

6 Long, *The New Space*, p. XIII.

7 It is in Zeller's Introduction where it is said to be his translation of Raumplan, but that term dates from 1931 and Fischer attended the Bauschule in 1920 and 1922, so it seems more likely to be Fischer's own term.

8 Maison Cook had a double-height studio overlooked by a balcony and the curved wall of the front terrace, a three-dimensional element that originated with Citrohan II, but the structure of the floors remains essentially two-dimensional. I owe this 3D observation on Le Corbusier to a conversation with Tim Benton.

9 One more level on the top floor is hidden and there are two levels on the ground floor, making nine in total.

10 The Villa Heim (1927–30) by Guevrekian, and "Les Peupliers" (1930) by Otto Bauer, who worked on the Tzara house for Loos, show some influence, but apparently not including Raumplan elements.

11 The plan drawing shows three steps, the finished house had four.

12 Dates given in Zeller, p. 107, presumably from the taped interviews he conducted with Fischer, now lost.

13 Benedetto Gravagnuolo, *Adolf Loos: Theory and Works*, Milan: Idea Books, 1982/1995, p. 194.

14 His remote instructions to Kulka for the 1932 Vienna Werkbundsiedlung houses. https://www.werkbundsiedlung-wien.at/en/houses/houses-nos-49-50-51-and-52

15 Martin Welz was my source for this, relayed to him by his mother Inger. Loos often stayed with Jean and Inger 1928–31 on his occasional visits to Paris, so Inger was well-placed to make that observation.

16 Kulka was born in 1900, like Welz, and briefly attended the same university in Vienna in 1919, and may have known Welz then.

17 A variant of the box idea was incorporated in Loos's 1931 Villa Winterniz (see Christopher Long, *Adolf Loos, The Last Houses.* Prague: Kant, 2020).

18 Andrew Ayers, *The Architecture of Paris*, Edition Axel Menges, 2003, p. 322.

19 This last observation I owe to Tim Benton.

20 It can be usefully compared to the funeral monument of 1930 for Marx's daughter — see Chapter 26, "A Tale of Three Monuments" — and will be compared to Welz's South African monument from the 1960s.

21 Christopher Long's work on the last houses of Loos put an interesting gloss on his thinking post-Muller. Loos seems to have preferred a simpler route, more transparent, a re-evaluation that parallels Le Corbusier turning away from his Five Points by the end of the 1920s. See Long, *Adolf Loos, The Last Houses.*

13

"UN NÈGRE VIENNOIS"

THE MAISON DUBIN IS CREDITED to "Raymond Fischer architect" on the plaque on the street. Fischer's generous comments about Welz's contribution, the "Collaborator" credit he gave Welz on this first project and the detailed look at the design for Maison Dubin suggest, however, that the main design elements came from Jean Welz, who after all had been appointed "chef de cabinet." Fischer included Welz among what were called commonly in Paris at the time "nègres viennois," brilliant young architects recommended to him by Loos. In this context "nègre" implies "ghostwriter."

That term brings up the question — was Jean effectively the main designer on all the Fischer projects he worked on during his tenure? According to Welz's family, Jean was wholly unambiguous: he was the designer, Fischer "the money-man."

Remember, Fischer gave Collaborator credit to Welz on two subsequent projects: the large block of "artisan" flats on the Rue Charonne (1930–32) (see page 85) — significant for an appraisal of Welz's abilities as a large-scale project that goes beyond the individual house — and the Montauban post-flood reconstruction works (1931) consisting of five small houses, a modest tenement and a slightly larger block of flats (further discussed in Chapter 16, "Inondation").

What did Fischer mean by the term *Collaborator*? In relation to the Montauban buildings, a dictionary entry on Fischer makes an interesting comment: "*L'influence de Loos est frappante dans les immeubles élevés à Montauban par l'agence Fischer, au point qu'il est permis de se demander si son collaborateur Jean Welz n'en est pas l'unique auteur.*"[1] (The influence of Loos is striking in the buildings erected at Montauban by the Fischer practice, to the point that it is permitted to ask if his *collaborator* Jean Welz is not the sole author. *My italics*).

Fischer himself confessed, "I do not hide that we feel the influence of Loos…the Tzara house…in the houses that he (Welz) designed for me [at] Montauban."[2] This suggests both that Fischer was not closely involved, but also quite happy that Welz let the influence of Loos play a part.

However, the Montauban designs are not even remotely comparable in complexity or sophistication to the Paris work — at least for the five modest houses and the small tenement. The houses were infill replacements for small flood-damaged two-story terraced houses, the tenement larger but just as modest. The small flat block is more interesting, especially the dramatic "flying roof" element that echoes the 1927 house designed by André Lurçat in the same street as a 1929 Welz design,[3] but the rest of the Montauban buildings do not approach the sophistication of the Paris designs.

Even if Welz was the sole author for Montauban, that does not mean the same would apply to Paris projects, where Fischer would have been much closer to them physically, but also in managing his clients for individual houses.

If we allow that it is possible that Jean Welz had a decisive input to the Collaborator projects, it is less clear in relation to a further seven projects completed between 1928 and 1932, during Jean's stay, all in and around Paris. For none of those does Fischer give *Collaborator* status to Welz.

It would stand to reason that either Fischer felt that Welz's role was a lesser one on these projects, or he had other reasons for keeping the credit, such as his standing with clients. It is still the case these days that the "name above the door" takes the credit for work done in his or her name in architecture. That has led to some famous ruptures where senior architects have felt they have received insufficient credit for their work, leading to them leaving and setting up under their own name.

Such a move would have been out of the question for Jean Welz, as he was not officially licensed as an architect in France, worked "on the black" and perhaps more importantly, he seems to have himself suggested that he was temperamentally unsuited to running an office. He appears to have been much more the "artist-architect" than the "entrepreneur-architect." He probably focused wholly on design-issues, leaving financial matters to Fischer, and was certainly aware that he would have been unsuited to taking on that management role.[4]

Fischer described his *equipe* as working as a team. He would come from the client with a list of their requirements: "Do you want to think from your side what we can do? Here is the terrain, the surface. Try to put it in the space."[5] That rather confirms Welz's version of the division into Fischer the "money man" and Jean the designer.

To reiterate, Jean Welz was Fischer's chef de cabinet, that means he was broadly in charge of design. The *agence* had Fischer's name on it, and it was he who went out to get commissions and dealt with the clients, and was the front man, with Jean the backroom boy. The explanation for the credits may basically be as simple as that.

However, the matter of credit is potentially complex, and the psychology involved can be at least as important as more practical issues. For example, in terms of personality was either man likely to claim credit where it was not due?

According to a grandson,[6] Fischer would entertain his two grandsons with tales of his exploits in the Resistance, but never made himself the hero. As an adult, this grandson, himself a leading business-man in France,[7] regularly had lunch with Fischer in the grand *bistrots* along the Boulevard St. Michel — not out of duty, but from the pleasure of his company as a highly-intelligent, very well-connected and very experienced politician as well as architect, and a charming man if perhaps less of a wit.[8] He never name-dropped and again never put himself at the center of his stories. Raymond Fischer, it seems, was not the kind of man to boast or make false claims.

In the Resistance, Fischer served under General Maurice Chevance-Bertin, the right-hand man of leader Henri Frenay. The General saluted Fischer "as an early collaborator of the clandestine Combat group [who] was entrusted by me with numerous important and delicate missions, which he always carried out, demonstrating calm courage and complete contempt for danger... In November 1943, he was assigned to the Secret Army of the Vercors... So he joined the 4th brigade and took part in the violent fighting of the summer of 1944. In short, a hero."[9]

However, Fischer's daughter, even in her nineties and with her own distinguished life and career, dryly declared her father was too young to admit having a family, always away on business and his rare time at home marked by broken pottery shards around the floor, as domestic arguments often involved the crockery. A researcher for a short bio on Fischer spoke to a post-war employee who was unwilling even to talk about his time with Fischer, as the issue of proper credit for the designs so infuriated him.[10]

According to those to whom I spoke that had met Welz in South Africa, even the idea that Welz would conceivably make claims for himself beyond what he had done, was the polar opposite of their experiences of his character (discussed in detail in Chapter 30, "A Solitary Adventure").

What can we deduce by looking at Fischer's work both before and after Jean Welz's tenure?

Before Jean Welz arrived, Fischer was credited with two modernist houses, the first a reconstruction of an existing building for the animal painter Jacques Nam. The building permit dates from early 1927, and it would seem likely that at least the design process pre-dated Welz.

The facade has the kind of plainness associated with the ideas of Loos (see page 83) but is raised on square pillars below and above has an element of asymmetry about the windows on the two floors above and a clear division from the top studio floor. The plan (see below) is very simple and would seem to be in Fischer's "Beaux Arts" hand.

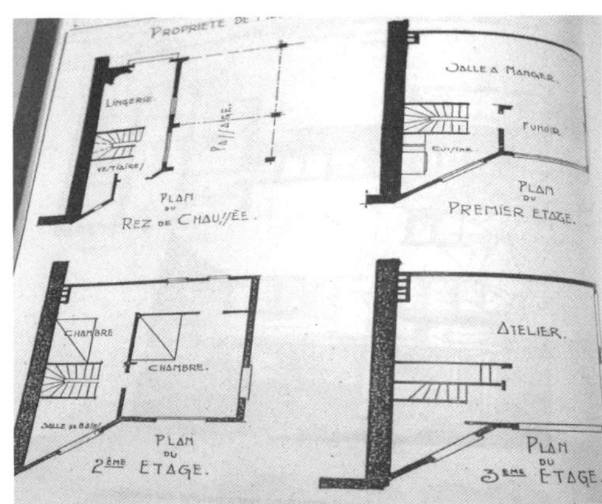

Left: Jacques Nam with cat. Source: *Jacques Nam 1881–1974*, ed. Jacqueline Cuzelin Guerret, babelio.com.

Right: Raymond Fischer, Nam House plan, 1927. Source: Raymond Fischer, *Villas et Petits Hôtels*, Paris: Charles Massin (1930).

As the project was a reconfiguring, it may be assumed that the floor plan could not be much changed.

The second project was the Maison Dury (1925–28, also known as Maison Carrée), a wholly new house. The facade again has a Loosian plainness and the windows are grouped symmetrically.

The design is neat but not exactly inspired.

The long gestation of the project suggests that Jean Welz may have come in at the end of the process, as there is a photograph in his portfolio of the Maison Dury roof terrace[11] (see also page 137).

The following five Fischer designs are, I would say, Fischer's best post-war houses. They are all broadly "modern," but in design-terms, to me, they are of quite a different order of sophistication to the pre-war buildings of 1929–32.

To the casual observer, it may be difficult to assess the post-war designs except for the obvious simplicity of the drawings, and Fischer's own house at least had the multiple levels we associate with Loos, although the only terms in which it has been described, rather sadly,

Raymond Fischer, Maison Dury (1925–28). Welz possibly worked on the roof terrace as images of the house were in his portfolio.

Left: rear-elevation; right, above and below: front view and roof terrace. All photos presumed to be by Thérèse Bonney, from the Welz portfolio, courtesy Jean-Louis Avril.

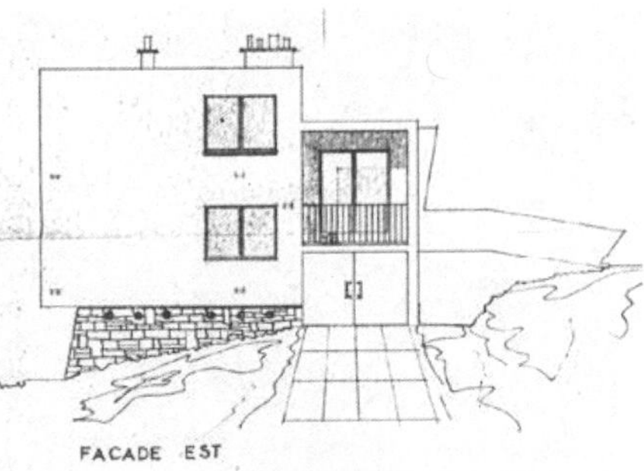

Raymond Fischer houses in Hirson. Source: Pierre-Yves Brest, "Raymond Fischer (1898–1988), Architekt," in *Allgemeines Künstlerlexikon (Thieme & Becker)*. Leipzig: Saur (2004). Courtesy Pierre-Yves Brest.

Top row, left: Maison Gerard (1952), Hirson.
Top row, right: Maison Brenon (1955–56), Hirson. Collaborator Paul Covez.
Center row, left: Maison Gontier (1957–59), Hirson.
Center row, right: Maison Foucart (1959–61), Hirson.
Below: Maison de l'Architecte (1964–65), Andresy.

Above: Villa Darmstadter (1932). Courtesy Welz family.

Below: Raymond Fischer, Villa Blumel (1938). Source: Gérard Cladel, Philippe Bodenan. *Raymond Fischer (1898–1988). Inventaires.* [Rapport de recherche] 574/89, Secrétariat de la recherche architecturale (SRA); Ecole Nationale Supérieure d'Architecture de Versailles, 1989, p. 57. hal-01905395.

is as "under the influence of Le Corbusier," which tends to be code in France for glass and concrete.

A perhaps more useful and direct comparison is between a house of 1932, the last one completed while Welz was still Fischer's Chief Architect, and one of 1938 that is after Welz's departure.

The framing device is similar, but the 1932 Darmstadter house has much better proportions and detailing so that the 1938 Villa Blumel looks like a clumsy copy of the idea, in contrast with the quiet elegance of the earlier house.

Any conclusions as to whether Jean Welz was the real designer has be provisional at this point — with only the first house-design looked at in any detail. However, the Maison Dubin does provide valuable clues, not least as it is the one that Fischer talked about most in his interviews in relation to Jean Welz's role.

We can recall that Fischer generously admitted that Welz both understood Loos's ideas better than he but also was better able to turn them into practice. The two skills are not synonymous. An ability to understand a philosophy of space is one thing. The ability to turn that into creative solutions, against the constraints and opportunities of a particular site, is quite another. The two go together much less often than the casual observer may imagine, and that would apply to any art form. The critic and the practitioner inhabit different worlds. It is an important point as it suggests that Welz, at the comparatively young age of twenty-seven, possessed both a strong critical intelligence and matching creative power, and that alone would make him stand out from the crowd, even among the Paris avant-garde.

Fischer was highly intelligent, but Loos's ideas are complex and many-sided, and can easily appear to be contradictory — adoring tradition and hating ornament, for example. However, it is to Fischer's credit that he grasped the Raumplan a decade before it got its name[12] to the extent that he seems to have actually came up with a more descriptive term for it in Le Chemin Aérien.

Fischer wrote a lot on architecture, whereas Welz wrote almost nothing. As discussed, Fischer's architectural ideas included favoring the vertical window over the horizontal, the use of color to replace ornament, the value of the penetration of light through the building, three-dimensional space-planning, the external massing of cubic shapes both projecting and receding, the free placement of stairs in contrast to the traditional straight route to the top of a building, and new construction methods making the well-designed "minimum flat" for workers more affordable.

Despite that range, there is a sense that most of those ideas are not his own, but adopted, like Perret's preference for the vertical window against Corbusier's use of the long horizontal window. On their own, they do not cohere into a personal design philosophy, and have more of the feel of a grab-bag among modernist themes. There is no doubt of his passion for modernism, and antipathy to the Beaux-Arts tradition but, for example, although he espoused the Open Plan as an idea, when it came to the crunch on arguably the most important design of his *agence*, even fifty years later he criticized Welz for wanting to take the Open Plan further than both he and his clients desired.[13] In this case at least, Fischer was a modernist on paper, but Welz was a modernist in practice.

This could be the nub of the issue — Welz was a designer through-and-through, his passion was to push ideas further, to create something new — in practice rather than words on paper. Fischer's skill was said to be in publicizing the ideas of others rather than originating his own.[14] The evidence from his houses, both before and after Welz, suggest the same in his architecture.

At this distance of time, and with the paucity of the kind of documentary and verbal evidence of which research can normally avail itself, it is well-nigh impossible to be definitive about who did what.

We have Fischer's list of his design themes, but they in themselves do not constitute the kind of coherence that we can see in the best designs of the period when Welz was chef de cabinet, and are absent from the period after his departure.

The approach in each case that follows is to work from the visual evidence provided by the buildings and plans, and the main reliance is upon what I have been able to extract from that. To my mind, I have to admit that the evidence favors Welz as the creative force.

At the Maison Dubin site a plaque credits Fischer as the architect, alongside Mallet-Stevens and Le Corbusier for the two earlier houses. Jean Welz, despite Fischer's credit to him as "Collaborator," is absent to this day.

NOTES

1 Brest, "Raymond Fischer (1898–1988), Architekt."

2 Zeller, p. 61.

3 Atelier Kielberg (1929), see Chapter 15, "House for an Artist."

4 In a 1972 talk Welz gave at the National Gallery in South Africa, he was very explicit that running a business was not his metier. He remarked that he saw that as at least half of architecture as a profession, so in that sense, he was a bad architect.

5 Zeller, pp. 62–63.

6 From a phone conversation in April 2017 with one of Fischer's two grandsons, who kindly called me from New York and we spoke for almost an hour.

7 With his brother, proprietors of Chanel.

8 In contrast, Corbusier described Jean as "a wit," with the sense of his being someone special.

9 Brest, and also published in the German dictionary *Allgemeines Künstlerlexikon* by De Gruyter.

10 Floreal Gonzalez. Information from a telephone conversation I had with Pierre-Yves Brest in 2016.

11 Confirmed by research in the Thérèse Bonney Archive, held by The Smithsonian.

12 In 1931, from Heinrich Kulka, Loos's main assistant.

13 Fischer's comment, quoted in Zeller.

14 Observation made in LR Cobos's dissertation.

OEUVRE
PART IV

Villa Darmstadter (1932), ground floor. The garden is to the left. Note the sculptural staircase with perforated metal sides and smooth underneath surface as well as the contrasting paint three-quarters up the pillars and walls. The three-quarter-height screen to the right shields the entrance door from the rear of the house. Courtesy Welz family.

14

THE PORTFOLIO

THE ONLY JEAN WELZ DOCUMENT that gives a clue as to what projects he actually worked on during the Paris years is itself something of a mystery. When he left Paris in late 1936, he had assembled a selection of black and white architectural photographs that he lettered from A to L, twelve projects in all. This was his portfolio, to show to prospective employers in South Africa.

Of the original twelve, there remain only eight in the folder, a loose-leaf affair. Over the years, the other four have been removed, but of those, three have since turned up in Paris. Some projects had two photographs, others up to four.

All the photos were mounted on thin card, a mid-blue for interiors and a mid-brown for exteriors. The letter-code was written on the backing cards, which were a larger size than the photos themselves.

The list order itself is a little enigmatic, as the logic is not immediately apparent. It is neither chronological, nor alphabetical in terms of the names of the projects. Neither does it seem to represent how big a role he played in the design, nor even which might be his favorite designs. Two of the twelve were his independent commissions aside from work for Raymond Fischer. I was stumped as to what he was thinking, until I went back to the list and suddenly I realized that I had probably been looking in the wrong place.

The first project in the list is the blocks of flats in the Rue de Charonne (1930–32). I had been thinking that he would have been most proud of the individual houses that would have given him more scope as a designer, and would surely therefore have listed them first. But his most impressive houses are at H and K in the list. Why would he have put them so far down the list?

The idea came to me that maybe the list was not about his favorite designs but perhaps ordered in order to appeal to what he thought might be prospective employers in South Africa. There might well have been no market by 1937, when he landed in Cape Town, for individual houses — however proud he might have been of their designs. It would, in that context, make sense to put the block of flats first. Perhaps someone had advised him that he would stand the best chance of work by showing his versatility in being able to design "minimum" flats economically and with the ingenious use of space he had demonstrated both in the Rue de Charonne flats and since his first opportunity at the Maison Dubin. The Rue de Charonne was also one of the projects for which Raymond Fischer had granted Jean *Collaborator* status, marking the extent of his contribution in his boss's mind, perhaps giving him plenty to talk about to a prospective employer; whether developer or architect.

That choice at least made sense, but returning to the letters that followed, matters were not helped by the letter B photo not being there — the first of the four missing letters. Furthermore, if there was an attempt at a commercial logic to the order, why would the only shopfront design be down the list at F?

Letters C, D and E were individual houses, but again not in chronological order, with the Maison Dubin, the first house he designed, at E.

Among the list were Welz's two independent commissions, but only his second, the Maison Zilveli (1933) remained in the file, at H, surrounded by three missing projects — and his first, the Maison Landau (1931) was one of those missing.

Perhaps, in the end, the order was random after the Rue de Charonne flats — a disappointment for the detective story and for expectations of fierce Teutonic organization.

The mystery of four missing slots was reduced when the first person to discover Jean Welz's work in Paris and who wrote the first article about him, Jean-Louis Avril, kindly showed me the documents he had been given when Jean's wife Inger visited him in Paris, with which he used to write his 1993 article.[1]

Three photos: of Maisons Landau, Dury, and St. Leger, had been taken by Inger Welz to Paris. Each one had the colored card backing that indicated they had been removed from the portfolio.

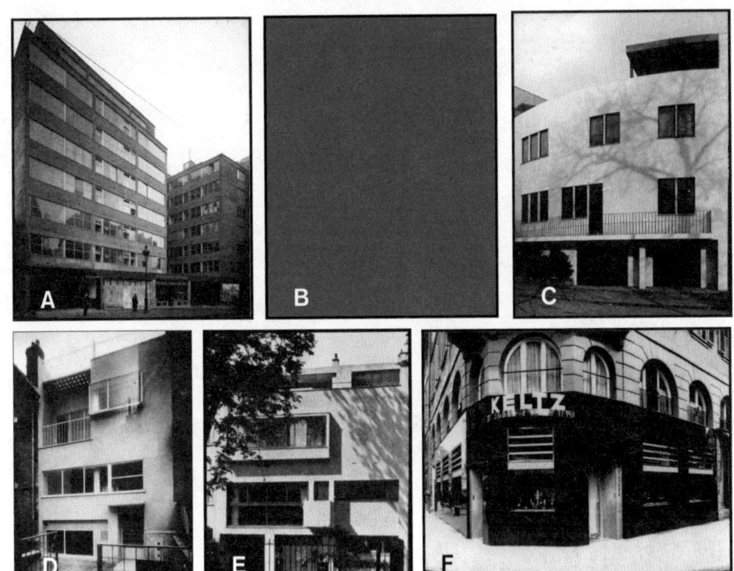

A: Rue de Charonne flats (1930–32) (two photos), Paris 11th arrondissement. **B**: ? (missing) **C**: Hôtel Godfray, Boulogne-Billancourt (1929)

D: Villa Kolpa (1929), Paris,19th arrondissement. **E**: Maison Dubin (1927–28), Boulogne-Billancourt (2 photos?) **F**: Keltz-Bloch shopfront, Strasbourg (1928?)

G: ? (missing) **H**: Maison Zilveli (1933), Paris, 19th arrondissement. (4 photos) **I**: ? (missing)

J: ? (missing) **K**: Villa Darmstadter, Vaucresson, (1932) (four photos) **L**: Gravestone for Karl Marx's daughter — Père Lachaise Cemetery (1930), (destroyed 1940)

Above: Maison Dury (1925–28). Possible contributions by Welz. Photo: Thérèse Bonney. From the Welz portfolio, courtesy Jean-Louis Avril.

Center: House at St. Cloud/Marnes-la-Coquette (1926–28). Possible contributions by Welz. Photos: M. Gravot. Source: Fischer, *Villas et Petits Hôtels*, Paris: Charles Massin (1930).

Below: Jean Welz, Maison Landau (1931). Welz's first independent commission. Courtesy Welz family.

These are the three photos that emerged in Paris via Inger:

1 Maison Dury (1925–28, also known as Maison Carrée): Jean could only have been involved in the latter stages after the exterior was designed, possibly on the roof-garden — and this one, in fact, had been left with Jean-Louis Avril in Paris.
2 House at St. Cloud/Marnes-la-Coquette for M. St. Leger (1926–28), later lauded for interior economy — as a "maison minimum." The exterior was designed by 1926,[2] before Welz worked for Fischer, and so if he was involved in the design it must have been on the internal layout — which was, interestingly, recently praised for its economy by a Greek architectural historian.[3]
3 Maison Landau (1931): Jean's first independent commission.

That left only one slot to be filled in the portfolio. It seems likely that was the Atelier Kielberg (for reasons discussed in the next chapter), for a Mr. M.F.K. Kielberg (1929): a dramatic front elevation, and drawings in Welz's hand of the interior plan.

A further enigmatic factor is that beside the "lettered" black and white photographs, there were also a number of others that were loose, not mounted on card, nor with a letter-code written on them. It would seem likely that also they represented projects Welz had worked on in some capacity, but perhaps not as principal designer.

The best-known of that group was the Mallet-Stevens house, which is the architect's own house, completed in 1926. That would tally with Welz working there for three months after the *Art Deco* exhibition of 1925, which closed that October (and from Guevrekian, we know he was to work with Loos by April 1926), but as some kind of relatively-lowly assistant, as the design was by Mallet-Stevens and predating the period Jean could have worked on it. It may have also been that he worked alongside his Vienna classmate, Gabriel Guevrekian, who had already worked for Mallet-Stevens for some years.

Keltz-Bloch jewelery shop, with detail of corner entrance, from the Welz portfolio. Courtesy Welz family. Photographer unknown.

The rest of the "loose" photographs cover six projects, two or possibly three were on the lettered list:

1. The Maison Zilveli (1933), his last work in Paris.
2. The Keltz-Bloch shopfront — a further four photographs.
3. A view through a twenty-five-panel window onto a roof terrace with trees beyond — which could possibly be the Hôtel Godfray (1929).
4. Another possible is an interior photograph that is an artist's studio, which is the Atelier Kielberg (1929).
5. One not on the list is an interior for the newspaper *La Liberté* — there are drawings by Welz as well as the photo of the completed interior (1929). The connection to *La Liberté* is also important as it was in that newspaper that Welz published his only article, also in 1929, one which praises Le Corbusier's Salon d'Automne interior to the skies, and gives some rare, in fact, unique, hints of Welz's own philosophy, such as the phrase "any addition without a use harms pure form."
6. The last items are two photos of an apartment interior (see Chapter 3, "The Tradouw Pass"). Inger Welz said that Loos handed smaller jobs like that to Jean on occasion, and there is the story from Jerome, the oldest boy, of meeting a Mr. Oppenheimer, for whom he was told his father had designed a double-flat in the Avenue Foch, although there is no other confirmation of the story.

When Inger Welz visited Paris in the 1990s, she also took with her a third independent but unbuilt project with a plan and a sketch, the Maison Rire (1933), a discussion and images of which follow at the end of this chapter.

In addition, there was the splendid large drawing for a sanatorium at Mont d'Or, a hotel sketch — for Loos — at Juan Les Pins (1931) (see page 308), and the set of drawings Jean did for his entry for the 1937 Paris exhibition's Austrian Pavilion, which was not selected (see Chapter 21, "Mont d'Or and Pavillon d'Autriche," featuring these two buildings).

If we assume that Jean took with him photographs of all the important projects he worked on, with the twelve on the lettered list,

Above: Welz drawing (deduced from the style), *La Liberté* newspaper offices, redesign, 1929. Courtesy Welz family.

Below: Welz interior for *La Liberté*. Courtesy Welz family via Jean-Louis Avril.

the seven in Montauban,[4] the Maison Dury, *La Liberté* newspaper offices, and the unidentified flat conversion, that brings his total oeuvre to twenty-four projects,[5] plus drawings for a further three.[6] Twenty-seven projects in Paris between 1928 and 1936, with twenty-four of those between 1928 and 1933.

MAISON RIRE

The drawing for Maison Rire is dated 1933, which possibly suggests it post-dated the Maison Zilveli, which was built in that year.

There are detailed plans for a two-story house and a pen and ink drawing by Welz (see following page). The shape is rectangular, twenty meters long by 6.7 meters deep, and the drawing features a view of the open-plan nature of the dining/living/"hall" area, with eight full-height glass windows (including double-doors at the far end of the drawing) onto the garden.

The house appears to be a modest one, the layout not unlike the Maison Landau (to be discussed), but with a greater open plan area that takes most of the ground floor, and the feature given the emphasis in the drawing. Almost the whole of the rear of the house is open onto the garden and with the full-height windows and doors, would bring a great deal of light into that ground floor.

The dining and living areas flow into each other on the front side of the house, leaving the large "hall" area, as it is called on the plan, facing the garden. The only feature on that side is a sofa, enclosed on three sides, echoing a Loosian feature of the kind found in an ingle-nook, but here, as it were, updated to provide a comfortable seating area diagonal to the garden but with views of it down the eight full-height doors and windows.

The double doors are by the sofa, and at the opposite end of the house another pair of doors, facing the sofa, that let onto a covered terrace, which has above it a larger open terrace that would overlook the garden.

The Maison Rire is a deceptively simple design whose focus appears, like Darmstadter, to be towards the garden, in this case to the rear of the house.

The big open-plan layout on the ground floor, complemented by the double height over the dining and living area would have created dramatic spaces from simple means and an openness that again moves away from the main body of Loos's work towards the Corbusian openness, extending from the double-height space in the Villa Cook to the larger Villa Stein-de-Monzie, and culminating in the Villa

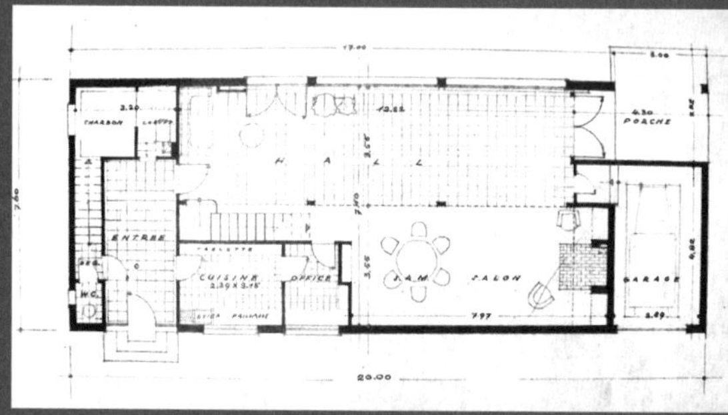

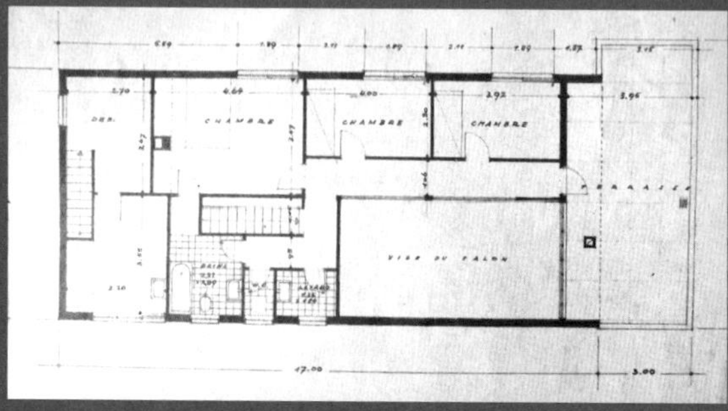

Above: Jean Welz, Maison Rire (1933), interior sketch. Unbuilt. Courtesy Welz family.

Center and below: Jean Welz, Maison Rire (1933), ground floor and first floor plans. Unbuilt. Courtesy Jean-Louis Avril.

Savoye. The Maison Rire, in a simple rectangle, like the Maison Landau, created vertical height and horizontal distance — both featured in the simple pen and ink drawing Welz no doubt used to show the client how the house would look internally.

We have no facade renderings, but the simplicity and thoroughness of the conception all work to create a house conceived from the inside out, as it were, with the facades being the functional outcomes of the internal creation of spaces, and in that one might see it as applying Loosian thinking (from the inside out) to a Corbusian philosophy (of the Open Plan).

NOTES

1 Jean-Louis Avril, *Le Moniteur Architecture — AMC*, no. 38 February 1993, pp. 35–38.

2 See maquette photo dated 1926 in Chapter 11 "Raymond Fischer."

3 Anthony C. Antoniades, "Masterpieces/Meritpieces," *Mag11/ Hydra*, Nov. 2005.

4 See Chapter 16, "Inondation — Montauban, 1931."

5 The Loos hotel excluded as it was a Loos design for which Jean prepared a sketch.

6 The Maison Rire, the Mont d'Or sanatorium and the 1937 Austrian Pavilion entry — all unbuilt. See Chapter 21, "Mont d'Or and Pavillon d'Autriche" on the last two large projects.

15

HOUSE FOR AN ARTIST

AFTER THE SUCCESSFUL COLLABORATION on the Maison Dubin, Jean worked for Raymond Fischer whenever he got commissions. He occasionally worked for others, such as Jean Ginsberg and Loos,[1] but Fischer was his main employer. Fischer had rented office space opposite Marcel L'Herbier, the film director[2] and would sublet when there was no work — his renting to a left-wing German newspaper apparently brought the Gestapo to the door the day after they arrived in Paris in 1940. His *agence* does not seem to have been a wholly permanent affair, and it depended upon young freelance Viennese and French architects. Unlike Le Corbusier, Fischer was not a star name and his commissions varied in terms of the potential for Jean Welz to suggest design ideas. There are three modern houses that seem to have been completed in the same year as the Maison Dubin, 1928, and with varied results.

The first, chronologically, began in 1925, before Welz arrived, and took three years to reach completion. The Maison Dury's facade, which seems to have been set before Welz started work for Fischer, can be seen as a kind of orthodox Loosian approach at least in banishing ornament.

Jean-Louis Avril pointed out to me the three main windows had some similarity to Welz's own Maison Landau of 1931, but my sense is that the latter's windows were more a result of practical limitations[3] and Dury's design would seem to predate Welz's arrival chez Fischer.

Jean came late to this project and perhaps the main suggestion of his involvement is a roof terrace photograph in his portfolio. The roof terrace as completed is arguably the most architectural feature of the house.

The circular glass inserts in the floor appear again in later designs, and this is the first where they appear (also in Dubin of the same year), but whether that is Welz or Fischer is hard to determine, although the timeline would support the idea that it was a Welz addition. (If the room below was dark, it could have been an afterthought to the main design, a finishing touch to the top floor.)

The second house was for a M. St. Leger and the maquette dates from 1926 when it was shown at the Salon D'Automne, again, some time before Welz joined.

There was an attempt, noticeable in the maquette, to emphasize the variation of planes through the use of color — darker on the recessed area (see Chapter 11, "Raymond Fischer"). Those ideas tie in with Fischer mentioning in his interviews of the late 1980s a similar theme as his notion of a kind of "cubism." As built, it seems the whole was finished in white which reduces the effect. It has been noted much more recently that the internal layout was a model for the "maison minimum" in its economy.[4] As economy of layout was the contribution Welz made to the Rue de Charonne flats, it may be that he worked on the layout of the St. Leger house at the Parc du Marnes.

The ground floor has an open-plan linking the dining-room (1) with the living-room (2). It is possible that through-flow was Jean's

Thérèse Bonney photograph, SIL-SIL-Bonney-GTE074-A, France, 1925–28. Maison Carrée, Marcel Dury residence, 11, rue de Belvédère, Boulogne-Billancourt. Roof terrace. Louis Raymond Fischer (1898–1988), architect, obtained from Smithsonian Libraries and Archives. © The Regents of the University of California.

idea, but Fischer was interested in Open Plan ideas to a certain extent.[5] There is also no double-height space, a theme in four Welz designs, but that could be that the bones of the design were already decided before Welz was involved — very likely given the maquette is dated 1926. For example, the upper floor has four bedrooms and two bathrooms, including a master-bedroom with dressing room and sitting-room attached in one suite. As a client requirement, that would not readily allow a double-height space without sacrificing bedrooms. The constraints of the (1926) external floor plan do not allow too much flexibility, but the final layout at least has clarity and concision.

Jean's contribution to both these houses would seem to be relatively minor, and the houses lack the visual appeal of what was to follow.

The third house is the Hôtel Godfray, which shows more flair, and on a difficult site, than the first two:

Although the front has the Loosian plainness, it has a visual appeal lacking in the other two, dividing the street level from the upper floors with a balcony around the first floor. As we will see, this may be a precursor of the Atelier Kielberg of the later year, although in this case the entrance is on the ground floor and the terrace would seem to have more of a visual role in reducing the massing of the three floors — separating the ground floor services from the upper floors — than a particularly practical one, as it is onto the street and not too attractive to use. The feeling of variety is greatly increased by a simple strategy: the windows on either side are stacked one floor above another, but the middle grouping has an offset, an asymmetry that has the door linked to a window above but the lower windows ranged left and the upper one ranged right. As the terrace is more formal than hugely practical, the door onto it also serves in the

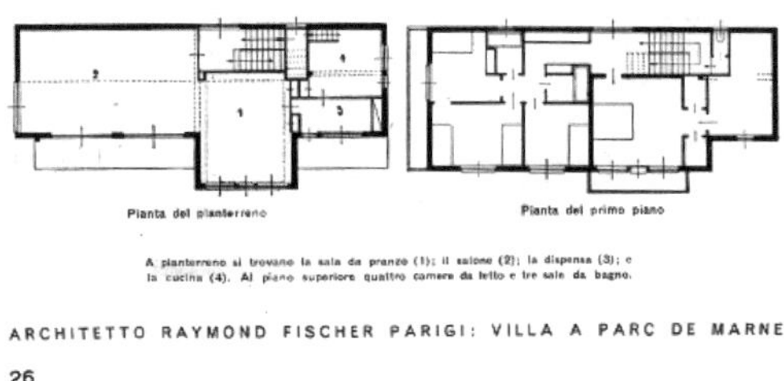

A pianterreno si trovano la sala da pranzo (1); il salone (2); la dispensa (3); e la cucina (4). Al piano superiore quattro camere da letto e tre sale da bagno.

ARCHITETTO RAYMOND FISCHER PARIGI: VILLA A PARC DE MARNE

26

House at St. Cloud/Marnes-la-Coquette (1926–28). Source: Bruno Moretti, *Ville*, Milano: Hoepli (1952). (Author collection.)

creation of the asymmetry that relieves what could otherwise be a monotonous facade.

The roof terrace is visible from the front and uses a contrast in color, which again reduces the massing from four floors to two — emphasizing the horizontal curve that is visually the best feature. Contrasting color was certainly a Fischer idea, although again that may be Welz implementing a Fischer theme.

The internal layout is very simple and probably predates Welz's involvement, as the lettering on the plan is more Beaux Arts than Welz's style, and similar to the Jacques Nam house plans that also predated Welz's arrival.

However, the discreet placing of the middle windows and door that just about departs from symmetry and in comparison relieves the tedium of the Dury facade, suggests that perhaps Jean had a role, including the balcony across the whole of the front, with small changes yielding worthwhile visual rewards.

The following year, 1929,[6] saw two contrasting houses, the Villa Kolpa and Atelier Kielberg, both featured in Fischer's publication, a

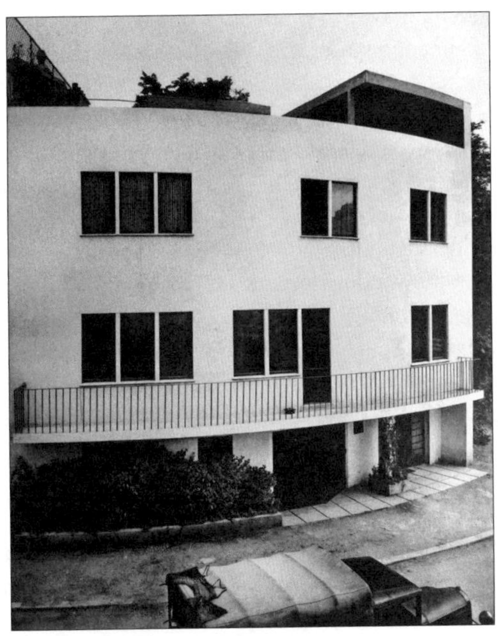

Hôtel Godfray (1928–29). Note: differing dates given by Fischer.
Source: Roger Poulain, *Villas Modernes*, Paris: Vincent, Fréal et Cie (1931).
The image of this project from the Welz portfolio is from the right.

prestige folder *Villas Modernes*,[7] of 1930. Kolpa was described as "a mid-priced house" and was one of a terrace, like Dubin, except the terrace was longer and the plot appears to have been an infill site, set among traditional designs.

The key point here is that these two houses were designed during Welz's era chez Fischer, and the differences, to my mind, are both substantial and important.

Villa Kolpa combined Loos with Corbusier in the sense that the first floor, or piano nobile, had a fenêtre-longue/long window, whilst featuring two levels of floor joined by a few steps. The placement of the long window so that it served the two levels was a unique feature.

Where the Maison Dubin had full-height windows on the first floor next to Corbusier's neighboring long window, Kolpa had no such neighbor to set a precedent and therefore perhaps could afford to try a play with a long-window — but adding the design challenge of matching that external feature with a contradictory interior of two floor levels.

The internal layout on the first floor was open-plan (and the area featured in most photos of the house) aided by a single internal pillar replacing load-bearing walls. It is also worth noting the round pillar in the foreground of the interior picture. Where Corbusier used pillars in the Dom-Ino structure towards the edges of the floor, here it is in the middle of the floor, used in order to open the middle of the floor up, obviating the need for load-bearing walls, which can still largely play that role here in the outside walls.

There is also a square pillar just behind the long-window on that floor, permitting the window to continue uninterrupted Corbusier-style, but square rather than his favored circular type.

Both pillars suggest a lack of dogmatism on Welz's part — a willingness to use what suits a particular purpose without being constrained by a credo. The square pillar matches the verticals of the long window and the round internal pillar has no sharp corners to navigate around in the open space.[8]

The "box" window of Dubin appears again in Kolpa, and the recessed balcony on the floor above has a ceiling perforated with circular glass inserts (cf. Maison Dury), bringing light from above whilst preserving the flat roof as an open terrace — which, again, makes a contrast with the traditional designs of both the rest of the terrace and the terrace opposite (not pictured), across not a road but a narrow pedestrian impasse.

Above: Villa Kolpa, Paris (1929). Note the roof terrace with glass inserts.
Photo: M. Gravot. Source: Fischer, *Villas et Petits Hôtels*.

Below: Villa Kolpa (1929), interior.
Photo: M. Gravot. Source: Fischer, *Villas et Petits Hôtels*.

The combination of two of Corbusier's Five Points (long window and roof terrace) with Loos's multiple floors (six levels over a basically three-floor house) is not just well-achieved but adds considerably to the variety of the first floor layout. While the budget was mid-price and the site not of great depth, the design uses the front facade to show how the long window can be used in a different relationship with the internal layout than Corbusier used, for example, in the Maison Cook.

Kolpa is both freed from the constraints of a famous next-door neighbor and from the stricter plainness of Loos's houses that sets out to make the exterior not an expression of the internal layout.

Where Loos, as Christopher Long writes,[9] privileges the internal three-dimensional design, with the exterior being consequential to those decisions; with Kolpa, the facade expresses the different levels — for example, the basement window next to the front door — while also achieving the trick of a long horizontal window that manages to accommodate two levels internally.

The ability to combine a facade that is coherent formally in itself, with a three-dimensional interior, is something that would mark Welz's achievement. Putting together elements of a Corbusian elevation with a Loosian interior is not something I am aware of other architects doing, and almost certainly not by the age of twenty-nine, as with the case of the Villa Kolpa.

Kolpa is also a "white" facade, with a resolutely modern appearance; the box window here serves to emphasize asymmetry in contrast to the surrounding facades that are in traditional red brick or stone. These strategies could be seen as a deliberate statement that was tailored to this particular location and site — an impasse of around twenty houses among which it sticks out as the only modern one — white among a sea of red brick and tufa stone. In other words, the design can be seen in contrast to what surrounds it — while Dubin followed Maison Cook's roof line but made certain variations in the facade in the very different context of the modernist houses by Mallet-Stevens and Corbusier.

The well thought-out reaction to the properties of a site — the disadvantages as well as the advantages — is a feature of Jean Welz's work, perhaps most extreme in his last house, the Maison Zilveli. It is also dramatically demonstrated in the Atelier Kielberg, also of 1929.

The original plot was in fact two adjacent sites, and the facade makes dramatic use of its available length by creating projections and

Above: Atelier Kielberg (1929).
Photo: M. Gravot. Source: Fischer, *Villas et Petits Hôtels*.

Below: Atelier Kielberg, rear facade.
Photo: M. Gravot. Source: Fischer, *Villas et Petits Hôtels*.

recesses with an elegant and commanding presence on the street, something that was altogether lacking in the St. Leger house, for example. The horizontality is emphasized by the terrace, as with the Hôtel Godfray, here to greater effect as the variety of projections and voids creates a stunning two stories above the terrace.

The scale of the facades would suggest it is set in extensive grounds to the front, whereas in fact it is directly onto the end of a short narrow cul-de-sac. It is a very commanding presence in the street scene and makes the most of the available facade length.

The artist's studio has a large glazed area with a sloping roof, all set back in a recess. A terrace runs all the way across the facade at the bottom of the studio glazing at first floor level, uniting the two sides of the building — the studio to the left with the residential accommodation to the right, and continuing across to a grand entrance. That is also recessed, with a canopy above formed from a projecting balcony effectively hooding the entrance.

The front entrance is noteworthy as an unusual combination of elements. Access to it is provided by the stairs to the ground floor, but instead of them jutting out from the front door to the street, they are attached to the longitudinal balcony/terrace and in the same plane, which is parallel to the facade rather than at ninety degrees to it. Formally, the staircase adds to the lengthwise emphasis the balcony provides, and uses the terrace as the access from the stairs to the front door arrangement.

The entrance and balcony are themselves quite wide with full height glazing to the balcony room, finishing at the same top height as the studio glazing to the left. A further window in similar glazing style is inserted to the right, with a similar window on the floor below it.

The terrace and diagonal stairs at ground floor level echo Corbusier's Villa Stein-de-Monzie rear elevation, but here create a grand entrance from the street to the recessed and hooded front door.

The ground floor facade was tiled in small square white tiles with dark grout and a wide folding garage door below the artist studio, with two narrow tall doors either side of it and a third further along to the right by the start of the stairs.

The ensemble of elements is both impressive visually and on the street and tightly composed.

The composition of the rear facade is also unusually varied, with a recessed plane across the whole of the non-studio area to the left of the rear facade. The aperture at ground level is filled with a series of full-height glazed doors onto the garden but also protected by the recess that is repeated above and forms a roofed area, again penetrated by circular glass inserts bringing light from above while forming the floor to an open terrace of the same width, divided into two wide glazed doors set onto it from the rooms behind, and with some protection against the weather from above provided by concrete projecting beams, which may have been intended to be covered by fabric when needed.

The clean lines of the rear facade composition are just as striking as the front, and together create a uniquely rhythmic pair of facades that have something of the reticence of the Viennese style, but given the play with projections and recesses, create a dynamic long facade that is interesting to compare to the Villa Stein-de-Monzie of Corbusier.

In terms of an alternative modernism to the Five Points, here we have a composition unlike any other contemporary modernist houses in Paris or indeed Vienna.

If we compare the front elevation of Kielberg to the rear of Stein-de-Monzie (see below), it can be argued that on a much more restricted site, the Welz design is both a tighter composition in the way it uses the stairs, and more complex in its massing — the recessed artist's studio and the projecting front door hooded entrance with balcony above.

The rear of Kielberg is again arguably a tighter use of the space and the open area to the left, more controlled than the same open area at Stein-de-Monzie — at least in basic visual terms. Of course, it would be fair to admit Corbusier had a much larger site with the ability to be expansive, compared to a very tight sight for Kielberg.

If we compare the front elevation of Stein-de-Monzie to that of Kielberg, it is much lesss relieved and varied in terms of massing.

Le Corbusier, Villa Stein-de-Monzie (1928) left to right: rear and front elevations.
© Fondation Le Corbusier.

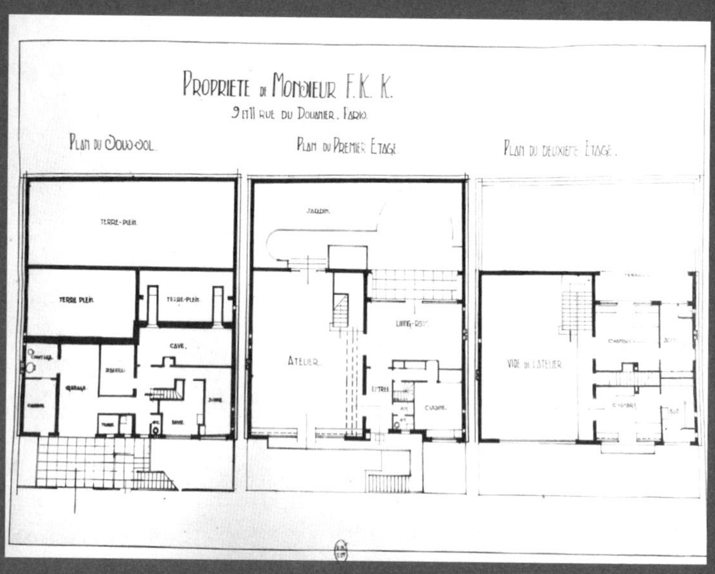

Above: Floor plans for Atelier Kielberg (1929), drawn by Jean Welz.
Below, left: the Kielberg Studio; below, right: the Living Room with furniture by Thonet.
Photos: M. Gravot. Source: Fischer, *Villas et Petits Hôtels*.
Originally published in *L'Architecture d'Aujourd'hui* no 3, Jan–Feb 1931.

Stein-de-Monzie is basically a flat facade whereas the whole rhythm of Kielberg is really more lively and expressive. The use of glazing is likewise much more varied and not restricted to the long windows that take up the first and second floors at Stein.

Both front and rear, the greater variety at Kielberg creates an arguably more satisfying composition of masses, and on a much tighter site — on a visual level at least.

If we move to the interiors what do we find? The Kielberg house as having been designed for an artist[10] features a profusion of double doors on the main floor — the entrance to the house and to the studio; the hallway to the studio both at the front and through the double doors to the living room also has a further set of double doors to the studio; and finally the living room has double doors to the rear onto the garden.

Although the Kielberg first floor is "open" in the sense of a large studio area without pillars[11] and a large living room the same, it is not Open Plan in the Corbusian sense and the interior does not have the expansive layout. That may have been a client requirement to have doors between rooms.

The Kielberg site seems to have been built on fully in that it was dug out at the rear for a void or storage area at the lower level, and the raised first floor at the front is on the same level as the garden at the rear, seemingly created on top of the storage area below.

The front staircase and balcony serve as the entrance to the main floor of the house and its two main rooms — the Atelier and the entrance hall leading to the Living Room. However, all these elements are accessed by the series of double doors rather than the conventional single door, and there are no changes in level, no small flights of stairs linking different levels on the same floor, no Chemin Aérien.

From the point of view of the Five Points, then, the Kielberg house is more Viennese, one might say, with banquettes under the front windows of the Studio and another in the living room, a familiar feature of Loos interiors. Two sets of double doors into the Studio, one from the front hall and one from the rear hall, separated by a further set of double doors as entrance to the Living Room close off the rooms — instead of the open flow in the Corbusier plan from the front Library to the rear Living Room and then into the Dining Room.

None of the Five Points appear in this house, which is clear from an initial glimpse from the street, with its large glass expanses — not a Viennese feature, although of course, it is functional rather than stylistic here in serving the artist's studio. (The interior photos on completion also suggest it is being used as a living-room rather than as an artist's studio.)[12]

The external staircase, balcony and white painted walls might suggest it is a Corbusian design. A little longer inspection would suggest otherwise — the massing and use of projections and recesses, the functional role of the balcony and stairs, the double doors (more for a sense of spaciousness than a practical feature for an artist), the hooded entrance functioning as a balcony above, are all tightly composed but with load-bearing walls, no horizontal windows, no pillars below or roof garden above.

The Kielberg is a large white house but one that has the quality of exterior visual flair we will see in two later key houses — Zilveli (Welz's second independent commission) and the Villa Darmstadter.

Raymond Fischer said, as late as December 1987, that he had taken from his Viennese trips a sense of the use of massing in a "cubist" sense, by which he seems to have meant the relief and recession of blocks within a design to create a facade that was not flat but had cubes of various sizes and shapes projecting or receding. In Loos's houses the only sense of that, for example on the Moller and Müller facades, was the use of a balcony at first floor level with an element of recessed wall behind it.

One may imagine Fischer talking of this theme to Welz, who then had the license to come up with his own variation on the theme, which can be seen rather more clumsily at the St. Leger house at Parc du Marnes (see the 1926 Salon D'Automne maquette in Chapter 11, "Raymond Fischer," pre-Welz), and in a much more elegant and refined version at the Kielberg atelier.

Le Corbusier, Villa Stein-de-Monzie (1928), Open Plan interior.

The difference between these two designs arguably speaks volumes in comparing Welz's period with Fischer, with those before or after. It also may tell us something of the relation between Fischer's themes and Welz's designs.

Jean would have had no objection to the "cubist" idea, taken from Vienna, but certainly in Kielberg he made it very much his own, unlike anything in Loos or indeed from his two tutors, Strnad and Frank. Here, he develops the blocky cubes of the St. Leger maquette into a much more sophisticated, dramatic and tightly-planned sequence of shapes and functions.

The interior is more conventional than an Open Plan layout would dictate. The large double-height Studio, the two balconies serving the two bedrooms on the second floor, and the rear one sheltering the full-height and full width glazing to the garden entrance,[13] and the front one sheltering the double front-door, all have a functional elegance that goes beyond the limits Welz had on the Maison Dubin, and suggest a different set of modernist rules rather than merely falling away from the Five Points.

Even though there was perhaps no opportunity to vary floor-levels internally, the idea of raising the back garden to the level of the living-room, and giving that room full-width and full-height glazing with another double-door onto the garden, is a smart functional variant of the use of levels, with the void below available for use as storage.

This combination — of how well Jean was able to integrate function and the efficient planning of internal space with a striking external composition — raises the quality of the Kielberg design to quite a height. It is a distinctive creative combination of Viennese and Corbusian elements, but goes well beyond that to create what appears to me to be one of the best-looking modernist designs in the Paris of its time.

A rich client and the freedom to design a house "for an artist," perhaps in reality for a businessman with an art collection, seems to have allowed Welz to show an originality and flair that the various constraints of the earlier houses did not permit.

NOTES

1 For Loos, 1931 Hotel design at Juan Les Pins, unrealized, the drawing has Welz-style trees (see page 308). Also see the photo of Ginsberg & Lubetkin's 25 Rue de Versailles flats of 1931, in Chapter 1, "Jean Welz Does Not Exist," as referred to in Chapter 17, "The Maison Landau."

2 A friend of Mallet-Stevens, whom he asked to do the decors for *L'Inhumaine*, which Loos helped at a screening of, in the company of Tristan Tzara in 1924. Loos was so impressed by the decors of the film that he wrote an article for the Viennese press on the potential of cinema in relation to modern architecture.

3 Welz's tight budget meant he used the largest off-the-shelf windows available, probably to get as much light in as possible for the money, and that would have determined their facade layout — more windows might well have required a steel joist above to support the roof, whereas with three, the masonry pillars between them could take the load.

4 By the Greek architectural historian Anthony Antoniades.

5 He criticized Welz for taking it too far, in his opinion, as he favored rooms that could be shut off — see Chapter 18, "Villa Darmstadter."

6 Dates are drawn from three Raymond Fischer sources: Zeller (1992), "Inventaires" research paper based on Fischer interview from November 27, 1984, by Gerard Cladel & Philippe Bodenan (Feb 1989, Ecole d'Architecture de Versailles), and the Pierre-Yves Brest dictionary entry. The first two show some variations in Fischer's memory of dates e.g. the Hôtel Godfray in this chapter.

7 Roger Poulain, *Villas Modernes, Raymond Fischer*, Paris: Vincent, Fréal et Cie, 1930.

8 A feature that appears again in the Maison Zilveli.

9 In Christopher Long, *Adolf Loos, The Last Houses*, Prague: Kant, 2020.

10 (Sir) (Ferdinand) Michael Kroyer-Kielberg was in fact chairman of United Molasses. It seems his wife bought a Pissarro in the same year as the house was completed, but also that year they began the biggest country house built in Britain between the wars (completed 1938), designed by an English architect of an earlier generation (William Curtis-Green, 1875–1960), responsible for the Dorchester Hotel and Wolseley car showroom on Piccadilly (now a famous restaurant). The "studio" may have been intended to show off their collection, with the light it would have allowed in, but Raymond Fischer does not seem to have discussed the commission beyond the barest facts. I have found no reference to the house in accounts of the Kielbergs.

11 There are two slim pillars centrally placed, one alongside the staircase entrance, the other below it in the same position (but only shown in the plan of the floor above — in the "void"), and another in a similar position in the living room.

12 *L'AA* December 1930 no.2 has two interior photos — the studio and the salon.

13 The photos suggest the living room was divided, creating a narrow loggia onto the garden with the shallower living-room area behind perhaps used as a dining room, as it was off the kitchen. If the studio was used as a large living-room that would make more sense. Perhaps the glazed wall onto the garden was felt to be too cold for a living room?

16

INONDATION — MONTAUBAN, 1931

I TRAVELED TO MONTAUBAN in the summer of 2016, visiting the city archives, a trip that paid off a full two years later when I inspected photos I had taken — of faded plans that looked as though they had not been touched since they were deposited in 1931. I only made a small discovery, but in the way that things have somehow constantly tied in with other little clues along the way, this one spoke to me of something about Welz's ideas, and for example his differences from Le Corbusier.

Montauban, in Southwest France, north of Toulouse, suffered flooding in 1930 from the river Tarn that runs through its center. Raymond Fischer was called in, presumably through his political contacts, to rebuild seven houses and flats near the riverbank and a dozen or so houses in the countryside nearby.

One point of particular interest about the seven is that Fischer credited Jean Welz as collaborator, and (as quoted in Chapter 13), "The influence of Loos is striking in the buildings erected at Montauban by the Fischer practice, to the point that it is permitted to ask if his collaborator Jean Welz is not the sole author." That is the first mention I had seen in print of the notion that Fischer credits might in reality belong to Welz, underlined by Fischer's notable accreditation phrase, "...the houses that he [Welz] designed for me [at] Montauban."

The houses and flats concerned were modest and clearly on a very limited budget, perhaps with the exception of one small block of six flats — of which decent photographs were taken at the time.

The one bit of architectural flair is the flying roof in the center of the roof terrace, flanked by chimneys. It is reminiscent of a feature on

Above: Jean Welz (for Raymond Fischer), flats with flying roof element (1930–32), 137 Quai Adolphe Poult, Montauban. Street facade. Source: Cladel, *Inventaires.*

Center: André Lurçat, Villa Guggenbühle, Paris (1927). Source: *L'Architecte*, no.1 1928, Plates 11–13, via portaildocumentaire.citedelarchitecture.fr.

Below: 137 Quai Adolphe Poult, rear elevation from the courtyard. Source: Zeller.

the (1927) Lurçat house at the end of the street where the Atelier Kielberg was built in 1929 (see Chapter 15, "House for an Artist").

Le Corbusier used a similar shape over the front entrance of the Villa Stein-de-Monzie in 1926.

A more modest feature is the variation of the windows on the upper-floor middle facade. It was this element that struck me when I looked at a rather faded facade drawing in the Montauban archives. The window-panes are all a uniform square shape and on the upper floor create a long line of twelve panes all the same. The drawing also does not have the flying roof between the chimneys above.

The block as built has panes taller than they are wide and in groups of four rather than three. It is only a slight, subtle difference, and could have been brought about by a simple practical matter such as that the narrower frames may have been available off-the-shelf locally whereas the square ones would have had to be custom-made and therefore more expensive.

However, it was the difference in appearance, the feel of the facade, that struck me. The oblong panes look right where the square ones, at least on the drawing, look too blandly uniform. Again that could be just the difference between a simple facade drawing without frames shown and how they would have looked on the building with frames. The result on the drawing is that the upper line of twelve panes, with equal gaps between the four sets of three begin to look like a fenêtre-longue à la Le Corbusier, and as a result efface the differences between the function of the rooms behind. In the Maison Cook (next to the Maison Dubin) the continuous window hides what different kinds of rooms are behind as they all look the same.

In one of the only articles Welz wrote, in 1929, he expressed the hope, ironically about a Le Corbusier interior set at the Salon D'Automne of that year, that the exterior would be a faithful reflection

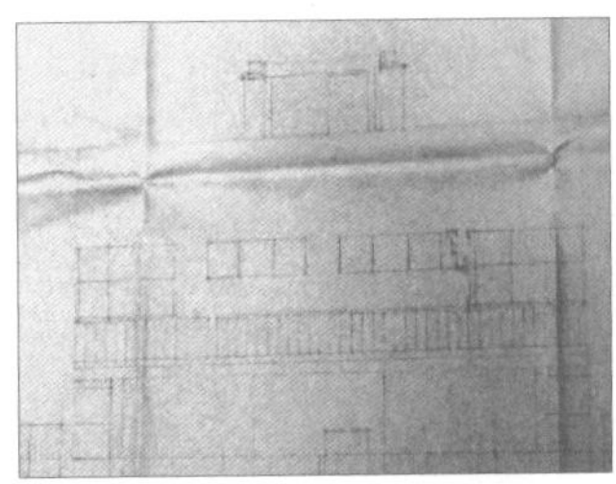

Left: Jean Welz, 137 Quai Adolphe Poult, Montauban (1930–32). Montauban City Archive.

Right: Le Corbusier, Villa Stein-de-Monzie (1926–28). © Fondation Le Corbusier.

of the interior. In fact, Le Corbusier often did the opposite, as at the Maison Cook, whereas perhaps for Welz it was an article of faith that the facade signifies what was inside (as with Loos's principles, and incidentally also those of Palladio, as we will discuss in Chapter 18, "Villa Darmstadter"). Certainly, as built, the block middle facade makes it very clear that different kinds of rooms lie behind the middle groups of three windows (shown as kitchens on the plan) against the living rooms with the taller two-pane windows. That simple difference helps to bring character to the facade.

At Montauban, it could have been that the facade drawing was by a local architect and Welz came in and made changes — the most obvious being the flying roof — or it could be simply that changes were made by Welz between drawing and building?

Whichever it was, I had the feeling that perhaps Welz saw that Corbusian echo, and made sure it didn't transfer to the block as it was built. The impact on the facade is that it looks Viennese rather than Parisian, as it were. The window apertures are simple holes in the wall, but the windows are set back within the aperture and given a simple ledge below the window-frames. The windows themselves look traditional but treated in that manner look modern in the Loosian way.

The more obvious interest lies in the overall design, which is probably Welz, which makes a dynamic ensemble from the two wings with central staircase block and a courtyard between the wings. As a solution for a relatively deep site with buildings on either side, it offers windows onto the yard front and rear internally to the site.

The rest of the Welz designs at Montauban are six modest houses and flats — but all with one noticeable feature that harks back to the Loos house for Tristan Tzara. Welz takes a feature of that house and adapts it to the very different situation of these small properties.

These five (171, top left, is two plots with a central entrance) all share the feature of the recessed balcony. The idea is familiar from the grand Tzara house but seen here in much reduced circumstances.

Quai Adolphe Poult runs along the river Tarn and the small terrace/balconies give each property a small outside space protected from the sun — Montauban is rather warmer than Paris — and a view of the river. Another house was built one street back from the river (Avenue Hamcher) and also featured the recessed balcony — still giving valuable protected outside space if without a view of the river.

Each of the recessed balconies is of a different format — the Hamcher one is fully glazed, whereas 161 Quai Adolphe Poult has

Above, left: 171 Quai Adolphe Poult; above, right: 163bis Quai Adolphe Poult.
Center, left: 161 Quai Adolphe Poult; center, right: 79 Avenue Hamcher.
Below: 151 Quai Adolphe Poult.

Photos courtesy of the author, 2016.

Above: Glass block and angled window-ledges at 89 Quai Adolphe Poult (1931).

Center: Welz family house, Worcester, Western Cape, South Africa (1950) with angled window ledge and glass blocks. Courtesy of the author from a visit in July, 2014.

Below: Floor mosaic and stair details at 89 Quai Adolphe Poult, Montauban with grill and ledges like Adolf Loos had used.

All Montauban photos courtesy of the author, 2016.

only a small window — perhaps representing the different wishes of different clients.

In common is the provision of a balcony in streets that mainly do not have projecting balconies. The recessed idea from the Tzara house is here adapted to give a functional feature that adds to the practical features of these modest houses and flats, and in fact bears very little relation to the Tzara house version which seems in the main to have had a monumental rather than practical function.

An even plainer house shows an elaboration from plan to building on the balcony surround that would have been costly but relieves its very basic design. A few small touches suggest Welz's hand at Montauban: The window ledge at 163bis has been angled downwards, (as at Welz's own 1950 house in South Africa, see the Appendix, "After Architecture").

The tiling to the entrance hall of the flats at 171 has an elaborate design, and the staircase has a stepped rail familiar from Loos's houses.

Another feature from Welz's South African house, a high-level horizontal aperture allowing light from one living-room to another, also showed up at the flats at 171 Quai Adolphe Poult, between the front room onto the street and in the wall letting onto the room behind.

Fischer would not have been hostile to these "Loosian" elements at Montauban, but with these modest houses they tend more to show the designer's consideration of the residents in providing a terrace in a town usually with hot summers, where the standard houses on that street do not have that luxury.

Such a concern overlaps with the "minimum flat" interests of Fischer and Welz's contribution to the Rue de Charonne flats. Here a Loosian element is adapted to a functional use to serve much more modest accommodation (see the Tristan Tzara house as discussed in Chapter 9, "The Guevrekian Letter"). Jean Welz used his experience of sophisticated design to create an imaginative outside space, a recessed balcony with a view and access to the exterior — an ingenious way to fulfill the modernist idea of bringing the outside in. It seems that his employer was not even aware of what he was doing until after the fact. If Raymond Fischer here mainly took the role of entrepreneur, Jean Welz was the designer, and one for whom the most modest project deserved his best attentions.

NOTES

1 Zeller, pp. 62–63.

17

MAISON LANDAU
A MINIMUM HOUSE

WITH HIS FIRST COMMISSION under his own name, Jean Welz makes a significant contribution to modern architectural design — by turning a Le Corbusier technique on its head.

Although it was clearly a low-budget project, built in a suburb just outside Paris where land was cheaper, and had to make use of off-the-shelf materials from the local builders' merchant, he shows the quality of his thinking through the development of what has been claimed as a unique approach to the mezzanine.[1]

Corbusier had been inspired by his local café's layout to create a mezzanine design. In the Esprit Nouveau house, which Jean saw at the 1925 *Art Deco* exhibition, Le Corbusier used a mezzanine — inserting such a floor to the rear of a double-height space. Jean Welz lavishly praised a similar layout in the article he wrote on the Salon d'Automne in 1929 on an interior layout Le Corbusier presented — with his new tubular furniture designed with Charlotte Perriand and Pierre Jeanneret: "The most perfect design that can be imagined with research pushed as far as possible."[2]

The simple variation that Welz proposed partly came about from the nature of the site, one with a long frontage to the street but fairly shallow in depth, the opposite of city-center sites with narrow frontage but considerable depth due to the high cost of being on a city street.

Jean Welz's solution was to turn the mezzanine around ninety-degrees to run it along the long side of the site, facing the street frontage, and creating a double-height space along the whole length of the modest building, allied to a full-length mezzanine. Although essentially a simple strategy, it elegantly turned the Corbusier solution around and created a dramatic interior for a modest building.

The design appeared in the second issue of *L'Architecture d'Aujourd'hui*, November 1931, in a brief article generously written by Raymond Fischer, who recommended the design as an example of the "maison minimum":

> "Jean Welz has built, in the Parisian suburbs, a small villa which, from the point of view of composition, cost and materials, can be considered as a 'minimum house,' all the materials and construction elements are from the local builders' merchants catalogue.
>
> "The lighting fixtures are goosenecks with porcelain reflectors; the boiler contributes directly to the heating, many cupboards — in plywood — were fitted nearly everywhere — for kitchen utensils as much as cloakrooms. The occupants therefore need the minimum of furniture, which contributes to reducing the purchase price of the house. The kitchen itself forms a large "cupboard" within the living-room. The main space, which goes up on two floors, creates a large cube of air, and gives the latter a long, very pleasant proportion. In my opinion this is one of the best attempts at a low-cost house.
>
> — Raymond Fischer"

Fischer was on the committee of the prestigious new magazine alongside Le Corbusier, Mallet-Stevens, Pierre Chareau, Auguste Perret, Jean Ginsberg, Berthold Lubetkin, André Lurçat, Willem Marinus Dudok and thirty others. It shows how well-connected he was, but also an article in only the second issue would suggest that Welz's name would at least have been known to a fair number of the thirty-eight architects on the consultative board.

The simple facade is a result of cost-constraints, but one that allows maximum light through the use of the largest windows that could be bought off the shelf — but also would not need steel beams the full length of the facade to support the roof, only over the windows themselves (and perhaps in wood rather than steel at those lengths). Steelwork along the whole facade would have raised the budget significantly, so here Welz uses off-the-shelf elements in a cost-effective way.

The interior photographs show that the sacrifice is not too constraining inside as the gaps between the windows can accommodate the curtains, and the overall area of glazing is still high.

Above: Jean Welz, Maison Landau (1931), interior view. Unmounted photo.

Below: Maison Landau, interior view. Photo mounted on blue card, assumed formerly from the portfolio. Unlettered. Both courtesy Welz family.

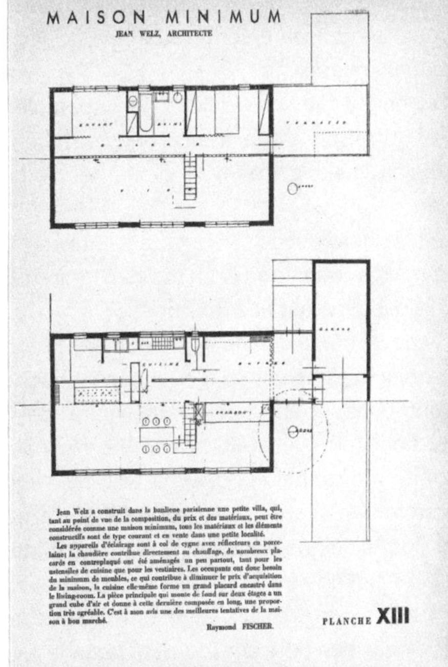

MAISON MINIMUM

JEAN WELZ, ARCHITECTE

Jean Welz a construit dans la banlieue parisienne une petite villa, qui, tant au point de vue de la composition, du prix et des matériaux, peut être considérée comme une maison minimum, tous les matériaux et les éléments constructifs sont de type courant et en vente dans une petite localité.

Les appareils d'éclairage sont à col de cygne avec réflecteurs en porcelaine; la chaudière contribue directement au chauffage, de nombreux placards en contreplaqué ont été aménagés un peu partout, tant pour les ustensiles de cuisine que pour les vestiaires. Les occupants ont donc besoin du minimum de meubles, ce qui contribue à diminuer le prix d'acquisition de la maison, la cuisine elle-même forme un grand placard encastré dans le living-room. La pièce principale qui monte de fond sur deux étages a un grand cube d'air et donne à cette dernière composée en long, une proportion très agréable. C'est à mon avis une des meilleures tentatives de la maison à bon marché.

Raymond FISCHER.

PLANCHE XIII

Above, left: Maison Landau facade. Photo mounted on brown card, given by Inger Welz to Jean-Louis Avril in 1985. Courtesy Welz family.

Above, right: Maison Landau, rear facade. Mounted on brown card, assumed formerly part of the portfolio. Unlettered. Courtesy Welz family.

Below: Maison Landau floor plans. Source for plans and interior photos: *L'Architecture d'Aujourd'hui*, October 7, 1931, Planches XIII–XIV, via portaildocumentaire.citedelarchitecture.fr.

It is the interior, both its layout and the economy of the plan, that stands out. The photographs reveal a much more dramatic interior space than the plain external facade would suggest.

The first-floor layout looks particularly modern, with both bedrooms closed off by corrugated folding shutters, a flexible use of space that in particular makes the parental bedroom a space strictly for sleeping as there would be no space to walk around the end of the bed.

Despite the constraints the design offers a spacious terrace off the mezzanine and a garden terrace sheltered by the garage. The ground-floor layout includes a further maid's bedroom and a spacious entrance off-axis to the main body of the building, supplemented by an open entrance area under the mezzanine, which together would create a very open feel as you enter through the front door and turn left towards the main space.

The double-height interior would be only revealed with a ninety-degree left turn from the entrance hall, and the turn is largely under the mezzanine, making the reveal of the double height all the more unexpected.

The kitchen fits neatly under the mezzanine towards the opposite end, next to the maid's room, and both the dining area and living-area benefit from the double-height space. For such a modest building, it offers quite a range of practical and aesthetic features, which is due to ingenious planning and use of space — hence Fischer's description of it as a contribution to the "maison minimum" debate.

The upper floor four-pane window to the right illuminates the child's bedroom, of a size that suggests it was also intended as a daytime playroom for which the additional light would be useful.

The lower floor also has a four-pane window (hidden behind the bush, the right side just showing the right-most pane) which provides illumination for the kitchen, again useful as it is located under the mezzanine and would benefit from the dual-aspect natural light coming from the rear.

Among the four letters in the portfolio that were missing their photographs, it made sense that the Maison Landau was one of them. The four photographs with coloured paper backing, two interior and two exterior, of Landau, were among the documents that Inger Welz presented to Jean-Louis Avril — again, the first to write about the architecture of Jean Welz — when she visited Paris in 1985.[3]

The intriguing clue to the source of this first independent commission for Jean Welz, given in the opening chapter, ties Jean

Ginsberg's 25 Ave de Versailles of the same year to Ginsberg's chemist-uncle, Joseph Landau, "President of the Polish Union of chemical industries. He was a founder of 'Chemistry House' in Paris, and a Knight of the Legion of Honor."[4] Although it is possible it is another M. Landau, the connection seems too great to be coincidental, especially considering his Paris links. As a modest house, it may or may not have been for Joseph Landau, himself, but perhaps for a close relative.

Raymond Fischer's article in *L'Architecture d'Aujourd'hui* shows that Jean Welz was not completely unknown, not totally in the shadows. Fischer knew virtually everyone in the Paris of his time, and for Jean to have his first house positively reviewed in such a prestige publication suggests he and his work would have at least been known to the Parisian coterie of modern architects, from the generation of Auguste Perret, to that of Le Corbusier and young Turks like Berthold Lubetkin.

Although the Maison Landau appears a deceptively simple design, its use of space has remarkable clarity and concision, while at the same time creating a rather grand and dramatic interior from the most modest of resources, of which the plain facade gives little expectation. Jean Welz opens his own account with a remarkable combination of reserve and innovative drama, and all on a low budget.

NOTES

1 The view of Jean-Louis Avril, who wrote the first article about Welz's architecture, in 1993.

2 Jean Welz, "Pour Vivre Heureux" (To Live Happily), *La Libérté*, December 4, 1929.

3 Although the photos did not have a letter written on the backing cards, as did the ones that remained with the Portfolio in South Africa.

4 "*Neveu de Joseph Landau, président de l'Union des industries chimiques en Pologne. Il compte parmi les fondateurs de la Maison de la Chimie à Paris, Chevalier de la Légion d'honneur.*" ("Nephew of Joseph Landau, President of the Union of Chemical Industries in Poland. He counts among the founders of Chemistry House in Paris, Chevalier of the Legion of Honour.") Cité de l'Architecture et du Patrimoine, Institut français d'architecture, Centre d'archives d'architecture du XXe siècle.

Villa Darmstadter (1932), photo from the Welz portfolio. Courtesy Welz family.

18

VILLA DARMSTADTER — 1932

TO MY EYES, THE VILLA DARMSTADTER[1] is beautifully simple while also being highly sophisticated. I see it as one of the most noteworthy designs of its era. That is quite a claim, however, I feel that it not only lays out an alternative modernist route to that of Le Corbusier, but I sense that it invokes the greatest architect of all time, Palladio, and in a contrasting way to Corbusier. In so doing, Darmstadter suggests a rich path for modernist architecture, a different one from that taken by the Paris avant-garde, which, some argue, had run out of steam by the early 1930s. Le Corbusier reinvented himself more than once after his "white period" of the 1920s, but other lesser figures did not match the level of his creative energies, which can be seen, for example, in his Chapel at Ronchamp (1955) (see page 323).

My feeling is that for Jean Welz, this is the point at which all of his Viennese background and creative intelligence comes together to create a real masterpiece. Although it is an essentially simple design, it has a rare elegance that fuses the rationality of his Viennese intellectual and cultural inheritance with an implicit critique of Corbusier. On its own, that could produce very little, but it is what he makes of these themes that is both original and highly creative.

For a 1935 article by Pierre Chareau, architect of the famous Maison de Verre, three houses were chosen to illustrate the best of modern architecture.[2] The first was Le Corbusier's Villa Stein-de-Monzie (1926–28), the second André Lurçat's Villa Hefferlin (1932), and the third was the Villa Darmstadter. While Stein-de-Monzie is white period Le Corbusier, and the Villa Hefferlin broadly white and

Corbusian, the Villa Darmstadter is neither, and clearly takes a different path to the other two designs.

The credit in the article was to Raymond Fischer. Where Fischer had given Collaborator credit to Jean Welz for the Maison Dubin and others, he had apparently not done so for the Villa Darmstadter.

As one of the most important designs in which Jean Welz was involved, it is crucial to assess to what extent it was by him, but first let us look at the elements of the design.

We see before us a two-story building visually defined by a central section bordered by a concrete frame and glazed to full height on both levels. The upper level has an integrated recessed balcony to the right.

Surprisingly, for Paris at that time, the areas to either side of the concrete central frame are in plain brick. There are no windows or doors, only solid planes of brick. Brick was used by Mies van der Rohe in the Wolf house of 1926 and more recently by the Dutch modernist Dudok in 1931, but here it makes an uninterrupted blank plane to either side, brick "wings" as it were. Its use could hardly be simpler or, one may say, purer.

Large areas of glazing were not common in 1932, but at a practical level one could see how they would be necessary to allow sufficient light into the interior, when there are no windows to either side.

In contrast to the vertical emphasis of this central area of glazing, the side facade visible in the photograph in the article has a long horizontal strip window, again simple and elegant in conception.

Left page: Le Corbusier, Villa Stein-de-Monzie; right page: Villa Darmstadter above and Villa Hefferlin below. From Pierre Chareau, "Artistic Creation & Commercial Limitations," *L'Architecture d'Aujourd'hui*, 1935 no. 1, pp. 58–59, via portaildocumentaire.citedelarchitecture.fr.

The other end has two strips, one at each level. It is worth noting that these strip windows do not go to the edge of the wall, which is load-bearing, but do extend to the full length of the internal walls, from wall to wall.

The roof is flat, but that is a feature of later Loos buildings as well as the "Paris" modernists and, for example, the Bauhaus and other German modernists.

The interior is equally distinctive — in its radical exploration of the Open Plan. The ground floor is basically one open space with a separate kitchen and dining space, although apparently without doors. The staircase is placed centrally in the open plan area, a sculptural spiral, curling up from the floor (see next page).

The front beam behind the glazing is lower than the rest of the ceiling — that could have been made flush but a modernist conception of honesty to materials perhaps insists it is visible. The rear entrance door shield on the right is a panel that does not extend up to the ceiling — making it furniture rather than structure and again a modernist "honesty" as a simple plane of what looks like steel.

The spiral staircase, instead of having just the simple banister visible either side, uses perforated metal, a material familiar post-war from the furniture of Mathieu Matégot, in order to create a swirling sculptural shape in the open space of the middle of the room. The underside is also a smooth sculptural surface, instead of the more common stepped finish.

The upper floor is unusually open, a feature worth particular note as "bedroom floors" are not normally an area for spatial experiment. Here, it is possibly the most interesting feature of Welz's design, and one without parallel since the Renaissance, in which time it was itself an echo of Roman and Greek precedents.

In order to discover its significance, we need to make more than one detour, beginning with the fortunate discovery of what I take to be the original design.

The first detour requires us to compare the original plan with the house as built, a comparison which brings in a story of its own. I had not seen the Darmstadter floor-plan until I came across an article by a Greek architectural historian, Anthony Antoniades.

He had been leafing through a book that he had almost forgotten in his library, one that he acquired by chance in a second-hand bookstore in Athens, left there by a German officer during the war, a rare Italian volume of 1934 featuring one hundred and ten architects'

Villa Darmstadter (1932).

Above: View of the interior left to right. Mounted on blue card, assumed formerly part of the portfolio. Courtesy Welz family.

Below: View of the interior right to left. Courtesy Welz family.

work from seventeen countries, including Gropius, Mies, Breuer and Rudolf Schindler.

Antoniades, historian and architect, declared that what interested him "throughout the whole book were five projects," two of which were "By Raymond Fischer," including the "Villa in Vaucresson" and the house at the Parc du Marnes for M. St. Leger — which he discussed earlier. The "Villa in Vaucresson" is the Villa Darmstadter:

> "I consider them pioneering in the idea of minimal housing, even though they are part of the suburban single family house mentality. Both are extremely frugal in plan, openness and economy of means, messengers of the possibility of modular housing complexes of higher densities; I always thought that were Philip Johnson to make his glass house two story, he would have followed the Villa Vaucresson model."

The comparison is interesting, as the Philip Johnson house (1949) is a famous exercise in pure architecture, indebted to Mies van der Rohe's purist Farnsworth House (1945–49). The comparison highlights that the Villa Darmstadter could hardly be more "minimal," employing an extreme "economy of means."

The article reproduced a page from the Italian book (see next page) with photographs but also the plan of its two floors.

The plan at ground floor level shows clearly that the glass doors open across the full width of the central area and onto a small plinth with circular ends (as the rear garden at the Atelier Kielberg). The upper floor, however, shows a contrast between the house as built and this plan. On the plan there are again opening doors across the glazed area. The photograph of the finished house shows those doors have been replaced by fixed windows.

To the right, the bedroom is closed off via three doors, one from the rear hall by the staircase, one onto the recessed balcony, and a third from that balcony to the central area. In the plan that area flows into the left-hand room and into the hall to the rear, all without doors.

One other small change, just about visible from the photographs, is that the back wall of the middle space has been moved back behind the chimney, giving a narrower hall. The dotted line on the plan along the hallway and then turning at right angles to meet the wall enclosing the staircase suggests perhaps a movable partition, like that at the Maison Landau.

The plan seemed to suggest that the upper level was also intended to be more open-plan than normally seen on a bedroom floor — and it was that thought which brought into focus an apparently casual remark that Raymond Fischer had made in his December 1987 interview: "If I had listened to Welz, I would have made houses with much more developed Open Plans. Personally, I considered that to live in a house one had to be able to close off the rooms."

That comment, apropos of nothing in the context of the interview, suddenly became rather pointed when looking at the Darmstadter plan and also gave rare evidence of a disagreement between Welz and Fischer. Further, it suggested that this plan, from the rare Italian book, was a fortunate discovery in that it represented the original intentions of the designer, later modified by either the client or Fischer, or both. In other words, it seems likely that this was Jean Welz's original plan and intentions.

If that was the case, what was the purpose of the open room to the left, and even more the open central space? It occurred to me that the right room, the only one with doors, might have been intended as a parental bedroom, closed off by doors for reasons of privacy. If those parents had small children, the left-hand room may also have

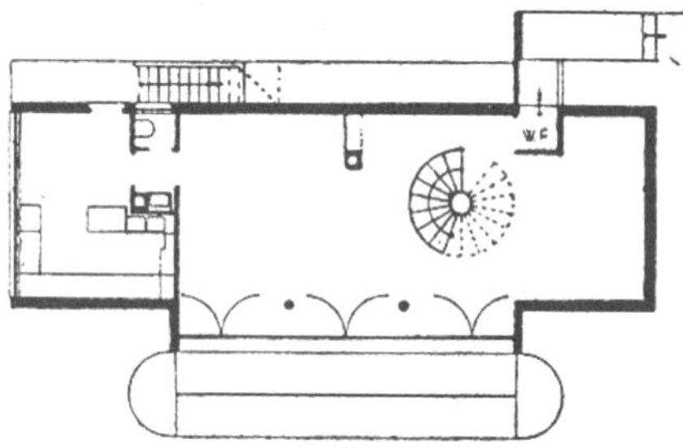

Pianta del pianterreno
Cucina, Sala da pranzo e Soggiorno

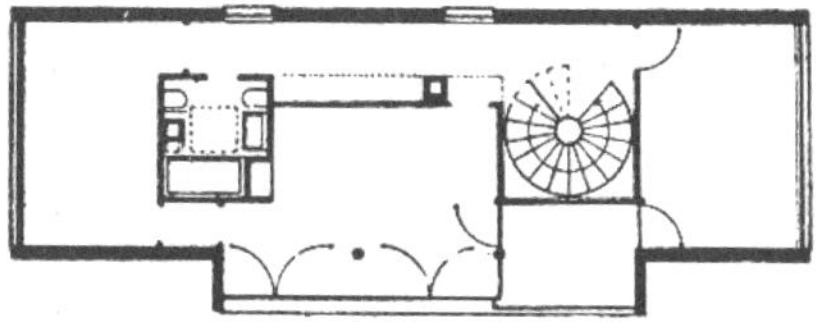

Pianta del primo piano

Villa Darmstadter floor plan (Moretti, *Ville*, p. 18. Author collection). Various discrepancies between the plans and the as-built house give a clue as to the designer being Jean Welz.

been a bedroom, but left open so that the parents could hear any crying during the night, and if the children were small enough, they would be in cribs and not able to wander out of the open doorways of their bedroom. This is only a speculation but offers one of what could be several practical explanations.

That still left the puzzle of the middle room. That too came into focus through a comparison, a second detour, that I happened to come across by chance.

At my desk one day from the corner of my eye, my attention was caught by the cover of a small book on Palladio showing the Villa Chiericati. What struck me at that particular moment was the basic structural principles of the design.

The Villa Chiericati, as with all Palladio's designs, is symmetrical. There is a small wing either side of a central portico. Those features are in common with the Villa Darmstadter.

The early phase of modernist architecture had a particular attraction for asymmetry. It was part of what was "modern," and favored by many architects and designers. The early "white" phase of modernism culminated in the Villa Savoye by Corbusier, completed the year before

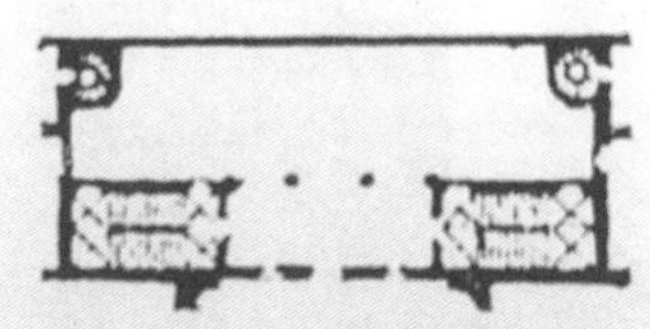

Andrea Palladio, Villa Chiericati (circa early 1500s). Source: Manfred Wundram and Peter Gossel, *Palladio* (Taschen Basic Architecture Series). Los Angeles: Taschen (2009).

Darmstadter, in 1931. The facade of the Villa Savoye was, if anything, something of a return to symmetry, although its sun-terrace continued the tradition of asymmetry.

The Villa Darmstadter was similar to the basic outlines of the Palladio house — a central entrance and two wings. Darmstadter was like a stripped-back version of Chiericati — the wings were plain planes of brick with no windows or doors — quite an achievement of design and planning in itself, in that it allowed enough light in via the central glazed doors to compensate for the pure planes unpunctured by windows.

The modernist version of the portico was just as stripped back — a slim "picture frame" around the top and sides. Two floors with two set-back slim pillars, fronted at ground level by full-height glazing comprising six opening doors and two fixed panels. These are mirrored on the left of the floor above by five glazed panels comprised of four opening doors on either side of a central fixed glazed panel, with the right end occupied by the internal balcony.

Further research suggested two Palladio villas as potentially relevant. One of his earliest, Villa Valmarana (1542), is very plain, perhaps under the influence of one of his patrons, Cornaro: "a building may be beautiful and comfortable and be neither Doric nor any such order"[3] — decoration is not required to be classical. The design is plain brick (if with ornate windows) either side of a simple central entrance.

The broken pediment was one that Palladio had "imagined" from the remains of a Roman temple he had seen and drawn.[4] There, the horizontal of the pediment was even more minimal. As with most of the villas, Palladio's design was only realized in a simplified manner, and, in this case, any elaboration, the broken pediment and fancy window-surrounds, were left out as-built (see photo opposite).

The lower pediment element is absent, and the open entrance has a shallowly-recessed panel extending to the roof line, recessing but not breaking the upper cornice. This is the plainest Palladio and the changes from the drawing, including the three "oculars," may suggest his hand rather than that of the builder, as the oculars also occur in a later house, the Villa Poiana.

This plain strand in Palladio looked to simple Roman structures, the basics of building. (One of Loos's favorite phrases was the aim "to build like the Romans.") At Poiana (see page 175), even the classical pillars of Valmarana are reduced to functional square shapes, the arch loses the moldings and the broken pediment is as reduced as the Roman temple drawing in his *Four Books*.

Above: Andrea Palladio, Villa Valmarana (Bressan) (1542). Courtesy RIBA Collections.

Below: Villa Valmarana (circa 1540s). Photo courtesy of the author.

It was said that Palladio personally preferred a lack of ornament and plain walls, externally and internally, and although no two designs are the same, the designs of his first decade bear that out. Poiana is ironically almost post-modern in the plainness of its entrance. It would be no surprise if this element of plainness in Palladio attracted Welz.

The second relevant theme can be seen in the Villa Pisani, which has a two-story portico with a loggia, important for our purposes on this detour, on the upper floor.

If you half-close your eyes, and focus on the structure of the portico, we can see a relatively modest projection from the main facade, fronted by the "engaged" pillars and two central pillars — similar to the Darmstadter design. Take away the side pillars and recess the central ones behind the glazing and the formal link is clear.

The double-height loggia also appears in the villa for Cornaro, being built at the same time.

In both cases the loggias are on the garden side, a further echo for Darmstadter.

If Welz, as I tend to think, studied Palladio in some depth, he would have quickly gone beyond the grandeur of the Temple-Portico image to see both a certain preference for the removal of ornament (an obvious echo to Loos), at least in Palladio's first decade, and traceable to the influence of Cornaro, and a mature theme from the second decade, of the double-height loggia.

The upper loggia is the focus of this detour-route. It was, in both Palladio and in Venetian Renaissance examples, a social area, a meeting area but also one for reading, thinking, contemplation, including the safe contemplation of nature in overlooking the garden, the sense of nature tamed, and pleasingly laid out for the owner and his guests to gaze onto from the upper floor viewpoint, one that meant the viewer could look over the extent of the garden, the tasteful civilized refuge from the untamed desert beyond, as it were.

The middle room on the upper floor of the Villa Darmstadter, deduced from the original plan, curiously discovered in the rare book found in the Athens second-hand bookshop, may have been intended by Welz to have a similar function to the upper loggias of Palladio's villas in the Veneto, and similar examples found here and there in Venice along the Grand Canal.

If that were true, the middle room being an open space, unlike the closed rooms that Raymond Fischer approved of, would make sense. It would itself be a kind of loggia, a modern version, where the

Above: Palladio, Villa Poiana (1548). Photo courtesy of the author.

Center: Palladio, Villa Pisani (Montagnana) (1552), garden side.
Source: Vicenza city website.

Below: Palladio, Villa Cornaro (1553). Photo courtesy of the author.

original plan with its sliding doors would open the space to the air when required, as the upper loggia was permanently open to the air in Palladio's examples.

Then the inhabitants could also look over the garden from a raised vantage point, or sit and read, or stand and talk by the windows, open or closed, with the view of the garden available at a turn of the head. Parents, coming from the right-hand bedroom, could join with their children from the left-hand bedroom, in that open middle-room, to play, read, instruct, or show the garden below — for example, listing the trees, plants and flowers in a relaxed fashion.

The Elysian dream, from the early photos of the house, was never realized. The sliding opening doors were replaced by fixed windows, and the middle room became one of, in Fischer's words, "the three bedrooms." The more prosaic needs of the client left the dream on the drawing-board.

With the Villa Chiericati, the portico and in particular the pediment, taken from the temple, adds grandeur to a farm-house and there is a long straight drive of two hundred meters or more to the facade, which builds the impression of grandeur on a stately approach.

For Welz, the pediment and the grandeur are not an issue, as the facade looks onto the garden and the entrance is by the most basic doorway at the back of the property, along the boundary.

Villa Darmstadter (1932), showing low steps to the rear entrance. Courtesy Welz family.

There is no driveway approach to require grandeur, although his design is impressive from its proportions and the purity of the sculptural brick wings.

Note on the photo opposite the two steps and low wall to the right, the path to the rear door — which is the only other entrance.

It is not just the idea that Welz went back to Palladio for these formal elements, even that he was able to see them, which is to abstract them from otherwise very different contexts. What is of most interest is the creative way that he transformed them for his own purposes.

The Mathematics of the Ideal Villa by Colin Rowe (1947) draws comparisons between Corbusier and Palladio, specifically the Villa Savoye and the Villa Stein-de-Monzie of Corbusier, and the Villa Rotunda and Villa Foscari of Palladio. Corbusier confided to the South African modernist, Rex Martienssen (who crops up later in this chapter), that his houses of the twenties were an attempt to recreate "the spirit of Palladio."

The Villa Savoye was completed in 1931 and the Villa Darmstadter in 1932, and it possible that Jean Welz was both looking for a way forward in the wake of the Villa Savoye and had turned in his own way to Palladio. It is, of course, further possible that the subject of Palladio was in the air, even that Welz could possibly have discussed Palladio with Corbusier, as the Rowe article suggests Corbusier's active interest in Palladio for those two houses (1926–28 and 1929–31).

However, what is really fascinating is the notion that Welz might have taken Palladio in a different way, creating an (implicit) dialogue between himself and Corbusier — on Palladio.

The Villa Darmstadter could be seen as a further repudiation of the Five Points of Modern Architecture that Corbusier first elaborated in the Maison Cook. With his first design, the Maison Dubin, Jean was more or less forced into a dialogue with Corbusier as the houses were literally attached.

There are, in fact, six or seven elements to the Five Points — and five of them are contradicted by the Villa Darmstadter — pilotis,[5] free facade, the long/free window, concrete pillars to avoid load-bearing walls, and the roof garden. None of these strictly appear in Darmstadter.

One important exception is what Corbusier described as "*l'intérieur muni de casiers et débarrassé de l'encombrement des meubles*" (the interior equipped with sideboards and freed from the encumbrance of furniture) — the interior with fitted furniture. However,

Welz seems to be taking this open plan interior beyond Corbusier in Darmstadter, through, as it were, Palladio — and also Renaissance architecture in general, as seen in Venice[6] and the Veneto.

If this was indeed, broadly, the thought-process of Jean Welz, it would suggest the kind of intellectual seriousness, combined with a breadth and depth of (architectural) thinking, that was readily echoed in the view of him held by family and friends.[7]

It is possible that Welz's inspiration for the extension of the open-plan theme to the upper floor and the "loggia" of his original plan was also Palladio. The latter's rooms lead one from another without corridors, and apparently the concept of privacy was different in Palladio's time.

The kind of free-flowing space suggested by Welz's plan for the upper floor has echoes of that idea, but in this case almost as though Welz was offering an alternative economy of space, a rejection of the closed room, which is precisely what Raymond Fischer had objected to in Welz.

On the ground-floor, Welz's radically Open Plan has another possible Palladio inspiration, in that the master always designed a void rather than a solid at the center of his plans, culminating most dramatically with the Villa la Rotonda that extended the void upwards to a dome, normally the reserve of sacred buildings. Here we might see Welz as taking Fischer's attraction to having the staircase in the center of the house, but for his own reasons, creating an asymmetrically placed sculptural spiral in the midst of the open-plan, with a circular hole to accommodate it in the ceiling, an imaginative variation on the void, at the same time solving the problem of accessing the upper floor.

Welz's opening up of the upper-floor space is perforce a different matter, with bedrooms at either end, but we might be able to see something of the imaginative leaps that mark Palladio, in the way Welz proposed the use of the space between them.

It might also suggest that dialogue — implicit or explicit — with Corbusier on Palladio. Whether they in fact discussed Palladio in person I do not know, but there is sufficient evidence on the Darmstadter plan and facade to suggest at the least an implicit dialogue.

Le Corbusier described Welz as "un drôle," a special person, and a few years later wrote a recommendation for him, when work had dried up. Le Corbusier was not one to give out compliments, especially to other architects, without reasons that were important to him. He was also one of the very few contemporaries with the ability to see clearly what Welz might have been up to, playing with Palladio in these kind of ways.

As Rowe points out, where Corbusier favors the curtain-wall and long horizontal windows, Palladio insists symmetry requires a load-bearing wall and the traditional window. Welz takes up the question of symmetry, has load-bearing walls of brick, but makes them an abstract plane without windows, and instead relies for light on a modernized version of the portico, sans pediment, and filled with vertical opening glazed doors.

Welz does in fact use pillars, but in a different way than Corbusier. The large full-height glazed doors on both floors in his original plan are only made possible by replacing the load-bearing wall there with recessed pillars taking the load of the floor or roof above. While that echoes Corbusier's 1914 Dom-Ino structure, it does not to permit a curtain-wall with long horizontal windows, but full-height glazed doors that both allow light inside and give access to and a clear view of the garden in front of the house, the main feature of the site.

This points towards a functional use of modern techniques and materials against the programmatic and formalist ideology of the Five Points. Corbusier wants to dispense with the load-bearing wall, Welz — like the Viennese second-wave modernists — only does so when there is a very specific purpose, one yielding benefits appropriate to the particular building and the particular site. In terms of the best use of the site, the Darmstadter house is set back against the boundary wall, in order to have the largest area of garden as the view from those glazed doors, simply a matter of sensitive design.

There are particular echoes in the strip-windows on either end of Darmstadter with a similar feature in the house considered Josef Frank's masterpiece, the Beer House (see following page). Jean's old girlfriend, Carmela Prati/Haerdtl, wrote an article on the house that year for the Italian magazine, *Domus*.[8] As he did not visit Vienna, the intriguing possibility is that she sent him the article (perhaps in a German translation) and he took the window idea from that (not forgetting that Frank was his tutor for two years in Vienna and so he might have followed his work with interest).

The contrast at Darmstadter is perhaps more with Le Corbusier than Palladio, part of Welz's "dialogue" with his contemporary.

The plainness, indeed sculptural simplicity of the facade, and his particular use of brick both echoes the Loosian theme of the neutral exterior, but takes it further, towards a sculptural quality in creating two planes of pure brick uninterrupted by windows or doors. These are load-bearing walls taken to an ultimate of a plain/plane wall. To attract enough light into the interior, the whole central area is open and/or glazed from floor to ceiling — another contrast with the Corbusian horizontal window.

Rowe wrote on Palladio and Corbusier in 1947, some fifteen years after the Villa Darmstadter, but his comments throw an interesting light on the comparisons I saw with the Palladio house (Chiericati) and Jean Welz's relationship with the Open Plan theme of Corbusier. In his own practical but nevertheless theoretical approach, Welz applied a Palladian facade to a Corbusier-plus internal layout. Welz's impressive strength as an artist here is that he takes certain elements of Palladio — the necessity of a load-bearing facade wall — and instead of contradicting that view he works with it and takes it further, using pillars where it makes the full-height glazing possible, and in so doing adapting the Palladian (or Corbusian) load-bearing pillar for this particular design.

Welz's load-bearing wall is a double-departure in that he employs brick — not one of the new materials demanded by an orthodox modernism. But, having done that, his brick is radically modern — a

Josef Frank, Beer House, Vienna (1931). Note the shallow depth and the upper strip window, both seen in Darmstadter. Detail from photo by Julius Scherb, Vienna, 1931.

pure plane uninterrupted by any apertures — framing either side of his New Palladian centerpiece.

In his rejection of a lumpen-Palladianism, Robert Adam may well have admired Jean Welz's replacement of a heavy Pediment with the light "picture-frame" device with which he encircles his garden-entrance.[9]

If, for example, Welz is conducting a dialogue with the Villa Savoye's Palladianism, it can be argued that Darmstadter is closer to Palladio in the sense of building on his formal innovations whilst retaining certain traditions such as the load-bearing wall. The Villa Savoye departs further from the letter of Palladio, as in the pillars all around, more reminiscent of a Greek temple. Both are beautiful to behold, but Welz might have felt himself that in Savoye there is more novelty, and that Darmstadter is closer to the Romans, as Loos (and perhaps Palladio) would have wished.

Returning to the question of whose design this was, Fischer did talk of Darmstadter in some detail. On the exterior design he said: "The idea, was this frame… in my first modern houses, I had no more dark corners, no more falling-back. The floor served as a lintel and I recessed the window-frames."

There is a definite sense of ownership here — "I" had no more dark corners, "I" recessed the window-frames. "The idea" is less personal, but it may be reading too much into the absence of the "I," although one could perhaps expect the designer to say "my" idea.

However, the emphasis on relatively small details is odd in the context of such a ground-breaking design. There is no sense in those words of the scale of the achievement it represents, the imaginative clarity and rigor to produce something so different from the trend of the times.

About the interior, Fischer said: "The concept was very simple: a large living-room, a kitchen, some bathrooms and three bedrooms. I asked myself the question of the position of the staircase, where to put it? Against the wall, as in the traditional way? I estimated that in this large room, it would make a positive decorative element."

Again, "the" concept could suggest a lack of ownership, but it could also be a straightforward description of the client brief. It could be said that "I asked myself the question" is not quite the same thing as declaring he had solved the problem. "Estimating" where it should go is not quite as strong as coming up with the idea. It could mean it was his idea, or that he approved Welz's proposal. Much more than that though, is again the concentration on a detail rather than any sense of the overall conception, which in this house is so strong.

Fischer's description of how he ran his office was that he would give the brief to the designer and then the design would be discussed. He had certain *parti pris* — vertical rather than horizontal windows and the "Bow Window," for example — but by his own account would leave the design to the designer. Rather than a broader statement about the overall strategy to achieve this striking design, Fischer's input, at least from his own words, appears to be around the edges.

He had, however, campaigned for full-height windows against the long-windows of Corbusier, taking the side of Auguste Perret in that debate on the pages of *L'Architecture d'Aujourd'hui* in 1931. The floor-to-ceiling doors in Darmstadter could be seen as a Fischer feature or, perhaps, again as Jean Welz adapting an approach his boss preferred — but using it for his own ends.

These abstract discussions are not particularly satisfactory at giving a strong sense of whose mind lay behind this design. Looking at comparable buildings is a far better guide. For example, Fischer's design most closely related to Darmstadter dates from around 1938, the Villa Blumel, completed after Welz had gone to South Africa.

While the photograph I have of the Villa Blumel is of poor quality (see page 118), it shows that some of the same elements are present, but the composition has little of the clarity, economy and elegance of Darmstadter. The picture frame is uneasily raised up a floor and the stripped-back clarity of the earlier house is replaced by heavier window frames below and heavier again above.

On the other hand, there is a design by Jean Welz for the 1937 Paris Exhibition, a proposal for the Austrian Pavilion, that shows similar boxed windows (see next page). This design is a few years later than Darmstadter so it does not establish precedence, but does show a certain continuity in Welz's approach, and a development of the box window of the Maison Dubin (1928) and the Villa Kolpa (1929).

In terms of the authorship question, the 1938 Fischer house demonstrates a wider fact. None of Fischer's designs, before or after Welz, approach the quality of designs during Welz's era. In relation to Darmstadter, the most obvious circumstantial evidence is that there is nothing in the periods either before or after Welz worked for him, in the work of Fischer, that is remotely near the quality of Darmstadter.

The idea that Welz felt strongly about the design is suggested by the fact that he included four photographs of it in the portfolio he took with him to South Africa, more than for most of the houses in which he was involved. Then there is the general view that Welz said to his close family that he was the designer and Fischer the money-man. There is no doubt that Fischer created the opportunity by gaining the commission, but overall it seems likely that it was Jean Welz who was responsible for the key qualities of the design. The ability to come up with such an innovative and deeply thought-through concept is not evident in any of Fischer's work, or indeed in his discussions of architecture in general or his own "credits" in particular, but is consistently evident in both of Welz's independent commissions as well as his work for Fischer.

There is a further interesting matter, related to the South African, Martienssen, after whose death it was said by Fernand Léger: "He ranks with Le Corbusier, Mies van der Rohe, Oud, Aalto, Wright, the great pioneers of modern architecture."[10]

Martienssen met Le Corbusier, and through him Léger, in Paris in 1934 and struck up friendships with both. One of the outcomes of that was a loyal-address to Corbusier in the summer of 1936 from the small group of South African architects keen on modern architecture, centered on the University of the Witwatersrand at Johannesburg, and printed in the first volume of Corbusier's *Collected Works*.

Shortly after that, Le Corbusier suggested South Africa to Jean as somewhere he might find work and congenial colleagues, and gave him the handwritten note Jean presented to Martienssen and the others at Witwatersrand in early 1937 (see page 247).

Martienssen came to see Jean during the latter's year of employment at Wits,[11] in the hut on the University campus that Jean was working in, and asked him to explain the principles and practice

Jean Welz, project for the Austrian Pavilion (1937). Courtesy Welz family.

of Corbusier's "Module"[12] system, which Jean was said to have used in the Great Hall entrance he designed for the University.

Martienssen had the reputation of being heavily influenced by Corbusier, and there is an echo of Jean explaining Loos to Fischer in his explaining Corbusier to Martienssen.

The resulting house, Martienssen's best-known design, has little to suggest a strong influence from Le Corbusier, but there are at least four features that relate to one of the designs Jean included in the portfolio he took with him to South Africa — the Villa Darmstadter.

Both feature a picture-frame surround, a section of full glazing on the ground floor with another above it on the first floor, including a balcony to the right, an internal open-plan layout, with a very open ground-floor plan, and the intensive use of brick on the facade. The house and contemporary reactions to it are examined at length in Chapter 25, "The Martienssen Affair," as well as the marked resemblances to Welz's design and philosophy.

While Martienssen inflected these elements in his own way, principally in shifting Welz's return to symmetry towards the earlier modernist attachment to asymmetry, I simply do not know if Martienssen saw Welz's portfolio, but it seems likely that Welz presented it to the Wits modernist group upon his arrival in early 1937, and it may well have made an impact at the time and been referred to in later discussions with various South African architects.

An irony is that I would argue that the Villa Darmstadter is in effect a critique of Corbusier rather than bearing his influence, and the idea that it was passed on — overtly or covertly — to Martienssen,

42. (Left) Photo of young South African visitors in Le Corbusier's atelier, pasted into Martienssen's copy of the 1937 edition of the Oeuvre Complète 1910–1929. (Wits Architectural Library)
House Martienssen, which th
The Martienssens had be
Continent they had rushed u
Beaux-Arts. The date of the

Photo of young South African visitors in Le Corbusier's atelier, pasted into Martienssen's copy of the 1937 edition of the *Oeuvre Complète 1910–1929*. Source: University of the Witwatersrand architectural library.

is an intriguing one. Although Martienssen's main interest seems to have been in theories of architecture, this house is his strongest design. I am not aware of any previous mention of connections with Welz's work. That Martienssen was spoken of so highly is a further irony in comparison with Jean Welz's anonymity.

I did not know a lot about Palladio before I saw the connection to the Villa Darmstadter. The more I learned and the more of his architecture I visited,[13] the more it felt that Welz's design for Darmstadter came not from a passing acquaintance but from a deep engagement with him. It may have come through Welz's relationship with Adolf Loos. The common factor is Vitruvius.

"His Bible was Vitruvius," Kokoschka said of Loos.[14] In his 1913 statement for his private architectural school, Loos insisted upon the duty creatively to rise to the occasion in changing circumstances and dare to do what the Vitruvius of antiquity would have done here and now (which is ever more demanding than just reiterating precedents): "Since mankind has come to recognize the greatness of classical antiquity, the great architects have all had the same approach. 'The way I build,' they thought, 'is the way the Romans would have gone about it in my situation.' This is the approach I want to instill in my students."[15]

Vitruvius, 1st century BC, is the only surviving work on architecture from Roman times. Palladio visited Rome five times in the 1540s to study and measure the surviving fragments of Roman architecture

Martienssen House, Johannesburg (1939). Source: *South African Architectural Record*, February 1942, p. 34. (University of the Witwatersrand architectural library). Photo: Heather Martienssen.

and contributed crucial drawings and thinking to a 1556 revised edition of Vitruvius by Barbaro, a mentor and client.

The creativity in Palladio's contribution to the Vitruvius edition, to whose importance Barbaro paid fulsome tribute, was at one with his overall approach to the legacy of the ancients. Like any artist he plundered it as a storehouse of wonders for his own purposes, taking this and that element in order to pursue his own goals.

He turned the Five Orders or pillars of Roman and Greek architecture into the basis of an integrated modular approach to design that used the height and distance between pillars as a way to determine the height and dimensions of rooms behind the portico. That unique effort of integration was combined with a rationalization of the components of the facade, bringing together the design of windows and other openings, pillars and horizontal elements into perfect symmetry, the unity of form that he was constantly striving towards. It was this degree of unity that distinguished him from other architects of his time and was his constant goal.

Palladio had indeed taken the approach recommended by Loos in relation to Vitruvius. At Darmstadter, Jean Welz seemed to have taken to heart that suggestion to "do what the Vitruvius of antiquity would have done here and now ... more demanding than just reiterating precedents."[16] He did it in a most intelligent and penetrating way, but in his case in relation to Palladio.

The Villa Darmstadter is a highly creative rethinking of Palladio, and in a similar spirit to Palladio's selective borrowing from Vitruvius and the Roman architecture he measured and drew in Rome.

In his use of brick as a plane, for example, Welz parallels Palladio's drive to unity and creates a purer version of Palladio. Loos's war on superfluous ornament is extended by Welz deep into antiquity, actually deep into Palladio's High Renaissance version of antiquity.

Welz shows a modern architecture can have load-bearing walls rather than curtain walls, use brick instead of concrete, have vertical windows where they bring advantages and strip windows that don't need to go around a corner, have symmetry rather than its opposite, yet embrace the open plan interior and extend it to the bedroom floor. By implication he suggests the Five Points were a false unity whereas Palladio's module of the High Renaissance has longevity.

Beyond all, that he created a thing of beauty that updated Palladio and showed that, as Loos asked, architects should not afraid to be "out of date," even if the date is almost four hundred years ago.

Welz's strategy is both radical and conservative, but the crucial Loosian point is that value does not reside in originality for its own sake, but always the context is "good building" "like the Romans."

Welz achieved an ingenious regeneration of the modernism of the 1920s through an updating of Palladio's pursuit of unity. His return to Palladio is the opposite of a search for novelty, a profound pursuit of the fundamentals of architecture, much in the way that Palladio had foraged in Vitruvius and the Romans. Over four hundred years before Welz, the great Inigo Jones introduced Palladio into England in The Queen's House, around 1619, the queen in question being Queen Anne. Jones used the feature of an upper floor loggia to the rear of the house, as with Palladio's Villas Pisani and Cornaro.

Credited with bringing the Enlightenment to England, Inigo Jones was a great admirer of Palladio, touring his houses and meeting his assistant, and he had a highly-annotated copy of Palladio's *Four Books.*

In my view, all great art is classical in its disciplined return to fundamentals. Palladio plundered Rome, Inigo Jones plundered Palladio for The Queen's House, and Welz plundered Palladio for the Villa Darmstadter.

There is a link between the stoical side of Roman architecture and the Loosian attitude to ornament. In his adaptation of Palladio, Welz not only brings the best of Vienna to bear upon Paris, but echoes the timeless validity of pure architecture through a restrained beauty that is his own.

"There will always come a great mind, I like to call him the super-architect, who will free architecture of foreign elements and

Inigo Jones, The Queen's House, Greenwich, London. Begun in 1619.
Photo courtesy of the author.

return us to pure, classical forms. And the public always greets this man with rejoicing, for our hearts and minds are imbued with classicism."[17] A young Loos wrote that as early as 1898. Welz's pure classical forms at the Villa Darmstadter qualify him, in my opinion, as "a great mind."

NOTES

1 The form of the name suggests Jewish origins from Darmstadt, a city where chemicals were an important industry. In the light of the Ginsberg/Landau connection, it is possible Mr. Darmstadter was a friend of Landau.

2 The choice of illustrations was most likely editorial rather than necessarily by Pierre Chareau. Although there is an interesting connection with Chareau in that Kertész took a portrait of him in 1927, the year of the latter's one-man exhibition, perhaps just a reminder of how small a world the Parisian avant-garde was, but it is possible Jean knew Chareau.

3 Cornaro: *Treatise on Architecture*, quoted in Ackerman, *Palladio*, 1966, p. 21.

4 *The Four Books*, Book Four, p. 37.

5 Internal pillars feature in a strictly functional context.

6 The upper loggia is found in many canal-side Venetian palazzi from the gothic period onwards.

7 Reports from his later life in South Africa, from family and architectural colleagues, emphasized this depth and breadth in relation to art in particular when he had become a painter, but also abiding in his discussions of architecture.

8 Carmela Haerdtl, "Una Nuova Casa di Josef Frank," *Domus* 4, August 1931, pp. 48–51, referenced in Long, *The New Space*, p. 233.

9 It is not strictly a picture frame as the bottom horizontal becomes a ledge, and the whole is bisected by the first-floor horizontal.

10 Tribute to RD Martienssen after his death in 1942 by Fernand Léger in the *South African Architectural Record*, January 1943, p. 22.

11 Information from Martin Welz, June 2017.

12 Corbusier's "Modulor" was published post-war, however he had used "*tracés régulateurs*" since before the First World War, a tradition that began around Palladio's time in the Renaissance, which was possibly also the reference for Welz's use of a "module" in his design of the Great Hall foyer.

13 I fulfilled a long-held ambition in July 2018 and visited nineteen of Palladio's Villas from a base in Vicenza.

14 Loos, quoted in Münz and Künstler, *Adolf Loos, Pioneer of Modern Architecture*, London: Thames & Hudson, 1966, p. 11.

15 *Adolf Loos, On Architecture*, edited by Adolf Opel and Daniel Opel, translated by Michael Mitchell, Riverside, Calif.: Ariadne Press, 2002, p. 120.

16 Loos, quoted in Joseph Maschek, *Adolf Loos: The Art of Architecture*, London: Bloomsbury, 2013, p. 37.

17 Loos, quoted in Mascheck, p. 121.

19

OSWALD HAERDTL
— 1932

IN 1932, THE SAME YEAR DARMSTADTER was completed, there was an important exhibition of modern architecture in Vienna, the Werkbundsiedlung Wien, with houses by seventy architects. Among those invited were all of Jean Welz's teachers; Hoffmann, Frank and Strnad, plus Fellerer, his supervisor at Hoffmann's, Gabriel Guevrekian, classmate and friend from Paris, and Oswald Haerdtl, his classmate rival at University and later at Hoffmann's.

At university, Haerdtl came top of the class and Jean second,[1] and a few years later Haerdtl won again when his design for a room at the *Art Deco* exhibition beat Jean's design in a Hoffmann-organized competition. Finally, twelve years later, Haerdtl's Austrian pavilion design for the 1937 Paris exhibition was built and Jean's design did not even figure on the shortlist — a final blow that probably hastened Jean's departure from Paris for good.

Haerdtl went from university to become Josef Hoffman's trusted assistant and then partner, and had a successful career until his early death in 1959. Two books on his work were published posthumously, one in 1978 under the auspices of their old university co-written by his wife, Carmela (Jean's old girlfriend), and a comprehensive large-format book of almost three hundred pages under the auspice of the Viennese architecture center in 2000.

The Vienna Werkbundsiedlung design was the last house on the site to be built, in fact a pair, and was Haerdtl's first design to be built, despite his progressing at Hoffmann's to become his partner by 1929.

That perhaps suggests the kind of difficulties faced by even the best-connected young architects at that time to get their designs built, and that in turn suggests that Jean's decision to stay in Paris in 1925 was less of a wild gamble than a sensible calculation about the relative chances for modern architecture in Vienna and Paris. Despite the disadvantages of his status as a "nègre viennois," Welz probably made the right decision, for him, in leaving Vienna behind for Paris. By 1932 he had been involved in at least six important houses plus other designs — the block of flats in the Rue Charonne, the gravestone for Marx's daughter and the seven designs in Montauban — whereas, judging from Haerdtl's career, he may well not have had any opportunities, let alone those of the kind he got in Paris.

The negative side is that although Oswald Haerdtl had the status of assistant, then partner to Josef Hoffmann, and was invited to the Werkbundsiedlung, Welz was unknown in Austria, and was not invited. Guevrekian, for example, had completed a large house in Paris in 1927 for a couturier, featured in magazines and books, and even if it was perhaps less interesting than the Maison Dubin of 1928, the latter was credited to Raymond Fischer in publications. Informally, he jointly-credited Jean Welz as 'collaborator' but that did not create a public profile for Welz.

It is instructive to compare the two men's designs, using Haerdtl's studio at the Werkbundsiedlung as an example. Haerdtl's is modern in that it has a flat roof and an absence of decoration, but compared to the Darmstadter design, while perfectly competent, it appears somewhat dull and unimaginative. The blockishness of Haerdtl's design is not uncommon among the Viennese moderns, not excluding Loos. It is an example of the difference between the 'visually' conservative

Haerdtl studio at the Werkbundsiedlung, Vienna (1932). Collection Architekturzentrum Wien. Source: werkbundsiedlung-wien.at/haeuser/haus-39-und-40.

Austrian modernism and the more adventurous Parisian variant. In such Viennese company, the Villa Darmstadter is in a different league.

Haerdtl had a successful career under Hoffmann until 1939, when they fell out over politics. Although Hoffmann had been considered avant-garde thirty years earlier, by then he was conservative in his views, and much too prepared, for his young partner, to accommodate the new Nazi regime following the Anschluss in 1938. Haerdtl re-established the modern architects' association after the war in Austria and, unfortunately for Welz, perhaps Haerdtl's best design was for the 1937 Austrian Paris exhibition stand. The story of Haerdtl getting that commission is an example of realpolitik, as it appears political influence and antipathies played a deciding part in taking the commission away from any other architect.[2]

Haerdtl and Welz appear to have had some mutual antipathy. Their relationship may have been colored by Haerdtl jumping in on Carmela Prati when Jean was banned as too bohemian, and Welz is not mentioned in either of the books on Haerdtl, who was honored by the Austrian state and given the commission for the Vienna museum in the late 1950s. Again he features in the Vienna architectural archive whereas there is understandably no mention of Welz.

The contrast in what they produced and their public profile is illuminating. Haerdtl was more than competent if rarely inspired, he was recognized by the state and his work has been well-covered. Welz found the freedom to pursue his own vision despite the constraints, but at the price of recognition. Haerdtl took on the management role with Hoffmann and had a successful career, producing interesting and modern commercial designs. Welz stayed in the backroom, where he could focus his energies on design issues, his passion. It was clearly no sacrifice to avoid the responsibilities of running a practice, and he was never concerned with fame or fortune. His luxury was to be able to spend his time pushing the boundaries of modern architecture in the nexus between Le Corbusier and Adolf Loos. I doubt he would have wished to swap that for a recognition he seems never to have sought.

NOTES

1 This information from the Welz family via Jean.

2 Meder, "Fragmente zu Leben und Werk des Architekten Otto Bauer: 'Ihr Platz ist in der Welt.'"

Jean Welz, Maison Zilveli (1933). The two women in the window remain unidentified as of this publication. The woman on the left could be Mrs. Elizabeth Kertész. The child in the sandpit is probably Jerome Welz, Jean and Inger's first-born, and the photo may be by André Kertész as Jerome appears in Kertész's photo of Jean and Inger inside Zilveli (see page 211).

Courtesy Welz family via Jean-Louis Avril. Image restoration Hugh Wyeth.

20

MAISON ZILVELI
— 1933

JOSEPHINE BAKER EXEMPLIFIED the avant-gardes' passion for the "exotic" in the Paris of the 1920s and 1930s and provides a curious connection between Le Corbusier, Adolf Loos and the Maison Zilveli. Baker met Corbusier onboard a liner between Buenos Aires and Rio de Janeiro and a flirtation ensued.[1] Adolf Loos was delighted when Baker called him the best dancer in Paris, and came over to him one evening in a Paris night-club, remembering his dancing-skill.[2] Loos famously designed a house for Baker with a pool having glass sides, where she could perhaps be seen swimming naked.[3] It is not quite clear whether she commissioned it, or it was a result of his fascination with Baker.

When the quarter where the Maison Zilveli was built was devoted to housing, having hosted an Olympic football stadium since 1912, a ceremony was held marked by cutting a tape — and Josephine Baker was the celebrity invited to do the honors. That more distant link comes alive, however, with the Maison Zilveli design and its links to Loos and Le Corbusier.

Jean's second independent commission resulted in a remarkable building on a site that could hardly be more different from the first. Where the Maison Landau was flat and suburban, Zilveli was on a precarious urban hillside with direct distant views to the hilltop basilica of Sacre Coeur at Montmartre to the back of the site, and to the Eiffel Tower from the long side-facade. Both tourist-attractions are marked on the simple hand-drawn plan, indicating they were important to the design.

The triumph of Maison Zilveli is that on a difficult site and with a low budget, Welz creates a daring and exciting building, one that carries on the dialogue with Loos and Le Corbusier, but again — as at Darmstadter — goes beyond that to achieve a building that is very much his own.

Zilveli strikes out in an avant-garde direction that bears comparison with the most adventurous work in Europe, and in so doing arguably moves beyond both Loos and Le Corbusier in that regard. However, it also remains consistent with many of the ideas of Adolf Loos, and what I would see as Welz's continuing critique of Le Corbusier's formal program of The Five Points.[4]

In the same year that Loos died, Zilveli pays tribute to his themes both externally and internally. Externally, he arguably takes the principle of plainness further than Loos ever did, and internally he develops a complex version of what by now had been christened the Raumplan[5] — Fischer's "Chemin Aérien" — of varying floor levels.

The dialogue with Le Corbusier carries on with a building that has certain superficial similarities to his ideas — the long side elevation raised on pillars being the chief one — but departs from them in four of the Five Points of Modern Architecture. Where Welz developed his own approach to the Open Plan in the Villa Darmstadter, here he proposes alternatives to the other four "Points": pillars, the long window, the free facade and the roof garden.

Zilveli is striking in visual appearance, but also has great coherence as an architectural project. Welz creates a *dramatic* building, but he does so from a rigorous attention to the possibilities and limitations of the site, which he overcomes with practical, functional solutions that — while literally airborne — keep both feet very firmly on the ground, in functional terms. The most obvious example is the use of the pillars, with which he raises the long side facade off the ground.

Why lift it up? The answer is visible on the simple plan, the arrows and text indicating "Sacre Coeur" and "Eiffel Tower" — those two little indications are fundamental to the solutions Welz found.

It is a narrow strip of land, but deep. However, the depth also leads from the street to the hillside, and begins to descend quite steeply, as shown on Welz's hand-drawn plan. The positive aspect to the hillside location is that it raises the houses some considerable distance above the street level below the hill, and in so doing creates the potential for views right across Paris and to two major attractions the city has to offer. The back of the site looks towards the next hilly quarter, Montmartre, and at its highest point, the dome of Sacre Coeur, while the long side-elevation next to a small park, with the advantage of no buildings next to it, has a clear view to the distant Eiffel Tower, the number one sight in Paris.

Why raise the floor but not use the area beneath it to create more accommodation? There are nearly always planning limitations imposed to the amount of accommodation you are allowed to create on a site of a given size. In effect, Welz has swapped rooms on the ground for room in the air — a practical solution with a clear function, with the huge bonus of the views.

There is a difference between pillars as part of a formal system, as arguably the case in Le Corbusier's manifesto, and pillars to do what otherwise could not be done — which is how Welz uses them at Zilveli. Another small mark of Welz's independence is that his pillars are not the same as Le Corbusier's. Welz uses cruciform pillars, reminiscent of the shape preferred by Mies van der Rohe for the Barcelona Pavilion of 1929 and the Villa Tugendhat, completed in 1930.

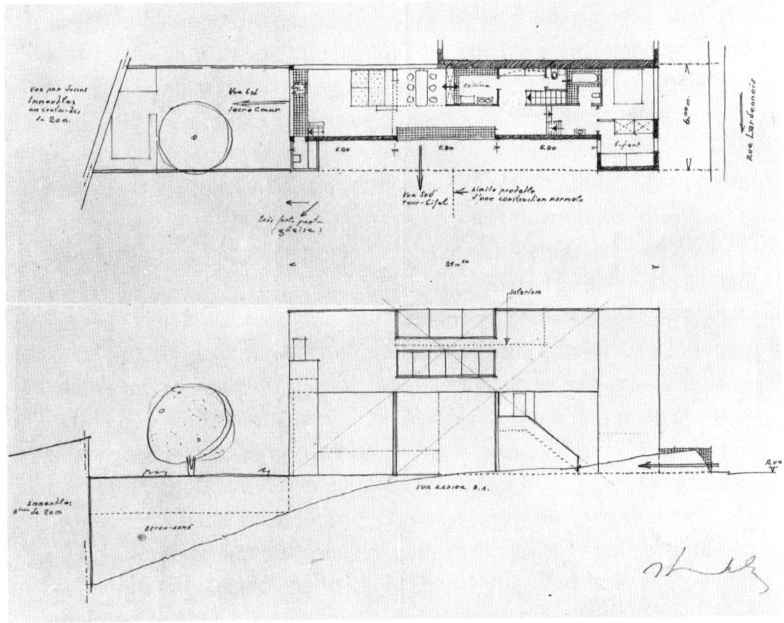

Jean Welz, Maison Zilveli plan, 1933. Note the two arrows pointing east and south to views of Paris attractions and the steep declination of the site, which was infilled to the dotted line. The lower elevation drawing features Corbusian "tracés régulateurs" connecting the staircase to the solarium. Courtesy Welz family via Jean-Louis Avril.

Where Le Corbusier wanted to give his pillars a strong visual form, Mies wanted to make the structure disappear,[6] and it may be a similar reason Welz chose the cross-shape over the round one, with an aerial floor on slim pillars.

Above the pillars, the walls are traditional load-bearing in type, with a concrete skim for the surface, made in sections on site as the construction process would have been artisanal and low-tech rather than high-tech and industrial. Throughout Zilveli, the walls are load-bearing, a contradiction of Le Corbusier's preference for the "curtain-wall" kind of construction, dating back to his Dom-Ino model of 1914, described in the Five Points as the Free Facade.

The pillars could, in theory, have carried on up, above the raised floor to form supports for the roof, but they do not, and that is consistent with the preference for traditional construction methods that we also see expressed in Loos, even in this most unconventional building.

The concrete skim in sections along the raised side elevation, as seen in the photograph of 1933, shows no apparent intention to cover the joins between the sections, where the concrete was applied. We may assume the builders only had access to one section at a time, perhaps to save costs on scaffolding. However, instead of applying a surface treatment to unify the whole facade, it appears that Welz left the marks of the joins showing, and that may well have been a deliberate intention (as the same idea appears in the terrace discussed further on). Pleasure in showing the marks of making was a feature of modernist thinking at the time, the desire to be honest about structure, rather than hiding it behind a coating that disguised the way something had been made.

The side elevation has a long horizontal window that is reminiscent of Le Corbusier's preference for the "fenêtre longue," but in his case that was part of his curtain-wall strategy, the lack of walls in the way meaning that a window could, in theory, stretch from one end to the other of a building, including around the corner, as first seen in the Fagus Factory of 1911 by Walter Gropius and Adolf Meyer.[7]

In this case, the window is long, probably because it has a view of the Eiffel Tower available from it. It is also the only window along that facade, and its length would help to bring light into the interior. In fact, the plain concrete with the central window is a minor echo of the layout of the Darmstadter facade, a symmetrical one.

The other window on the raised floor is at the rear of the site — the whole wall being window — a little like the Le Corbusier Esprit Nouveau house window that Welz would have seen at the 1925 *Art*

Jean Welz, Maison Zilveli (1933), end facade facing away from the street. The window faces towards Sacre Coeur. Courtesy Welz family via Jean-Louis Avril.

Deco exhibition. Again, it uses an expanse of glazing to make the most of the view, this time to Sacre Coeur at Montmartre. The end wall is divided into smaller panes, a reminder that this was a low-cost building — one or two big pieces of glass would have been very expensive at that time, even if it had been possible.

The last of the Five Points that has a reference at Zilveli is the roof-garden. Again, here Welz does something different. Instead of a roof garden there is a "solarium," and one of very precise dimensions, which is an exact echo of the long-window beneath it, in fact a mirror-image of that aperture. The cut-out in the shape of the side elevation (see Welz's hand-drawn plan) is a very definite one, emphasized on the plan by the "*tracés régulateurs*" which show its symmetrical design, and underlines the desire to make the most of the view to the Eiffel Tower by creating an outside equivalent to the view from the interior directly below it. So again, this is not a general notion of putting a garden on the roof but a very specific function for a very specific shape — providing a sitting-out or sunbathing area oriented towards the available Eiffel Tower view.

The only other of Le Corbusier's points refers to the Open Plan. Perhaps partly because of the limitations of the narrow site, the open area on the main Zilveli floor is limited to the raised floor and corridor outside the kitchen, which leads down a couple of steps onto the dining-area and living-room, both of which have higher ceilings than the rest of the house (see interior photos on the following pages). The echo in that arrangement gestures perhaps more to Adolf Loos's varied floor-levels than to Le Corbusier.

Loos's ideas feature more heavily, and more literally, in the Maison Zilveli than they did in the Villa Darmstadter. As Loos's final illness went back over a year, it is possible Welz was making his own tribute to his mentor at Zilveli, as the Chemin Aérien arguably takes the idea further than had Loos himself, and that can be said of more than one feature of this house.

First of all the street facade. It has a plainness that arguably exceeds Loos in its absence of ornament.

Among the Welz portfolio I could not find a period photograph of the street facade. All the photos were of the side elevation and the interiors were also of that floor. The immediate contrast is with the neighboring house in smart red brick. The windows are very plain indeed, and appear to be almost inserted in holes cut in the wall without much in the way of ledges above or below. It would appear that the facade was painted in a cream color at some point, but whether that is original or not is difficult to tell on sight. However, the joins in the panel of concrete skim that we can see on the period photos of the side elevation are absent here, as though a minimal effort was made to present at least a single plane of finish to the concrete.

The entrance is to the left, a tunnel under the block above it. To the right there are windows, but it may well be that was originally intended to be a garage, although what appears to be the original fence suggests that such a plan was changed before the fence was erected.

The short tunnel leads under the bedroom block, which has a wide room on the first floor and two smaller rooms on the top floor, including a parents' bedroom with the three window panels and a children's room with two. The nearest thing to ornament is the coping along the roof line.

It is particularly in the context of the neighbors that this radical plainness hits you in the eyes, and must have done so from day one, although the lack of maintenance in the intervening period has not improved appearances.

The Loosian features continue from the street facade to the interior, and in two main ways. Firstly, the route from the street to the furthest parts of the house, and the varied floor levels that we find in

Maison Zilveli street facade, 2013. Photo: Jean-Louis Avril.

the interior are both part of what became known as the Raumplan. I find the term Raymond Fischer used, Le Chemin Aérien, or Aerial Way, a more visually explicit term, and Welz took up that theme with enthusiasm and rigor from his first house, the Maison Dubin.

Here the route from the street emerges from the tunnel into the open, past a small circular pillar. I wondered why it was circular, à la Le Corbusier when the rest were cruciform, but it occurred to me that it may be a simple practical matter that a round pillar is less likely to catch things on when you are entering the building, carrying the shopping, for example.

The staircase is set into the main building, protected to some degree from bad weather by the floor of the raised section above. The angle of the staircase was originally defined by Welz's use of the "regulating lines" that Le Corbusier employed to rationalize the proportions of his facades, but apparently the angle was too steep for practical use, and so Welz reduced the angle as built.

The shaded area in the foreground shows that again the surface appears unpainted, although there is a suggestion of dark paint ahead at the top of the stairs to waist-height, which was perhaps a practical element to protect against wall damage, from baggage or furniture being carried past.

Approaching the front door at the top of the first flight of stairs is a window to waist height with another to the left and around the corner. They give onto the hallway, which is an enclosed staircase in terrazzo tiling, ascending to the right.

Internally, the enclosed staircase reaches a small landing with two options. First, if you carry on ahead, there are a few steps in front of you down to the large front bedroom that faces onto the street (its windows are obscured by a small tree in the street facade photo).

In the shaded area to the right of a side-on photo (see page 204) a three-paneled window to that bedroom is visible, with another similar window diagonally across the room. On the side away from the street and adjoining the neighboring house, there is a space off the bedroom with washing facilities.

The second option from the landing is to turn back ninety-degrees to face towards the back of the site; the staircase, still enclosed on either side, ascends to the main raised floor, with a landing and ahead, the kitchen door. Meanwhile to the left, there is another door onto the hallway of the top floor. (See the hand-drawn plan on page 195 for the details of this floor as drawn by Welz.)

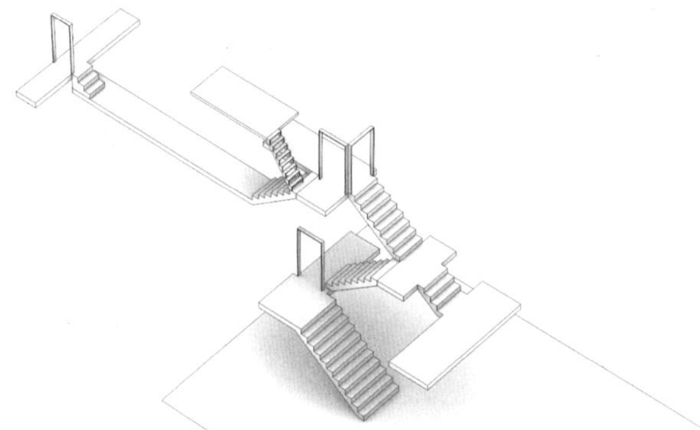

Above: Maison Zilveli (1933). Staircase to the "front door" to the right. This angle was published in *L'Architecture d'Aujourd'hui* that year, but without any text. It is also clear from this view and the side view (see page 204) that there are three or four play areas with divides between them, one or two possible sand-pits and a ledge/seat to the far left. Courtesy Welz family.

Below: Maison Zilveli interior axonometric 'aerial way' render by Hugh Wyeth. Note that the bedrooms do not appear here. Also see Plates, Figure 1 for a version with colored route arrows highlighting the two pairs of interior/exterior views.

Maison Zilveli (1933), raised floor with a view to the rear of the site. Note Jean Welz looking towards the camera from the external balcony — close-up opposite page. Courtesy Welz family.

As soon as one goes through that door into the hallway one can turn left, where there is first a bathroom and then the parents' bedroom, opposite the children's bedroom (again, these are shown on Welz's drawing). A tiled floor gives access to these spaces.

Facing along the side facade, one can turn right to look through the building to the rear of the site, as pictured in the photo opposite, the staircase to the solarium without risers to maintain the open view.

In the foreground, you can see the plain square dark tiles, to the left a hand-basin in front of the open stairs. If you walk forward, the level and the surface changes. Beyond the tiles are three steps down to the rest of the floor which has a wood-strip surface. There are two radiators at ninety-degrees to the wall (taking less wall space), one before the long window and one after it. A globe rests on the foreground of the window-seat, which extends the full length of the long window. The hinges of the door to the staircase landing are just visible to the right of the photo.

In the bleached-out area of the middle of the photo, through the long window there is a slightly crouched figure just about visible, actually standing on the external balcony and looking towards the camera. The crouch betrays that the tall figure is Jean Welz, standing on the extraordinary jutting-out balcony visible in the external photographs.

If one were to continue ahead, the space has the kitchen window to the right, opposite the long window, and then the space opens out in terms of width and of height.

The foreground, in the top photo opposite, reveals that this "living area" is a double-height space, as is the dining area to the left. The lower ceiling by the long window is an indication of the solarium above. To the left in the distance is a built-in shelving unit that gives onto the kitchen behind, also functioning as a servery for dishes to be passed through from the kitchen. The dining table is a massive wooden structure, built into the wall to the left. The Zilveli family story is that the table was made by a sculptor friend. On one visit, burglars of the then-empty house had wrenched it out of the wall, but it was so heavy that they gave up trying to remove it from the house.

The foreground of the image shows another open shelving unit, a simple piece that looks as though it was designed for the house by Welz. Note the side walls in the foreground are painted a darker contrasting color (a theme from Raymond Fischer that Welz adopted here, and in practical terms, leaving the upper area of the wall white as it would be dark without windows or other sources of light). To the right in the background are the steps up to the higher level corridor.

Turning again to the opposite direction of view, the next photograph is taken further into the room and is perhaps a little later, with rugs on the wooden floor. In front of the distant rear window it is just possible to make out a ledge. In fact, the photo foreshortens it as it is a meter or so deep and covered in the same dark square tiles as the hallway.

What is not visible from any of these interior photos is that there is a tall narrow doorway to the left of the tiled area, giving onto the external balcony (see the Welz drawing and the exterior photo of the long side-elevation), accessed by three steps up from the main wooden floor, another change of floor level. In the journey from the

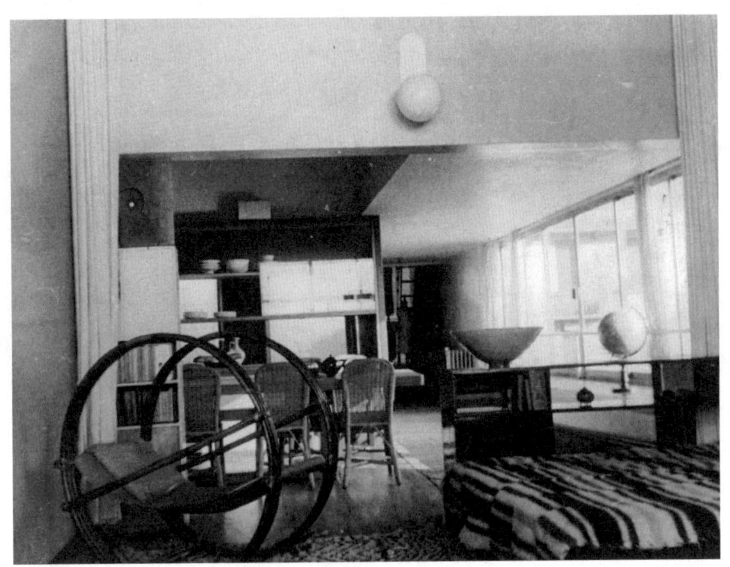

Above: Maison Zilveli (1933), the reverse view from the rear of the site towards the street. Note the contrasting colors on the walls left and right — color replacing ornament. Courtesy Welz family.

Opposite: side view. Courtesy Welz family.

Maison Zilveli (1933), edited photograph (possibly by André Kertész) with a focus on the balcony. Courtesy Welz family.

street to the back of the house, this is the final change of level, as if it were a final tribute to Adolf Loos. The balcony behind that door is the most extraordinary feature of the house.

The balcony (now destroyed, only the foundation elements of concrete and steel reinforcement bars remain in the ground) was one of the most fascinating elements of the design. It was supported only by a six-centimeter-thick wafer of reinforced concrete.

The imprints of the wooden formers remain uncovered, revealing the imprint of both the tall vertical planks and surmounted by horizontal ones. This may be the first time such a "brut" (brutal) finish was used anywhere externally, and Welz seems to have gotten the idea from working on the Rue de Charonne flats, where the lift towers had such a finish (see below) before they were covered with a smooth skim.

There was also another important element of the balcony design. It had a built-in seat and desk as part of the concrete construction (see plan page 195 and detail on page 234), with the ensemble providing another, external, view towards Sacre Coeur. That mirrored the sightline from the picture-window inside, providing an internal and external version of the same view.

That, in turn, was an echo of the internal and external views of the Eiffel Tower from the long-window and the solarium respectively.

Rue de Charonne flats (1930–32), internal courtyard lift-towers in béton-brut during construction. Photograph from Welz's portfolio. Courtesy Welz family.

With the simplest of means, Jean Welz made the most of a narrow site on a steep hillside at Zilveli, creating four views in all, in two pairs, two external mirroring the two internal versions.

This doubling of the view, matching interior with exterior view, was something that Welz did slightly differently at the Villa Darmstadter. There, the object of view was the garden, seen from the ground floor through the full-height glazing, and from the first floor likewise, but looking down on nature and perhaps ahead to tree level.

With Zilveli, Welz creates a more radical version of the interior/exterior mix, with the solarium and projecting balcony both fully external, both in the air, both providing different views. The first — reclining on a deckchair in the Solarium, with walls protecting you on three sides, enveloping you as you can look to the Eiffel Tower in the far distance, followed by the second — the balcony, afforded with a built-in seat and desk facing towards Sacre Coeur, where you are in a far more exposed position, out on a limb, and with the option in a standing position of turning one hundred and eighty degrees the other way to look back along the long aerial facade of the house.

That remarkable and precarious-looking balcony was the final destination of the Chemin Aérien, which in this case has become quite literal. It was a journey ending in the air, the climax of a most complex and varied way that begins with the ultra-plain facade onto the street and takes the visitor on an ingeniously varied path.

First outside, then inside, then outside again — but twice, first with the solarium and then the extraordinary aerial balcony. The route from the street involves more than a dozen changes in direction and level along the way. Jean Welz had conceived a promenade of great variety, with such modest means, and an even more modest budget.

He had combined the open air at the start (from the street gate, under the overhead block, to the external staircase to the "front" door), and doubly so at the end (Solarium and Balcony). In contrast, he had created the funnel of the tightly-enclosed internal terrazzo staircase, ascending one floor before turning back on itself in order to arrive at the main suspended-floor.

After that — opening out, first gradually, then more and more, until ending at the double-height space with the picture-window having the view of Sacre Coeur, twinned with the same view, but from the precarious open-air platform of the balcony, with its built-in desk and seat.

To achieve such a range and variety on such a narrow site is an extraordinary achievement in itself, and one that compares interestingly with the Raumplan layouts Loos designed in his final years. But where Loos relaxed the Raumplan by the time of the Villa Winternitz (1931–32), reducing complexity and the opacity of the route, Jean Welz at Zilveli creates a tightly-woven pattern, one that orchestrates the available dimensions of the outside, as well as enclosing, then opening, more than once, the inside, the interior route, as part of the range of variations offered to the promenader.

On his first outing, at the Maison Dubin, Welz tightly organized the path through the building, but in the Maison Zilveli he has upped his game a notch or two, to exploit every opportunity the site offers. To summarize, the long side-facade facing onto the hillside park provides an open-aspect he takes advantage of with the open-air stairs to the door on the next level, then offering a staircase twisting upward. Once at the top, another range of visual experiences offers itself — involving changes of level, touristic views to the two major Paris attractions, mirroring internal and external views, a low ceiling followed by a double-height one, and the picture-window comprising the whole wall as you reach the conclusion of the promenade — unless you take the left-hand side-door onto the gloriously perilous balcony. All this, despite the site constraints, is a remarkably energetic creative conception.

Two photographs were published in *L'Architecture d'Aujourd'hui* in the same year the house was finished (see following page). There was no text describing it, and both the address and Welz's name were given incorrectly.

Maison Zilveli was registered at the local Town Hall under the name of Raymond Fischer. In fact, that would have been a matter of generous support from Fischer as a registered architect, in order to obtain the permit to build that would not have been available to Jean Welz, as he was unregistered.

In this case, at least there is no doubt about authorship. Fischer lent support, but this was an independent commission of Welz, only his second. One unusual feature, again an adaptation to the site, is that while the street facade is ultra plain and discreet, the drama is reserved for the side elevation. That is very unusual in itself, but in the circumstances of this particular site, an end-plot giving onto a public space unlikely to be built over, it makes sense. More than that, it again makes the most of the potential of the particular site in terms of creating a striking building as well as one that functionally creates the doubled twin views.

A year after the Villa Darmstadter, the Maison Zilveli is proof of a remarkable versatility. Welz produces a house whose design is so avant-garde as to compare favorably in that respect with anything being built anywhere in the world at that time, and despite only being able to call on a very limited-budget.

Notwithstanding those major financial constraints, Welz manages to pack an awful lot of architectural features in to a very constricted and tricky site. Jean's design is very daring, and in terms of form it is both rigorous and elegant, whilst at the same time constituting a comprehensive riposte to the Le Corbusier Five Points. On top of that, his development of the Chemin Aérien is arguably the most sophisticated and extensive version that had yet been seen and, with the death of Adolf Loos in the same year, a fitting tribute to his influence on Welz.

Welz's apparently simple hand-drawn plan, the most basic presentation imaginable, is nevertheless, in its own modest way, a triumph of the kind of high-quality architectural thinking he had already displayed at the Villa Darmstadter. It goes to show that it is the mind behind the design in the end that is all that counts, and a pencil and scrap of paper is perfectly adequate if the ideas that it expresses are first-rate.

MAISON PARTICULIÈRE A PARIS, RUE LARDENNAIS
JEAN WELZ ARCHITECTE 1933
70 Georges Lardennois PARIS 19e
UNE VUE DE LA PIÈCE DE SÉJOUR
53

Photocopy from *L'Architecture d'Aujourd'hui*, 1933, via Jean-Louis Avril, who made the annotations correcting the mistaken address and misspelling of Welz's name. Note in the below image a shadowy figure on the balcony visible through the long side window — probably Jean Welz, who thus actually gets his image in the journal, if only in the background and hardly visible.

The Maison Zilveli shows a splendid depth of thought and creative imagination hand in hand and, to my mind, Jean Welz had created his second masterpiece in two years.

By the big picture-window to the rear of the Maison Zilveli, Jean sits next to Inger, with their first born (of five sons), on the raised tiled area adjacent to the window looking out to Sacre Coeur.

How proud Jean must have been to be portrayed thus with his young family at this peak of his achievement, less than a decade after arriving in Paris, and, when the house was completed, he was barely thirty-three years old. What future did he imagine for himself at this point? Maison Zilveli was to be his last house in Paris, his last commission, and an end rather than a glorious beginning to his career as an architect.

NOTES

1 Ellis Woodman, "Le Corbusier Burst into Tears When He Heard Josephine Baker Singer 'Baby,'" *The Architectural Review*, June 4, 2014. thearchitecturalreview.com/essays/

2 Claire Beck Loos, *The Private Adolf Loos: Portrait of an Eccentric Genius*, Los Angeles: DoppelHouse Press, 2020, pp. 37–39.

3 More about this idea can be found in Farès el-Dahdah and Stephen Atkinson, "The Josephine Baker House: For Loos's Pleasure," *Assemblage*, No. 26 (April 1995), p. 80. They write, "The house does not belong to the person of Josephine, but to the exoticized body she constructed and to Loos's design pleasure in imagining it."

4 By this time Le Corbusier had effectively abandoned the Five Points, but he never said why.

5 The term Raumplan was coined by Loos's assistant, Kulka, in *Adolf Loos: Das Werk des Architekten*, Vienna: Anton Schroll Verlag, 1931.

6 This last idea generously suggested by Tim Benton.

7 I recalled that building as I had written an article about it for *The Modernist*.

Inger, Jerry and Jean Welz in Zilveli, 1933. Photo: André Kertész. Courtesy Welz family.

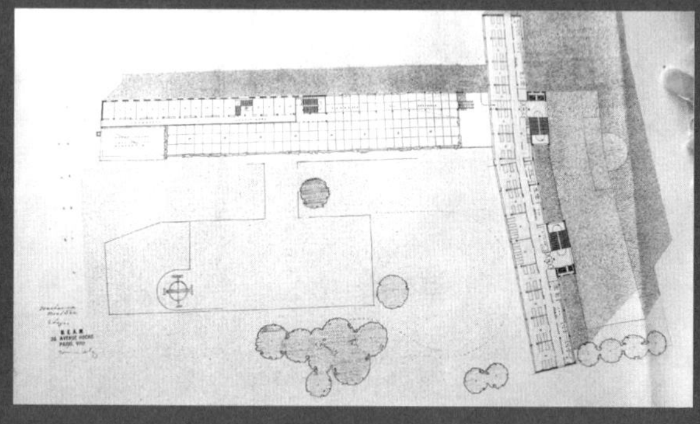

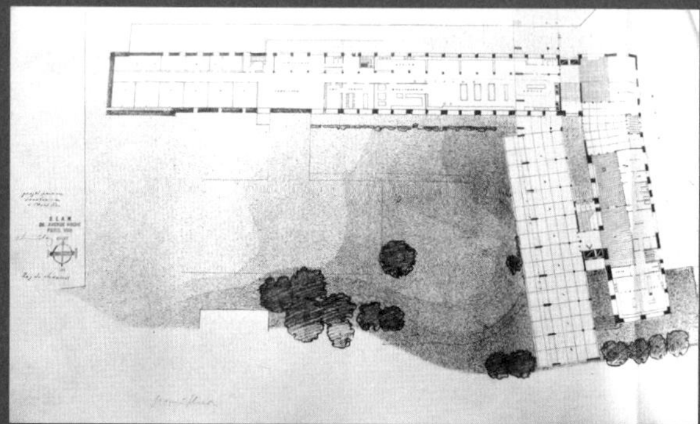

Jean Welz, Mont d'Or Sanatorium project (circa 1934–35). Courtesy Welz family.

Above: rendering, 65 x 30 cms; center: a typical upper floor; below: ground floor plan.

21

MONT D'OR AND PAVILLON D'AUTRICHE
THE UNBUILT

THE MOST IMPRESSIVE architectural drawing we have by Jean Welz is for a sanatorium project at Mont d'Or, southeast France. It was intended to be on the site of an existing hotel near the Alps, a location providing the benefits of clean air for tuberculosis patients.

The perspective is a high-quality drawing, with exquisite charcoal sfuso effects and suggesting a line of hills or mountains in the background. With this standard of skill, it is no surprise that Jean turned to art when his architectural career came to a premature end. The drawing is stamped S.E.A.M, with an address in the eighth arrondissement of Paris. That may be the client,[1] but the drawing is undated. It was an independent commission, and not under Raymond Fischer, suggesting one of the periods, rather the rule after 1932, when Fischer had no new work.

The drawings show a well-developed project that, like so many in the years leading up to the Second War, was fated not to be built. The plan drawings of the ground floor and a typical floor show how far the project design had gone, so that it was a practical prospect for building and must have involved months of work and perhaps site visits.

The obvious comparison to Mont d'Or is the famous Sanatorium by Alvar Aalto of 1933, "one of the most significant works of international Modernism in the inter-war period."[2] Whereas Aalto designed for one hundred and eighty-four, later raised to two hundred and eighty-four patients, most in single rooms, the Mont d'Or proposal was for over five-hundred patients in mainly four-bed rooms, twelve on each floor with two five-bed rooms: fifty-eight patients per floor over what would appear to be nine floors.

For Aalto, Paimio was a four-year project, from 1929 to 1933, and the planning and drawing stage of Mont d'Or must also have taken a considerable time. Paimio was the first such project for Aalto, as it would have been for Welz, and the complexity of issues to be taken into account at Mont d'Or — the distance of the kitchens from the bedrooms, with four dumb-waiter lifts from the kitchen area to the upper floors with perhaps trolleys from the lifts to the wards; the other lifts: two passenger lifts to the right of the entrance hall, which appears to have escalators down to the main entrance, approached on a curving road, as at Paimio, and at the other end of the main block, a larger lift perhaps to take beds, alongside another passenger lift; accommodation for nurses and doctors for over five-hundred patients; the exercise ground for patients in the enclosed area between the two wings of the L-shaped design — all would have taken considerable discussion with the medical and engineering specialists involved in the planning.

On visual grounds, at least, the Mont d'Or perspective bears comparison with the Aalto design. In fact, it can be argued to be more attractive, with a more unified facade compared to the bend in the main Paimio facade, with terraces only on the closest part (the most often-used photo) and a plain windowed facade for the rest. In contrast, Welz's Mont d'Or project has a large, open, full-length ground-floor terrace. The building is raised above it on concrete pillars, with another terrace above that with full-width glazing to the small wards, which is only interrupted by narrow load-bearing pillars, perhaps in steel.

The Aalto project put the patient at the center of the design process, leading to single rooms, whereas the Mont d'Or scheme has four- and five-bed rooms drawn on the plans. Welz was almost certainly working to a commercial brief, and the cost of single rooms would obviously have been considerably higher.

The Mont d'Or drawings show that Jean Welz was more than able to work at the larger scale, and in particular, his drawing skills were at the highest level. As an overall conception, Mont d'Or is an impressive project, showing his ability to combine functional economy — in the plans of the ground floor and a typical floor above — with a unified and striking exterior facade that bears favorable comparison with the best — as with Aalto's famous Paimio, described as one of the "three institutional buildings inseparably linked to the rise of contemporary architecture."[3]

Above: Alvar Aalto, Paimio Sanatorium main facade (1929–33). Source: Frederic Covre, via divisare.com/authors/2144734746-alvar-aalto/projects/built. Courtesy Fabrice Fouillet.

Below: Spingkell Sanatorium in Modderfontein (now closed), where Welz stayed when he had tuberculosis. Source: theheritageportal.co.za/thread/springkell-sanatorium-modderfontein. Photographer unknown.

It must have been a sad irony for Jean Welz to lie in sanatoria, in 1939 and again in 1940, that bore little comparison to the ultra-modern facility he had designed a few years earlier.

As his tuberculosis recurred a few years before Jean Welz died, it would not be surprising if while lying in another hospital bed for weeks on end, his mind turned back to the handsome scheme he had designed nearly forty years earlier.

The perspective drawing, a presentational tool that does not seem to have been required for his housing work for Fischer, demonstrates the high level of creative skill that Welz would have been able to bring to the work for Fischer in the relatively short, intensely active period between 1928 and 1932. It also adds to our understanding of the range of his abilities and, in its conceptual level as a complex and demanding project, adds strength to the idea that he was at the least more than capable of taking on the role of the effective designer of the key modern designs of those five important years.

One larger project that did get built overlapped with Darmstadter and Zilveli in the period 1932–33, a medium-size block of flats for Fischer, completed above two existing shops. Fischer did not discuss it and Jean did not include it in his portfolio, but it was featured in Fischer's short-lived magazine during 1933–34, *L'Architecture Rationnelle* (see photo opposite).

The facade is reminiscent of the Rue de Charonne block and has strip windows that would have brought in the maximum of light to the flats in a narrow street.

It appears to be three flats wide over the two shops below, and suggests an effort to maximize the use of the street windows in the layout, which presumably had access towards the rear, perhaps off a central corridor in the middle of the building which would allow flats to the rear as well, creating perhaps thirty flats over the five floors.

Aerial views show what looks like a rooftop studio set back from the facade and not visible from the street. I have no further details, but the facade style suggests the design was quite possibly by Welz.

The Pavillon d'Autriche was another larger project, this time in the public sphere. Welz's design was an entry to the competition for the Austrian pavilion at the 1937 Paris international exhibition.

His proposal for the facade includes a large flag of the Republic (red with a white stripe), and that is mirrored by the facade design

IMMEUBLE D'HABITATION
Paris (14 ème), 77 rue de l'Ouest.
1932-33

Permission de construire du 30 septembre 1932 et récolement du 5 décembre 1934 indiquant l'achèvement des travaux, in Fiches parcellaires des Services Techniques du Plan de Paris. Photo in l'Architecture Rationnelle , *hiver 1933-34.*
Bâtiment construit sur des boutiques existantes.

Raymond Fischer, medium-sized block of flats (1932–33), published in Fischer's *L'Architecture Rationnelle.* Source: Gérard Cladel, Philippe Bodenan. *Raymond Fischer (1898–1988). Inventaires*, op cit.

which would have been in red bricks top and bottom with glass between.

The detail of the perforated brick design (see the drawing opposite page) also had an Austrian national echo, reflecting the Austrian Cross of Merit. Welz's side elevation carried the theme through, showing the brick pattern in detail. The large-scale national flag again emphasizes that element of the design.

Next, we note the sections and side elevation, which can be seen on the following double page spread. The section shows the lie of the land and the roof arrangement behind the front facade. The full side elevation includes a projector and screen, with the sight-line towards the screen shown from either side for visitors approaching or leaving the pavilion, and the rear section shows the suggestion of a pond with an island, with a tall tree set on it.

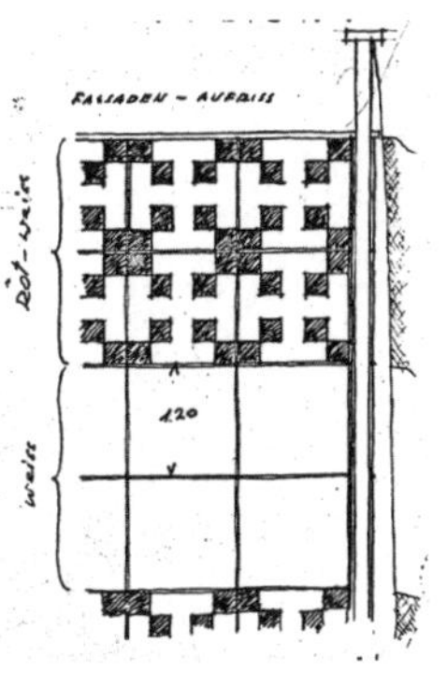

Jean Welz, Sketch of the facade for the Austrian Pavilion at the 1937 Paris Exhibition, with details of red brick design reminiscent of the Austrian Cross of Merit (example center right).
All sketches courtesy Welz family.

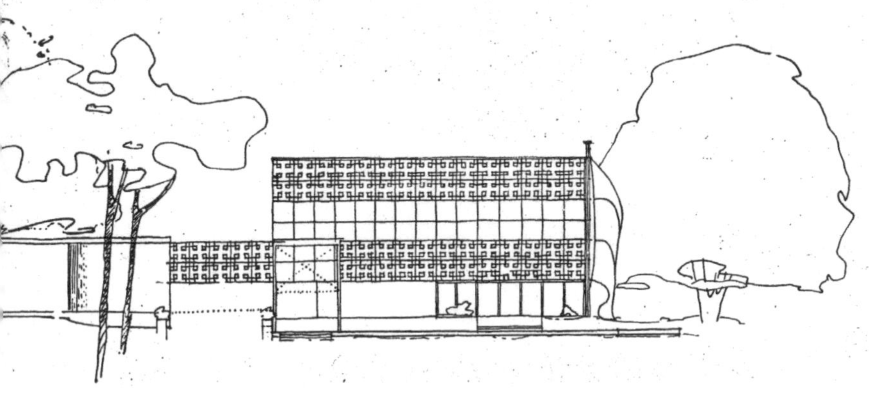

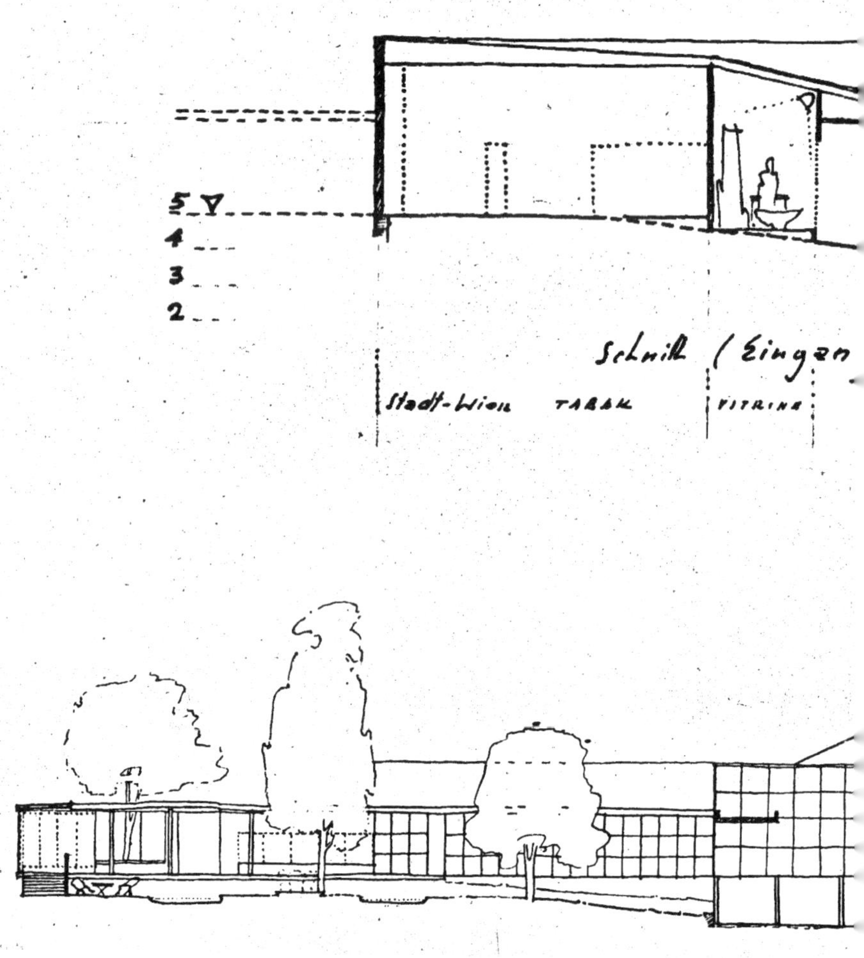

Jean Welz, side elevations for his Austrian Pavilion proposal of 1937, showing the integrated screen detail for projected images that could be seen by visitors on both sides and a reflected light source (dark dotted lines in the detail above) to illuminate the vestibule interior, probably through a translucent ceiling panel.

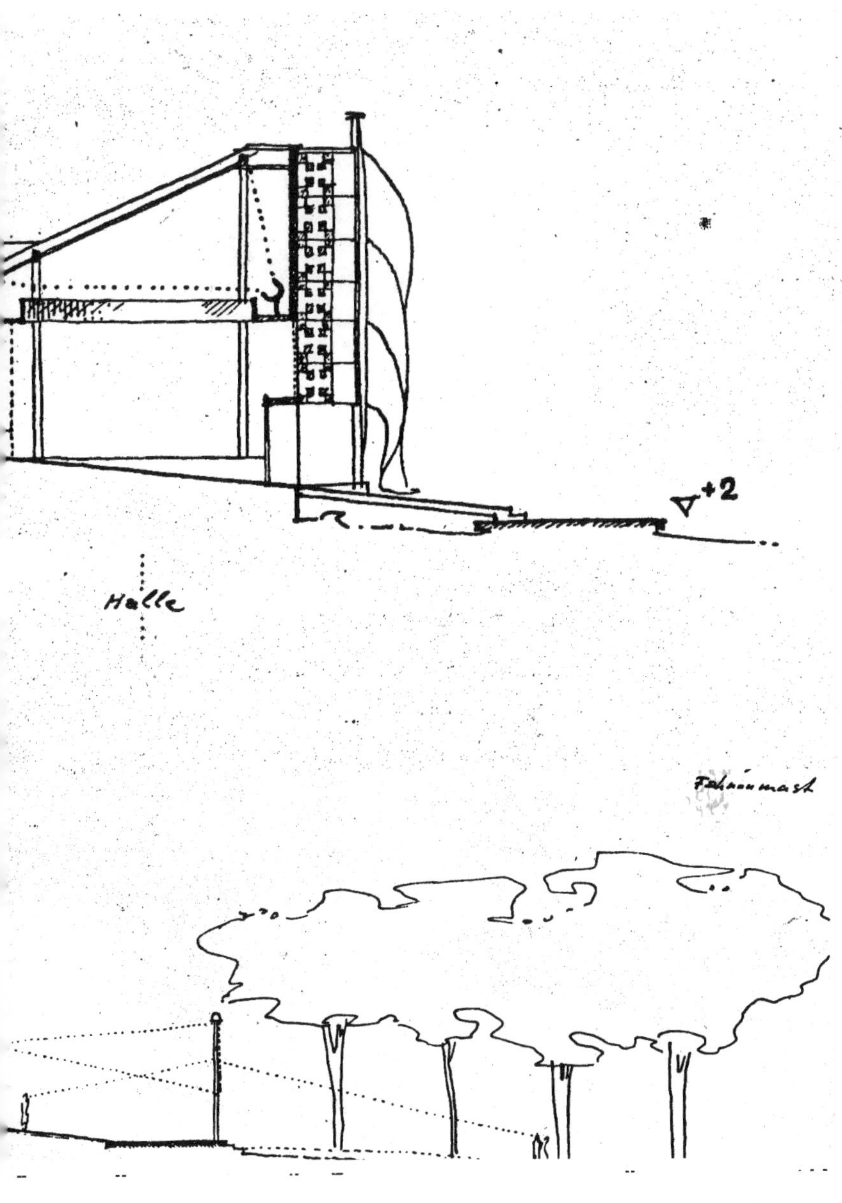
+2
Halle

110511
Insel
Schnitt
1:200
Garten und Wandelhalle
Ausstellungs-saal am Wasser

Ausstellungs-saal am Wasser

In the drawing opposite, the top left of the sketch (details of which are also enlarged below it) provides more detail of the rear section with the island and water. The lower right illustration shows an internal-garden view of the facades, with the box windows familiar from Welz houses and the Darmstadter facade, and again the lake, with a table and chairs on a terrace overlooking it.

On the upper left drawing, the few steps down remind us of Loos, and are an indication of the different levels in the Pavilion revealed in the plan.

The front facade is on the right of the plan view below. The arrows show the entrance and exit points and indicate the route through what is a varied path with changes of direction and level and a semi-circular section towards the rear of the site. Welz achieves a considerable range of effects, with views restricted by doors and walls that allow for a pleasing, meandering journey, and the semi-circular rear section with its internal pond and island, and at least a dozen trees of various sizes around the plot, provide a contrasting moment of nature, surrounded by a heavily-directed architectural promenade.

Within a relatively small site, Welz sets out to create a maximum of variety in the route taken by the visitor, an ideal challenge for such a building that basically has a one-way passage through it, allowing the designer to create that route in a way that could not be so directed for a house.

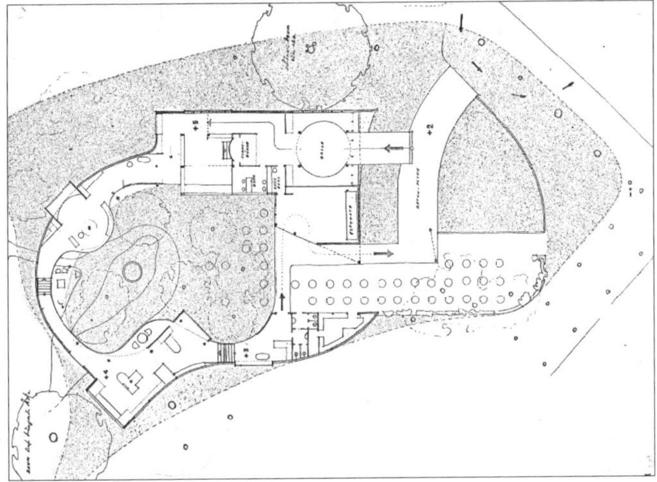

Opposite: Detail renderings of interior courtyard views.

Above: Austrian Pavilion plan, 1937. All courtesy Welz family.

The entrance (see detail opposite, top arrow) takes the visitor from the curved approach path to a concrete ramp at ninety degrees to it, under the "flag" and medal themes of the facade to a circular exhibition space, perhaps of double height. The route ahead is barred by a small stage with a curved backdrop, and that is followed by a zig-zag that begins the promenade through the building along a corridor and a step up.

The visitor passes under a threshold with a small room to the left, and ahead a change of direction is required by a glazed wall that looks onto the garden beyond, with a left ninety-degree turn, which becomes a curve into another circular space with views externally to trees and grass and internally to a pond. The path continues to curve, narrowing to a short flight of six stairs, and then opening onto a concrete curved terrace with chairs and table giving a view onto the pond. The path straightens and widens, carrying over the pond, before curving again and giving way onto a larger area with seating, boxed windows to right and left, and on the left side an external area onto the pond, curved again in outline and with a table and chairs.

The space then narrows again (see detail opposite, lowest arrow) and becomes heavily-constricted in a repeating theme of a flight of stairs down. At the bottom, another box window looks to the outside, and the route again bends in a widening curve to the left, through a narrowed threshold to a hall. Welz marks the path of the visitor with a dotted line continuing a circular route around a pillar, facing an exhibition case. The way out through a corridor has the visitors exit under a succession of three screens across the path, at different angles with images projected onto them. The route out is flanked on the right by an area of round tables under a tree or two, and otherwise in the open air.

It would seem likely that Jean couldn't afford to have a model made, and there does not seem to be a perspective drawing of the kind that makes such an impact with the sanatorium project. His entry was otherwise reasonably comprehensive, enough to create a three-dimensional rendering from his drawings (opposite, also see Plates).

By the time Jean decided to enter the Pavillon d'Autriche competition, his work for Raymond Fischer had dried up. He had now lived for over a decade in Paris and had cut his ties with Vienna. He had never really established himself there and, although he had a prestigious job at Hoffmann's, all that he had to his name was his work on the traditional country house that had occupied him for most of his time working under Fellerer. Although he was not one to get involved

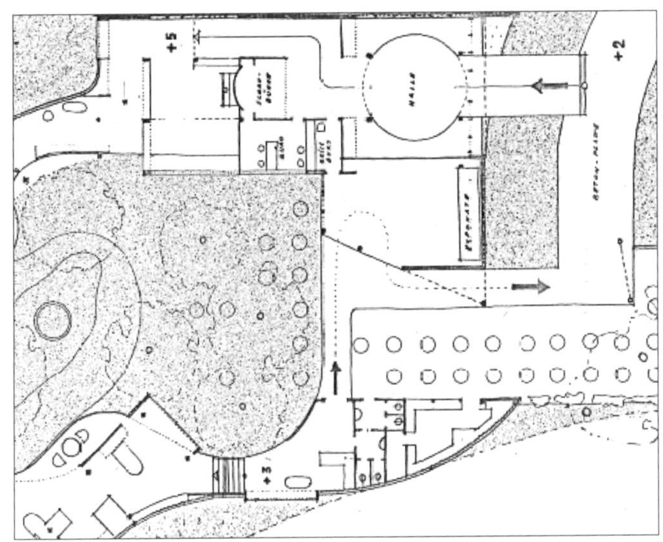

Above: Detail of entrance and exit (marked with arrows) on Welz's Austrian Pavilion plan, 1937. Courtesy Welz family.

Below: Jean Welz, Austrian Pavilion, 3-D render by Hugh Wyeth. See Plates, Figure 6 for an enlarged color version.

in jostling for position, he must have realized that this was a long shot. In the end, his design was not even shortlisted.

The competition was the focus of intense politicking, which in the end was won by Jean's old nemesis, Oswald Haerdtl. There were those who favored the entry by Otto Bauer, but he had a redoubtable opponent among the worthies involved, who very actively blocked Bauer winning when his entry received the most support among the jurors.[4]

Haerdtl, in contrast to Jean, was very-well established and closely allied with Josef Hoffmann, still the most powerful architect in Vienna. Haerdtl seems to have known everyone of influence and had his supporters, not least as his pavilion for an exhibition in 1935 for Austria had been considered a notable success.

His 1937 design was a development of the 1935 idea and took the use of large areas of glass further — again with considerable success, creating a dramatic facade of two stories entirely in glass and raised from the site floor. The 1937 pavilion was perhaps Haerdtl's best design, and the dramatic facade still has impact today.

The entry by Otto Bauer, a former pupil of Loos living in Paris, was only added to the final selection due to the high cost of all three of the shortlisted designs, and on the recommendation of the Austrian CEO and General Consul, General Guy Pascal Montmartin.

Entries from Erich Boltenstern, Oswald Haerdtl and Egon Fridlinger were shortlisted, but Bauer's was cheaper. Bauer was

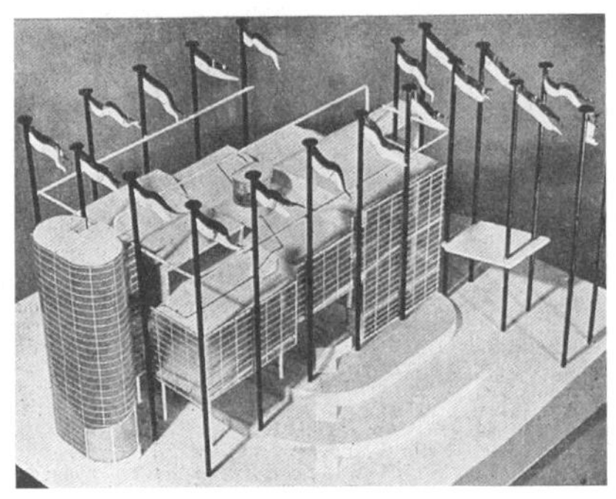

Opposite: Oswald Haerdtl, 1937 Paris Exhibition — Austrian Pavilion as built and model for the 1937 pavilion. Source for both: *Oswald Haerdtl, Architekt und Designer.* Collection Architekturzentrum Wien.

Above and center: Otto Bauer, 1937 Paris Exhibition, Austrian Pavilion proposal. Source for both: *L'Architecture d'Aujourd'hui* no 8 1937, p. 86, via portaildocumentaire.citedelarchitecture.fr.

Below: Otto Bauer, Les Peupliers, Garches, Paris, circa 1930. *L'Architecture d'Aujourd'hui* no 1 1938, p. 61, via portaildocumentaire.citedelarchitecture.fr.

established in Paris and had designed a large house with a circular glass tower at Garches. Bauer had developed the idea for his Paris proposal from the house at Garches, combining Loos and Art Deco with an economic and functional use of space.[5]

Bauer was also connected on a commercial basis to CEO Montmartin. "When a decision in favor of Bauer began to be made, Art Councilor Clemens Holzmeister, who favored Oswald Haerdtl, used his personal friend, the Minister of Trade and Transport Fritz Stockinger, to use all means from abroad to prevent Bauer from being commissioned. In the Austrian State Archives, a note with a telephone number can be found: 'Holzmeister requested not to commission Bauer under any circumstances.'"[6] In the end Haerdtl was commissioned.

Jean Welz's design creates a highly varied route on the tight site, with changes of level allied to different kinds of internal and external views — some with water, some with grass and trees. Welz's plan had a series of curves, against the squarer Haerdtl design, more organic, one might say than the Haerdtl, and the plan more flowing as an unfolding promenade. An elegant and complex design with Republican themes cleverly integrated into the facade. Admittedly, the Welz design had less immediate visual appeal than the Haerdtl proposal but was arguably more architecturally sophisticated behind the facade.

It would only be fair to say that the Haerdtl facade was a dramatic triumph — with its glass front suggesting an openness in the Austrian Republic that was one of the last optimistic throws before Hitler's Anschluss of 1938.

Anonymity in Paris would not have helped Welz in Vienna. His remarkable buildings there would have been both unknown, as they are today, and even if they had been known, they would have been credited for the most part to Raymond Fischer. He had no reputation to travel back to the selection panel in Vienna, nothing with which to build bridges where he had burned them a decade earlier. By 1936, there was no work in Paris and no hope of a triumphant return to Vienna.[7]

In terms of the competition itself, it is possible that nobody among the judges knew who Jean Welz was, and he would have been without a champion in the selection process.

Mont d'Or and the Pavillon d'Autriche were both elegant and highly sophisticated projects, providing strong evidence that Jean Welz's skills were far from limited to the single house. While the depth and breadth of his vision for the Villa Darmstadter and Maison

Zilveli suggested an architectural imagination considerably beyond that of most architects, the two bigger unbuilt projects suggest that here is an architect who would also have been capable of large-scale buildings of the highest quality.

Maison Zilveli was a triumph in many ways, and one may imagine Jean Welz's hopes that it promised at last what he had lived for — the chance to forge ahead with designs at the leading edge of modern architecture. However, it was a low-budget house completed in 1933, the year Hitler came to power, with the shadow of the 1929 crash looming ever-larger as fewer and fewer projects got built, especially modern ones. Realistically, opportunities would be few and far between, and Welz's 1933 house design for a Monsieur Rire,[8] similar to the Maison Landau but a little larger, joined the unmade projects.

In the end, the promise of Zilveli was not to be fulfilled, less a new start than the end of the road, at least in Paris. It was only Jean Welz's second personal commission, but destiny was not to hold a third.

NOTES

1 The drawing is stamped S.E.A.M, 36 Avenue Hoche, Paris, VIII, a building in a prestigious street near the Salle Pleyel which seems to let offices to companies in different industries. I have found no further information about S.E.A.M., but it could stand for something like Société Entreprise Alpes Maritimes — the location of Mont d'Or.

2 Marianna Heikinheimo, *Architecture and Technology, Alvar Aalto's Paimio Sanatorium* (dissertation), Aalto University, 2016.

3 Siegfried Giedion, *Space, Time and Architecture*, 2nd Edition, 1949. The other two were Gropius's Bauhaus and Le Corbusier's League of Nations entry, which was also unbuilt.

4 See Meder, "Fragmente zu Leben und Werk des Architekten Otto Bauer: 'Ihr Platz ist in der Welt.'"

5 See Franziska Bollerey (Case Study 7), in *Restaurants and Dining Rooms* edited by Franziska Bollerey and Christoph Grafe, Routledge, 2019.

6 From Meder, "Fragmente zu Leben und Werk des Architekten Otto Bauer: 'Ihr Platz ist in der Welt.'" My translation.

7 Although he passed through late in the year, en route to what he hoped was a new life. A family story had him commissioned to design a house for a wealthy relative, but I have been unable to find anything more.

8 For Maison Rire plans and comments, see Chapter 14, "The Portfolio."

TALES
PART V

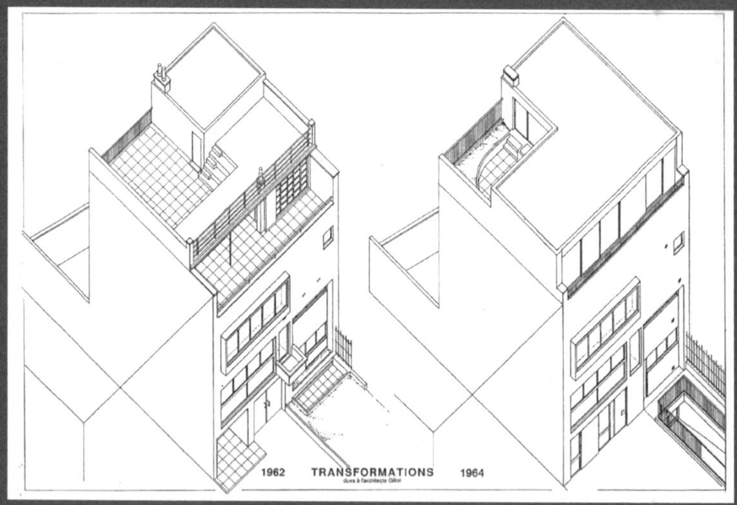

Above: Axonometric drawings of the Maison Dubin before and after the balcony reconstruction by the new owner. Courtesy Pascal Zeller.

Below, left: Maison Dubin as built in 1928, signed by Fischer to Welz. Photo: M. Gravot.
Below, right: Jean Welz playing guitar as a student, circa mid-1910s.
Both courtesy Welz family.

22

A TALE OF TWO BALCONIES

JEAN WELZ'S STATUS AS A "NÈGRE VIENNOIS" and the resulting absence of a public reputation as an architect had a price that can be seen in the fate of two keynote balconies he designed in Paris.

The first was on his debut at the Maison Dubin in 1927–28. Remember, he told his son Martin that the small cubic balcony on the front of the building was for him like the introduction of a theme in a piece of music, one that was to be developed throughout.

Welz had music in his blood. As mentioned, he played the guitar and the violin and was born around the corner from Mozart's birthplace in Salzburg; at eighteen, he was torn between an opera-singing career or one in architecture.

His first child, Jerome, had a memory as a small boy in Paris of his father returning home from a hard day's work bearing two copies of sheet music. The notes were printed on both sides of the paper, and to relax, Jean would paste first one side, then the other, along the walls of their small windowless basement flat. He would pick up his violin and walk around the room, playing from the two extravagant sequential copies. There was no money for toys for Jerry, but life without music was just not possible. Welz, as quoted by Miles: "I heard a Mozart concerto played by Busch in Paris, and my breath was so taken away that I had to grip the chair, and I will never forget it in my life."[1]

When Martin Welz visited the Dubin house in 1979, that balcony had been removed by the owner at the time, the President of the French architects' association, who said to Martin that he had no qualms about making alterations to the house (he also filled in the

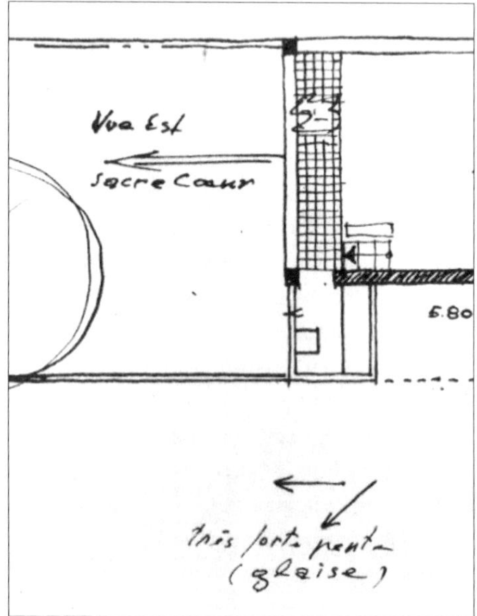

Above: Sacre-Coeur view from the Maison Zilveli location. Photo courtesy of the author.

Below: Maison Zilveli Plan, detail showing the balcony at the bottom edge. Two shapes can be seen there — a long built-in bench on the right and a small square "desk" to the left. Courtesy Welz family.

terrace on the roof, see page 232) as it was by "a lesser architect."

He meant Raymond Fischer, let alone the unknown Jean Welz, who would have received even less consideration from this distinguished fellow, who had also added the notable feature of brown patterned carpet carrying on from the floor via a small coving, up the wall for a foot or so. The aesthetic judgment of this leading bureaucrat is one thing, the arrogance of his attitude is another. Not just another architect, but nominal leader of the profession in France. Even this is simply further evidence of the price paid by Jean Welz for his lack of public profile, of reputation. This important fellow may possibly have thought twice about destroying the balcony had it been by a famous name, not just the chief architect to "a lesser architect,"[2] and, doubtless highly aware of the dignity of his leadership position among French architects, the 1979 incumbent felt not the slightest compunction in silencing Jean's keynote.

The final house Jean designed in Paris, the Maison Zilveli, also had a balcony integral to the design, one whose role was more important, as it marked the climax of the "aerial way," which built to a crescendo from the street to the furthest rear part of the hillside site and was an integral part of the conception of this extraordinary house.

The slim balcony, long rather than broad, that extended from the raised floor area by the picture-window at the rear of the house, and which featured a built-in small desk and long seat, could have been oriented inwards towards the rest of the house, or the adjacent community-garden, but instead it quite deliberately afforded a direct view of the basilica of Sacre Coeur, atop the next hill in sight, at Montmartre. It created an outdoor office as it were, where one could sit and contemplate the view, and use the desk to write one's thoughts, or sketch, provoked by that splendid view.

The balcony was designed to stick out so far from the house, I feel, as part of creating an outside view that would be separate from, but also an echo of, the inside one. As a result, the balcony could not cantilever from the wall, but needed an end support — the slim six-centimeter (roughly two and a half inch) blade of reinforced concrete bearing the marks of the wooden formers. It appears to have been built in-situ and, remarkably, in one piece — the support and the balcony itself have no joins. It was bonded into the wall with rebars projecting into the wall area, which would only then have been constructed around those bars.

It is inconceivable, to my mind, that Welz designed such a

structure without a deep knowledge of pre-stressed techniques, devising his own home-made version of those principles. Two 1933 photos (see below) show Welz's bravura with the "thin-wall" reinforced concrete method and with pre-stressing, perhaps adapted from the famous French engineer Eugène Freyssinet (see Chapter 32, "Zilveli Destroyed" for further elaboration). Both views emphasize its shocking thinness, the mark of a true master of structure. The support becomes a part of the visual effect of the building — a challenge to the viewer wondering how such a thin support could be safe — which keeps attention on the raised floor.

While the balcony may have partly been motivated by economy, the *brut* feature, inspired likely by the lift towers during construction in the Rue de Charonne flats (see Chapter 20, "Maison Zilveli"), marked Welz's artistic sensibility, which took a liking to the rough finish that tells the story of the use of the natural material to shape the concrete supporting blade. It also perhaps warranted a footnote in architectural history as the first example of an external *béton-brut* wall,[3] another point in the Jean Welz story that has gone unnoticed.

In 1986, the balcony was declared dangerous to public safety and destroyed by the local Police Authority. They submitted the proposal to the Architectes Batiments de France state organization, whose duty is protection of the Patrimony of architecture, but in their collective wisdom they failed to respond with any comment or objection to the demolition. Perhaps their knowledge of pre-stressed concrete

Maison Zilveli balcony details, 1933, showing the traces of the wooden shuttering on the end of the slim concrete supporting blade. The balcony was likely built all in one piece. Courtesy Welz family via Jean-Louis Avril.

or the history of beton brut was not quite *au fait*. From a 1973 photograph (see below), we know the balcony had already withstood the test of time for forty years. With such a sound structure, as I surmise it was, minor chipping or cracks to the concrete surface could easily have been repaired.

As a feature in a decayed modern building, by an unknown architect, and registered in the local Town Hall for sake of building permits under the name of Raymond Fischer, the balcony's fate is understandable, if ironic and sad. Its ruin is marked by the original foundations showing the steel reinforcing rods, observed by me in 2013. How differently the matter perhaps would have been handled if it had been by a prestigious name such as Le Corbusier.

Nevertheless, in 1964, Corbusier's masterpiece the Villa Savoye, then in a ruinous state, was only preserved from demolition by the eleventh-hour intervention of André Malraux, Minister of Culture. If the greatest name in modern architecture's most famous house was nearly lost only a year before his death in 1965, Welz has been comparatively fortunate with his first and last Paris designs. The Maison Dubin has got its balcony back. It would be splendid if that was to happen with the remarkable version at the Maison Zilveli.

NOTES

1 Quoted in Miles, p. 20.

2 A subsequent owner restored the balcony, although the interior has been altered and the top floor changes have not been returned to the original state.

3 Le Corbusier used a similar effect on the large pillars of the Maison Suisse in Paris, in 1931.

Maison Zilveli detail from 1973, showing only minor wear to the otherwise intact balcony. Courtesy Jean-Louis Avril.

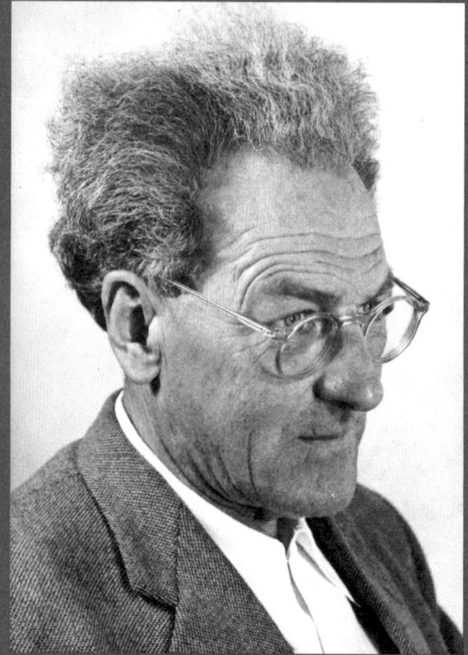

Above: Friedrich Welz at the Galerie Welz, 1963. Source: Austria Wochenschau (Austrian News reel) No. 35/1963. Courtesy Film Archiv Austria.

Below: Jean Welz, circa early 1960s. Courtesy Welz family.

23

A TALE OF TWO BROTHERS
THE DEALER AND THE ARTIST

FRIEDRICH WELZ IS DESCRIBED on the wall of the Leopold Art Museum in Vienna as a Nazi war criminal.

"Fritz" was Jean's younger brother by three years and never left Austria. After the war he became a powerful figure in Austrian Art, founding the Salzburg Art Festival that ran alongside the famous music festival, and became a close ally of Oskar Kokoschka, who was by that time no longer the pre-war "anti-fascist," but a conservative nationalist opposed to abstract art, donating most of his graphic art, along with Friedrich's private collection, to found a modern art museum in Salzburg, known today as the Museum der Moderne.

Friedrich was rewarded by the Austrian state and Salzburg authorities, and on his seventy-fifth birthday, in 1978, a celebration included an apologia by a returned Jewish exile whose father's pictures were shown in Friedrich's gallery in Salzburg in 1942. She took that as proof that "Fritz," as he was known in the family, could not have been anti-Semitic and presented him in the role of a victim whose motives were pure.

That so-angered a Salzburg historian that he wrote *Master of Intrigues*,[1] a book on Friedrich's dealings during the Nazi period, when Jewish property was aryanized for less than ten percent of its market value. In 2010, a legal battle begun in 1999 was settled, with nineteen million dollars awarded to the estate of Jewish gallery owner Lea Bondi Jaray, to recompense her heirs for the pressured acquisition, by Friedrich, of the painting *Portrait of Wally* by Egon Schiele, shortly after Hitler marched into Austria in 1938. In 2011, a forty-four million dollar Klimt painting bought by Friedrich was declared war loot, having been taken from its Jewish owner after she was deported to Poland, and later killed.

Friedrich was an SS officer, but he was not trusted by the Nazis, described in his file as not reliable, and first and foremost an opportunistic businessman. He had his official seal — to buy art for Hitler's proposed post-war museum — removed, following suspicions of fraud in his dealings with the Nazis.

Friedrich seems to have been, at best, a businessman taking advantage of circumstances. He could be very charming, and a highly-intelligent dealer, with considerable persuasive powers, whether with the SS, high officials in post-war Salzburg, or the daughter of a Jewish exile.

In 1945, he was arrested by the American authorities as a war-profiteer, but held for only two months. He was finally acquitted, in January 1950, of a series of accusations. From *Master of Intrigues*: "Swapping paintings with those publicly obtained as war loot, without inventory and subsequently allowing them to disappear, fiddling values in his own favor, fiddling values relating to estimates and to market values, covering up incriminating provenances and evidence of 'aryanization,' and deceiving the gullible into believing artworks had been purchased and paid for above-board and with correct receipts."[2]

"With the award of the title of Professor, through the appreciation of numerous national awards, but especially with the founding of the 'Rupertinum Modern Gallery and Graphic Collection' in 1977, which he served as its first director until his death on February 5, 1980, Welz achieved all the goals he had been pursuing since 1934," writes historian Gert Kerschbaumer.[3]

In 1934, when their father died, Friedrich took over his father's framing business, in Jean's absence, and is said to have visited Jean and the Paris galleries in 1936 — a memory that came in useful, suggests Kerschbaumer, when his Nazi bosses set out to plunder whatever art they fancied in Paris.

Jean's son Martin says that there was a falling out of the brothers on Jean's side, and Friedrich told him, when Martin visited Salzburg in 1979, that he did not understand what the falling-out was about. Jean felt he had been deprived of his inheritance by his younger brother. However, Jean's wife, Inger, had no patience with that idea, as the business was in a poor state at their father's death, and was only saved and improved by Friedrich's undoubted enterprise.

Friedrich's Nazi past was effectively buried post-war until the scandal of *Portrait of Wally* erupted in 1999, and the *Intrigues* book came out in 2000, followed by a film in 2012. After a hostile parting in 1936 (about their father's estate), there was no communication for thirty years between the brothers, until 1965. "Jean is unlikely to have known anything about his brother's politics. They simply had no contact. Jean never corresponded with his Austrian relatives, barring with his uncle Max, after the latter emigrated to America with his Jewish wife in 1938."[4]

Where Friedrich spent forty years executing a plan that would enrich him and raise his status to national hero, Jean was virtually the polar opposite, unconcerned with money or position.

> "In 1964, on their first brief return visit to Europe, Inger attempted a reconciliation with Fritz, who offered to host an exhibition of Jean's work in the Gallerie Welz, by then a highly regarded art establishment in Salzburg. Inger did the arranging; Jean only wrote a formal letter to Fritz, used in the brochure, that explained his philosophy of art and the impact of emigration on his work, describing his paintings as 'pieces of my soul torn from my existence.' After the 1965 exhibition, the status-quo of non-communication resumed."[5]

It is tempting to suggest that Jean left Austria for the kind of reasons that Friedrich stayed. Jean vividly remembered being told off as a child, by a neighbor in Salzburg, for playing with Jewish children, which must have been before the First War, a reminder of the deep-rooted anti-Semitism in Austria. According to Martin, Jean "was an anti-fascist," both in Austria and later. During his later life in South Africa, his children recalled him annually inviting a Black choir into the house at Christmas, something looked askance at by their neighbors. Jean went off cycling every day in the small town of Worcester, to talk art and politics with the only communist in the town, who ran the coffee-bar, and Jean readily volunteered to design improved drainage and toilet accommodation at the local mainly-Black school. He was disgusted when the students vandalized what had been newly built for them, but as an Austrian and of an older generation, that is no surprise. Preparing for the 1965 Salzburg exhibition, Jean told an interviewer: "In South Africa, any decent man can only walk the streets with a bowed head."[6]

If Jean was rather liberal in South African terms, Fritz was thought a savior of Jewish property by some and a Nazi war criminal by others — when perhaps neither was strictly true, though he certainly became wealthy from his bargain buys. The notice denouncing Friedrich in the Leopold Museum in Vienna was insisted upon by the New York prosecutors in the *Portrait of Wally* case, and agreed to by Rudolf and Elizabeth Leopold, whose own wider-ranging acquisition activities lay under not dissimilar clouds of suspicion — except they claimed the national interest rather than personal gain as their driving force.

Friedrich very adroitly welded together personal profit and professional ambition, to become a wealthy and eminent man — clearly without too-onerous a burden of moral scruples during the "National Socialist interlude." If he was not directly involved in sending Jews to their deaths himself, and never convicted of being a war-criminal, he did accumulate works of art at the expense of Jewish collectors whose belongings were "aryanized." It seems that he was possibly something of a daring opportunist who would profit from both the Nazis and the Jews, while claiming — when times changed — to be acting in the interests of the dispossessed.

He was able to get away with so much partly due to taking care not to have proper paperwork. As a result, little could be proved. It was also partly due to the climate in which he operated, which mainly sought to paper over the Nazi period, not least as the "de-nazification" that Germany underwent did not happen in Austria, as the Austrians could portray themselves as victims of Hitler.

Friedrich was driven by money and status, Jean appears to have been driven by neither; "a free thinker, an artist, in an age when that term implied general non-conformity," as Martin Welz puts it. However, Friedrich was also genuinely keen on modern art, in his own way, and there is one ironic connection between them.

Oskar Kokoschka was a protege of Adolf Loos as early as 1910, as the firebrand author of the first Expressionist play. Franz Ferdinand, heir to the throne, saw the play and as a result wanted "to break every bone in that young man's body." After the Second World War, as Kokoschka became a conservative nationalist and sought a specifically Austrian alternative to abstract art, he became a close friend and ally of Friedrich. While in Salzburg in 1965, Jean drew a charcoal portrait of Kokoschka, perhaps with the pre-war anti-fascist figure in mind, and unaware of that change of heart.

Friedrich seems to represent just the kind of hypocrisies that Jean hated about Austria, his son Martin recalling that less than a handful of times he ever heard his father speak German (usually, as with French, when he didn't want the children to understand what was being said). Jean, who memorably met Stefan Zweig at a black-tie event in Vienna, may well have shared his despairing sentiments:

"Never has a generation fallen from such intellectual heights to such moral depths as ours."

As against the public record, a more intimate view comes from their cousin, Herta,[7] who liked Hans but was "ambivalent" about Friedrich. To her, he had two sides: kind to her, but she observed "a lot of hatred in the family — a lot of anger — of conflict." She saw Fritz as a man torn between good and evil.

On the "good" side, Herta was certain that Fritz was "definitely trying to help when he bought the gallery of Lea Bondi (owner of *Portrait of Wally*) — even though he paid little for it and the other paintings he bought off other Jews. The market had crashed and modern art was not valued, quite the contrary, and he at least paid something for them rather than just taking them from fleeing Jews." In some circles, he was even called a "savior" of Jews, who would otherwise have probably got nothing for paintings considered "degenerate" by the Nazis, and who saw him as a caretaker to whom they could return after the war, should they survive.[8]

She concluded, "He was not evil, and there was lots of information about him being the place Jewish people went to when they had to leave... He paid because he felt like a savior trying to help, so when he bought paintings and drawings he paid little, but they could not get a lot of money from anybody at that time."

Herta felt Fritz "turned his neck both ways, depending on the prevailing winds politically." His gallery was "the most important one in Salzburg and arguably in all Austria. He was a big name and powerful in the art world — and like more or less everybody else, unwilling to rake over the Nazi past."

Friedrich Welz welcomes Oskar Kokoschka at Salzburg Airport for the Art Festival, circa mid–late 1950s. Cover of Kerschbaumer, Gert. *Meister des Verwirrens: Die Geschäfte des Kunsthändlers Friedrich Welz.* Photo: Votava / Imagno / picturedesk.com.

She went to stay in Paris for an exhibition[9] and found Jean "living in a very damp cellar. They were very poor," and she was shocked by the poverty. "They had a baby, a little boy sitting on a damp floor with no toys to play with."[10] In contrast, Fritz "owned a huge amount of Schiele and Klimt, via the Lea Bondi gallery he bought in '38." Instead of a comfortable job in Vienna with Hoffmann, Jean was living in relative poverty in Paris with his wife and baby boy in a small basement flat.[11]

Here, perhaps, is an example of the classic gulf between the mentality of the dealer and that of the artist. Fritz could feel himself to be a savior of fleeing Jews whilst getting rich from it at the same time, while Jean, having forsaken Vienna for Paris, paid the price for artistic ambition.

The contrast between the two brothers raises two interesting points. First, both were driven men — Jean by art, Fritz by wealth and power. Jean was often described, when a painter, as "difficult," but as a protection against fools rather than from the kind of divided personality Herta noted in Fritz.

Second, the younger brother almost stands as a model for the dark side of Austria, the queasy feeling so well portrayed in *The Third Man* (which still plays weekly in a Vienna cinema) that suggests underhand dealing and moral corruption. Fritz was happy to play along,

Jean Welz (left) and Friedrich Welz (right) at the Galerie Welz exhibition of Jean's work, Salzburg, 1964. Photo: Bayerische Staatsbibliothek München/Bildarchiv.

become an SS officer, and profit from aryanization, while perhaps astutely having one eye on creating an alibi that would at least get him out of trouble after the war, even if it took until 1950 for him to be cleared.

Jean would make twenty-five versions of one painting and still tinker with the twenty-sixth — and destroy over half his work as unsatisfactory. He was not easy, obsessive and preoccupied as an artist, distant and formidable as a father, utterly maddening as a husband. Naive in his dealing with people and innocent in money matters, he could also be utterly charming — and kind. Jean savored freedom from an early age, and instead of an interest in wealth and position like his brother, he thought only of art.

NOTES

1 Gert Kerschbaumer, *Meister des Verwirrens: Die Geschäfte des Kunsthändlers Friedrich Welz* (Master of Intrigues: The Dealings of the Art Dealer Friedrich Welz), Vienna: Czernin Verlag, 2000.

2 The Austrian authorities notoriously gave the benefit of the doubt in many such cases in the early post-war period.

3 See https://www.salzburg.gv.at/kultur_/Seiten/ge_plan.aspx. The same year, fascist police raided Stefan Zweig's house in Salzburg.

4 Confirmed by Martin Welz, January 2018. Quote from April 19, 2022.

5 This and later quotes in this chapter from Martin Welz, email, April 19, 2022.

6 Interview by Pamela Diamond, *Cape Times, Weekend Magazine*, July 19, 1965.

7 The information that follows including that in quotes came from Herta's daughter following a meeting at the Cafe Sterdl in Vienna, February 7, 2017.

8 The "savior" term may have come from an exhibition in Vienna around 2000 on Jewish History — information supplied by Herta's daughter.

9 Herta's daughter thought it was perhaps in 1933.

10 In fact, the basement was in a smart new block in the wealthy 16th arrondissement, built by Raymond Fischer in 1926, who perhaps made it available to the small family. It was small but not damp, according to Martin Welz, April 2018.

11 Inger was ill with an ectopic pregnancy and the medical bills impoverished the family, the reason for their move to the basement — Cousin Herta via her daughter, Vienna, March 2017. Martin Welz's close family account from April 2018 is that Inger had the miscarriage of her only daughter at seven months due to very severe coughing, which she had suffered from since a child in Denmark, and could not work as a journalist, one cause of their lack of money.

24

CORBUSIER'S NOTE

LE CORBUSIER NEVER VISITED South Africa, but his influence on the affairs of Jean Welz there was considerable, even at a distance of eight thousand kilometers from Paris.

Jean left Paris in the autumn of 1936, bearing two important documents — a scrap of paper with a hand-written note from Corbusier, and a portfolio of black and white photographs of the buildings he had worked upon. Both would play an important if irregular role in his fate in South Africa.

As work had finally dried up in Paris, it was urgent for Jean to find new pastures to support his wife Inger, and their first son, Jerome, born in 1930. Inger had placed advertisements in newspapers in likely territories — "Gifted Austrian architect. Aged 36. Looking for architectural work" — and had received seven replies from an ad in a Johannesburg paper.[1] He arrived in Cape Town from Hamburg on February 6, 1937, on the SS *Usambara*.

South Africa had been recommended to Jean by Le Corbusier. At almost the same time that Jean was making his rounds to say goodbye to Paris, Corbusier exchanged letters with a group of modern

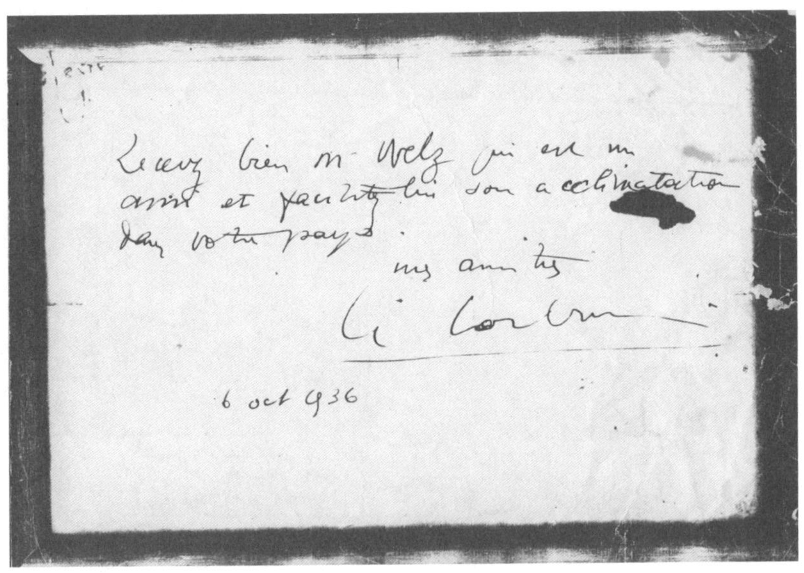

Recevez bien M. Welz qui est un ami et facilitez lui son acclimatation dans votre pays.

mes amitiés

Le Corbusier

6 oct 936

Above: "Receive well Mr. Welz, who is a friend, and facilitate his acclimatization in your country. My friendship — Le Corbusier — 6 Oct, 1936." Courtesy Welz family.

Below: Jean Welz's onboard drawing of the SS *Usambara*'s deck. Note the date on the drawing is the last day onboard, February 6, 1937. Courtesy Welz family.

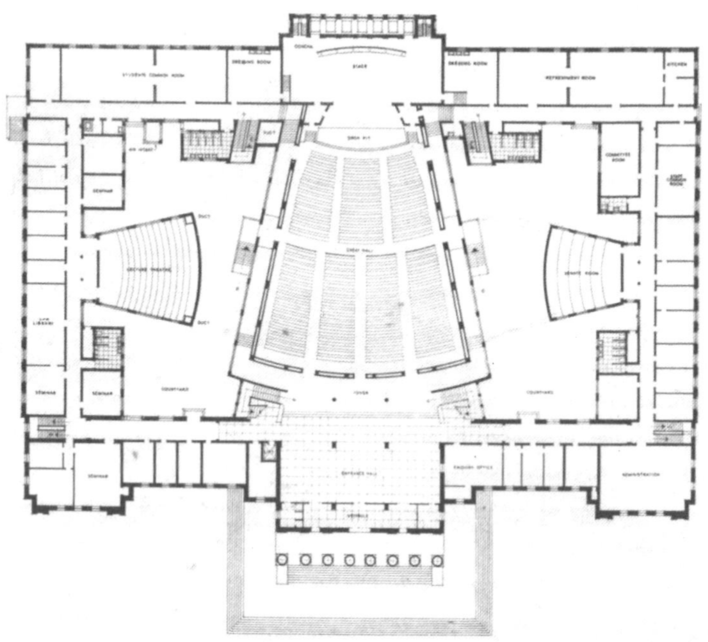

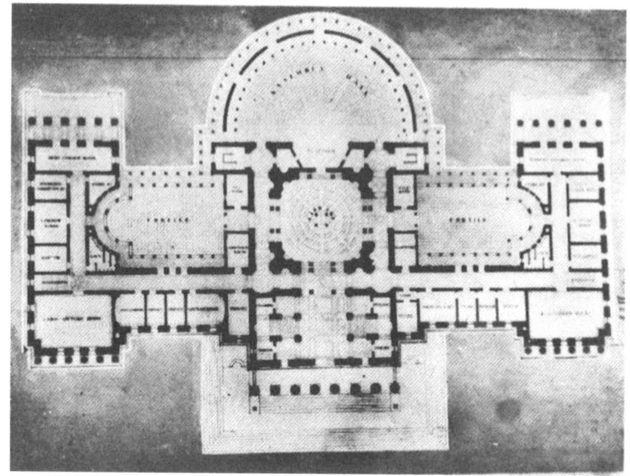

Above: Plan after reconstruction behind the Portico. Vestibule, Entrance Hall, Foyer and Great Hall (1937–38). Source: *South African Architectural Record*/University of the Witwatersrand, April 1941, p. 138.

Below: University of the Witwatersrand, Central Hall, original layout. Source: University of the Witwatersrand.

architects in South Africa, led by Rex Martienssen,[2] that he would christen The Transvaal Group. Corbusier must have thought Jean would find a good reception among these enthusiasts.

For those in the Architecture department at the University of the Witwatersrand, it may have been something of a surprise to have this six-foot-five stranger, with no English nor Afrikaans, standing before them, and although Welz was politely received by Professor Pearse, head of department, Martienssen immediately wrote to Corbusier to ask if the note was genuine, a portent of things to come.

Martienssen was the group's direct line to Corbusier, one may assume a matter of some prestige for him, and the arrival of someone with potentially superior connections to their hero might well have been a not-unalloyed pleasure for him.

Pearse, a classicist rather than a modernist, recognized Welz's quality, later calling him "a first-rate man," and became a friend and supporter for life. The blow for Jean was that there was no job for him, and he had to find work as a draftsman, first with a Danish architect[3] later ennobled for his sterling help to Danes in South Africa — who was a contact through Jean's wife Inger, herself Danish. He also worked for a prolific Johannesburg practice, Cook & Cowen, who had graduated from Art Deco to a "restrained modernism" by 1939 — which potentially sounds like Welz's style, but he was there for only a few months before Professor Pearse was able to facilitate Jean working on an important project on the "Wits" campus.

The main university building was a neo-classical facade but behind the central portico the structure had been burned down in a fire in 1931.

It was probably late in 1937 that Jean was given the task of designing the entrance area behind the pillars of the portico — the

University of the Witwatersrand Campus, Johannesburg, circa 1930. Source: University of the Witwatersrand.

Vestibule, Entrance Hall and Foyer — as marked in pencil on the plan of the reconstruction.

If, as I imagine, Welz had steeped himself in Palladio in 1931–32 for the Villa Darmstadter, it may have raised at least a private smile for him that he had traveled five thousand miles to be given a re-design behind a portico whose lineaments went straight back to the Vicenzan master, almost exactly four hundred years after his first villa, that had disinterred the Portico from the ruins of Ancient Rome.

The impact of this modern interior, behind a classical facade, was mentioned by a former Wits student, Gilbert Herbert, later author of the standard book on Martienssen and Modernism in South Africa: "In March 1942, I walked up the steps leading to the Central Block, passed through the portico's giant colonnade... and in the foyer entered a new architectural world, my first encounter with the Modern Movement...." Herbert goes on, "... thanks to the participation of members of the School's staff — mainly Professor Pearse and Duncan Howie — in the design process."[4]

There is no mention of the involvement of Jean Welz here,[5] although ironically what first showed Herbert "a new architectural world" was Welz's design of the three entrance zones. It was the Great Hall behind, entered from the Foyer through the three doorways shown on the plan, which was the responsibility of a young member of the Transvaal Group, Duncan Howie, who had only graduated in 1936. Only behind the Portico pillars lie the vestibule, then the entrance hall, then the foyer, leading to the Great Hall auditorium. The structural design is clearly evident on the plan — with three pairs of two pillars serving as the support for the open area, the first pair in front of the vestibule doors, the second pair towards the rear of the entrance hall and the final pair on the raised foyer platform, creating a large open area from the front doors to the Great Hall.

The "Foyer" design is significant as the first example of modernism on the campus, an impact of the Transvaal Group, for certain, though not through one of their number such as Martienssen or Fassler, but through this new arrival. Jean's appointment was facilitated by Professor Pearse, and the politics of ignoring the Transvaal Group in favor of the unknown newcomer may have been controversial at the time.

Martienssen had made contact with Le Corbusier in 1934, and in 1936 opened the way for other staff and students to follow in his footsteps. He had published one issue of a modernist journal, *zerohour,* in 1933, a copy of which he had given Corbusier, who had praised

T w o   v i e w s   o f   t h e   E n t r a n c e   H a l l

Two views of Jean Welz's Entrance Hall at the University of the Witwatersrand (1937). Above: with Foyer background and stairs to right of left-hand pillar; below: with Vestibule to the left and Foyer off to the right.

Source: *South African Architectural Record*, April 1941, p. 153.

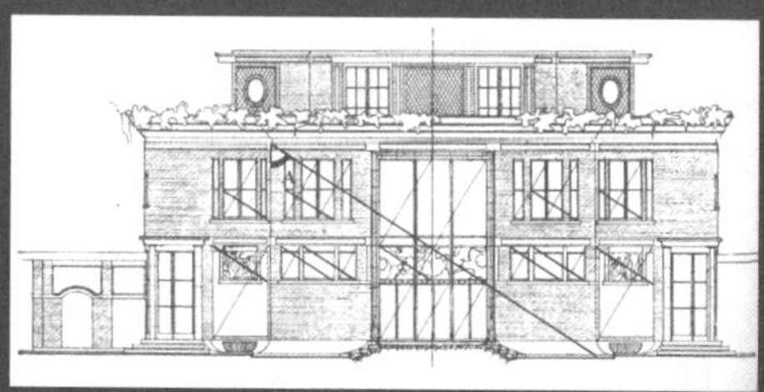

Above: Vestibule looking left towards the Entrance Hall, University of the Witwatersrand. Source: *South African Architectural Record*, April 1941, p. 160, advertisement image.

Below: Le Corbusier, Villa Schwob (1916). © Fondation Le Corbusier.

it, and formed two earlier modernist groups on the campus with sympathetic colleagues.

The struggle for modern architecture at Wits, at that time a very hierarchical and rather conservative institution, was a long and demanding one. A recent survey noted a tendency to tolerate modern design if it was hidden behind either classical facades (the Central Building) or a bland exterior (The Bernard Price Institute for Geophysics).[6]

In addition, there was a long-standing commitment to a University architecture firm not oriented towards the modern, and something of a power-struggle resulted, with the head of the Architecture Department fighting for modern design as a "consultant" to the established firm. Professor Pearse waged a successful campaign, in what must have required both determination and considerable diplomatic skills, to move design for the new campus buildings from the neo-classical towards the "International Style" of the Bauhaus and Le Corbusier.

Pearse held a high opinion of Jean, and felt "very fortunate to have him on my staff," as quoted by Gilbert Herbert, later writing on the "Golden Age" of architecture at Wits University. "Jean Welz... was responsible for the modern double-volume entrance foyer and staircases. It was a serious design problem and Pearse thought he made a very good job of it."[7]

Although Welz's work was limited to the entrance areas, it was tricky both in terms of design and structure, with rock in some areas and soil in others that had previously required digging down over thirty feet to reach a solid base for construction.

Jean produced a quietly elegant set of solutions, including the use of an exotic marble cladding to the double-height pillars and an eight foot dado of travertine, the favorite modernist marble. Both materials suggested Welz's Viennese, and indeed Loosian, background. Loos used marble on the pillars of the "Looshaus," the Goldman & Salatsch building in Vienna in 1909–11, although what gained the most notice at Wits was that "Welz redesigned the foyer using a module after the manner of LE CORBUSIER, allegedly among the first examples of the use of a module in South Africa.... Welz's modular design for the problematic Great Hall aroused great interest among those at the University, who were keen students of modern European architecture and disciples of LE CORBUSIER."[8]

Le Corbusier's Modulor, which assigned proportionality in architecture to human dimensions using the Golden Ratio à la Vitruvius, was in fact a post-war development, but since the Villa Schwob of 1916, Corbusier had used "*tracés régulateurs*" (mentioned by Raymond Fischer) and the Golden Section to organize the proportions of his facades.

The design of the Vestibule/Entrance Hall/Foyer is more reminiscent of Loos than Le Corbusier, but one has to remember that Le Corbusier was the hero of the Transvaal Group at that time, and Loos seems not to be mentioned at all.[9] With his relationship with Le Corbusier going back over ten years, and his English still developing, Welz may have preferred a discreet silence to mentioning that his "module" was in fact inspired by Palladio, rather than Le Corbusier, if that was indeed the case.

In terms of Welz's own work, the Foyer design was something novel as, apart from the Rue de Charonne flats, he had not built at such a scale, and this was a grand entrance to a grand public building. It is a tribute to his technical as well as aesthetic skills that Pearse, of a more traditional background, was so pleased with Welz's solutions. There is also the fact that the Loosian strand of modernism was more reserved than the Corbusian, which Jean probably realized would be more appropriate behind a neo-classical portico in a conservative institution. In that sense, Vienna and Johannesburg were not so many thousands of miles apart.

The next job Welz was involved in on the Wits campus was a small one-and-a-half-story building with a resolutely plain exterior, the Bernard Price Institute for Geophysical Research. Pearse seems to have had a hand in it again, and Welz was employed as a draftsman but was "responsible for the layout," that is, the ground plan. Unlike the Central Building, this was a completely new structure, if small, and had an uncompromisingly modern exterior, a first on the campus. The building was part-financed by the War Office in London and played an important part in the development of radar.[10]

The layout, which Jean Welz was reputedly responsible for, Pearse said "turned out very successfully." The plan is initialed "G.C." for Jean's fellow-draftsman, Gordon Chambers, although the lettering has Jean's familiar low-slung "R" that possibly suggests Jean's involvement. Jean's usual economy is apparent throughout with a minimum of circulation space.

"Welz claimed an involvement with the Hillman Engineering Block (1938–41), consistent with the design of the foyer."[11] That short sentence suggests he was involved in a third building on the campus, but his precise role in it is not otherwise noted. The phrase "consistent with the design of the foyer" is significant.

Bernard Price Institute of Geophysical Research, University of the Witwatersrand (1938).

Above: Rear elevation; the external staircase from the roof of the ground floor is similar to one at the House Stern of 1934 (Martienssen, et al.), earlier ones by Corbusier, and Welz's at the Atelier Kielberg (see Chapter 14, "House for an Artist"). Note the Central Building in the background. Source: *South African Architectural Index* (SAAI), March 1938, p. 71.

Below: Front elevation of the "BPI" building with radar mast, 1940. Source: University of the Witwatersrand.

Welz's use of some kind of module attracted attention on the Foyer and suggests why he was brought in to the Hillman building.

Duncan Howie, the nominated architect, wrote an eleven-page article on the Hillman design refreshingly free of rhetoric, in the Anglo-Saxon manner. Design questions are dealt with in terms of practical considerations.

There is an interesting side-panel and sectional drawing in the Howie article dealing with the idea of a module. There are three elements linked here: the external module or unit, the internal layout, and the stairs. These are not separate elements, but inextricably connected. In other words, the modular approach is not an isolated application as, say, in the design of the cladding, but fundamental to the planning of the height of the three wings and the ability to access them off the stairways.

The internal layout, the stair halls, and the external proportions are inextricably related. The module means you can have rooms of different heights, and still be able to design the stairs to give access to both a 12' high and 18' high floor. There are perhaps echoes, at least, of Loos and the Raumplan in that concept, in linking different room heights. In this case, it is likely the source for such an idea would have come from Welz, as Loos was very-little known at that time and in that place.

"The main staircase, so arranged as to serve these varying floor levels from the different landings, has an important secondary function to perform, that of providing the vertical as well as the horizontal circulation between the north and east wings. The importance of this link has been reflected in the general design and emphasis has been given to the staircase by setting it back from the main wall surfaces and by the contrasting character of the fenestration."[12]

The resolute plainness of the external design, and the way the practical requirements of the "unit" or module are carried through to the style of the facade, hint at the possible influence of Welz beyond the practical, a connection that may be sensed in the following comment: "Although the style of the Central Block is classical, if one looks beyond the exterior…, the interior is modernist and speaks to many of the features of the Hillman building."[13] Author Katherine Munro at least has realized the connection between Welz's work on the new interior of the Central Block behind the neo-classical facade, and the entirely new Hillman Building, although no one may know — yet again in his history — if Welz was involved and unnamed.

The external facing of the building is in units of 3 ft. 0in. height. The floor levels are related to these facing divisions, and all levels are governed by a 3 ft. 0 in. unit. Thus the ground floor level is the datum, and the office floors have an interval of 12 ft. 0 in. The laboratory floor to floor dimension is 18 ft. 0 in. This renders access from a common stair feasible.

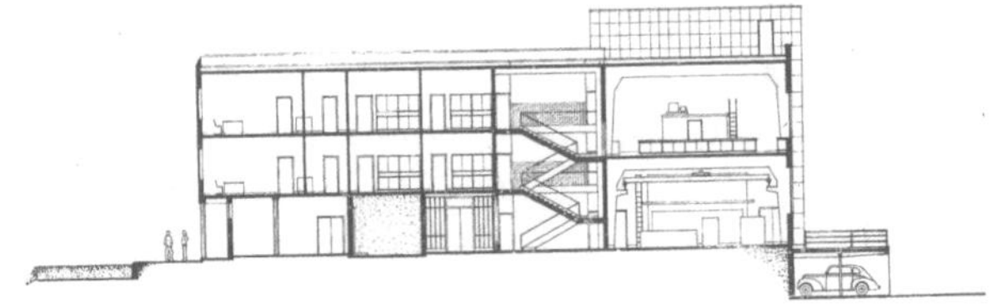

Above: Side panel in Duncan Howie's treatise on the Hillman Engineering Block design, with modular concepts related to Loos's Raumplan likely coming from Welz.
Source: *South African Architectural Record*, June 1941.

Center, left: Hillman Building main facade with staircase hall set back.
Source: University of the Witwatersrand. Photographer unknown.

Center, right: Hillman Building west courtyard entrance.
Source: *South African Architectural Record*, June 1941.

Below, right: Hillman Building pillar mosaic detail. Source: University of the Witwatersrand. Photographer unknown.

It would be potentially unfair to Howie to take any credit from him and give it to Welz, as the evidence is extremely fragmentary, but thin though it is, there is more than one reason for thinking Welz played a more-than technical role in the Hillman Building. Take the windows to the aforementioned stairways. The small square windows look more Loos than Corbusier, more Viennese than Parisian.

Howie had used similar square windows in the internal courtyard of the Central Building. That would suggest a continuity in style that was his alone. However, he was working there overlapping with Welz's work on the front parts of the building inserted behind the classic facade. It is just possible that the idea for the square windows came from Welz there and was carried on to the Hillman building — but that can only be guesswork, as I have no further concrete evidence.

A similar thought occurs about the finish of the round pillars. The roundness echoes Le Corbusier, but the application of square mosaic tiles is novel. It could be a Howie idea, but there is an interesting echo of the 1928 water-feature that Jean may well have been the designer of, in the back garden of the Maison Dubin, his first house. The four pillars of that design (see Chapter 26, "A Tale of Three Monuments"), and in fact the whole feature, was clad in small square mosaic tiles, similar to the pillars of the Hillman Building.

The three Witwatersrand buildings must have given Welz some hope, after exactly two years there, that he had a future in South Africa. However, his continued lack of profile made his opportunities more restricted, at that point, than he had managed to carve out in Paris. A reminder of those salad-days was yet to come, but not perhaps quite in the way he might have liked.

NOTES

1 Miles, p. 24.

2 Martienssen had met Le Corbusier in Paris in January 1934 and was revisiting in the autumn of 1936, the first of a stream of South African visitors from the Transvaal Group such as John Fassler, and some associated students, through 1937. The loyal address letter from Martienssen et al. was published in Vol 1 of Le Corbusier's *Oeuvres Completes*.

3 Gotszche, knighted for aid to Danes in South Africa.

4 Gilbert Herbert, "Recollections of the School of Architecture, Wits University — in 'the Golden Age,'" *South African Institute of Architects*, Architecture South Africa, 2011, pp. 62–67.

5 Herbert does mention Welz's contribution in a chapter on the University of the Witwatersrand in *The Collaborators:*

Interactions in the Architectural Design Process by Gilbert Herbert and Mark Donchin, Ashgate Studies in Architecture, 2013; Routledge, 2016.

6 "Working as a team," in Herbert and Donchin, p.171.

7 Herbert and Donchin, pp. 62–67.

8 *Artefact* entry on Jean Welz: http://www.artefacts.co.za/main/Buildings/archframes.php?archid=1866

9 That would go even more for other members of the Second Wave of Viennese modernism — Josef Frank and Oskar Strnad.

10 Despite the historical significance, the "BPI" was demolished and replaced by a larger building.

11 Artefact entry on Prof. GE Pearse: http://www.artefacts.co.za/main/Buildings/archframes.php?archid=1247

12 Duncan Howie, "The Wolf and Hirsch Hillman Building," *South African Architectural Record*, June 1941, p. 192.

13 Katherine Munro, "The Hillman Building: A Living Treasure," *Wits Quarterly*, Autumn 2010, p. 25.

Above: Rex Martienssen House (1940), Greenside, Johannesburg.
Photo: Roy Herman Kantorowich, taken in 1963. Courtesy RIBA Collections.

Below: Villa Darmstadter, Paris (1932). Courtesy Welz family.

25

THE MARTIENSSEN AFFAIR

THE LAST UNEXPECTED TWIST to Welz's two years' of work in Johannesburg relates to the Villa Darmstadter.

The affair of the Martienssen house, by "the King"[1] of South African modernism, of great repute as the outstanding figure of the architectural movement in that country, claimed by Fernand Léger to "rank with Le Corbusier, Mies van der Rohe, Oud, Aalto, Wright, the great pioneers of modern architecture,"[2] potentially strikes more deeply in Welz's anonymity saga.

According to Martin, Jean's son:

> "Jean recounted on more than one occasion how one day in that year at Wits, Martienssen came to see him, asking him to explain exactly how the Module worked. Jean obliged, drawing some sketches to demonstrate. The issue was discussed intensively, and at length [Jean] went on to recount how Martienssen went off with the notes and sketches, and nothing was heard from him until some weeks later, when he produced the plans for his house. The meeting between Jean and Martienssen... took place just at the time when the Martienssen house was designed. That much I know from my father, first-hand."[3]

Martienssen's house is very much key to his reputation and was the subject of much discussion in South Africa, and this account throws an interesting new light on the design-process.

As we have heard, Jean Welz had taken with him to South Africa his portfolio of the designs he had worked on in Paris, including the Villa Darmstadter.

When I first saw the Martienssen house, in the flesh, I didn't make a connection. It was only later, as with the Palladio example, that putting the two houses side-by-side made a number of similarities obvious.

Both feature a picture-frame surround, a section of full glazing on the ground floor with another above it on the first floor, including a balcony offset to the right, an internal open-plan layout, with a very open ground-floor plan, and the intensive use of brick on the facade. The overall proportions are fairly similar, a two-story flat-roofed oblong. It was the framing devices and the use of brick that caught my attention first. The Welz frame only encloses the central area, whereas the Martienssen encloses the whole facade, but the similarity of the device remains. The use of brick was unusual if not unique in modernist houses, but the degree of its use in the later house is a reminder of the striking brick planes in Darmstadter.

The windows on both buildings are double height, floor to ceiling, one on top of the other, and with a balcony to the right. Their position is quite different, but again, to call attention to the similarity of the device.

The use of the open-plan has been remarked in both houses, ascribed to Le Corbusier's influence at the time but, if you recall, the Welz house took the open-plan arguably further, which may have formed a part of the discussion between the two men that day in late 1938/early1939 — or possibly earlier.

I came across two further key pieces of visual evidence. The first was Martienssen's ground-floor plan.

Like Darmstadter, it is virtually one space except for the kitchen. The staircase is more conventionally placed but otherwise the whole ground floor is open. This plan dates from an earlier stage so the similarities may be purely coincidental — or perhaps the result of an earlier discussion with Welz.[4]

The second image is rather fascinating, taken from the same set of drawings, and is an earlier version of the facade, which is a very different facade from the version that was built, so different as to be almost unrecognizable. In addition, it has to be said that it is a rather clumsy ensemble of elements.

The differences are the long strip window, à la Le Corbusier, and the square first-floor window, a little reminiscent of the Esprit Nouveau house, but the elements together make an ungainly and poorly-composed facade.

The black and white photo of the finished house at an angle suggests another influence, Lubetkin (and/or Jean Ginsberg) in the way the side of the balcony is left open (see photo page 260).

The elements carried over from the earlier drawing, are the square windows, and the doorway with its angled steel support and ramp. What has been added is a projecting balcony with open sides and railings — a signature of Lubetkin first seen on the Ginsberg & Lubetkin block of flats where Jean Welz was photographed on the nautical roof, except there it has a more elegant curve on the balcony front wall.

There are differences between the facades, but even those redound to Welz's credit.

Martienssen takes the Welz elements in Darmstadter and replaces their symmetry with asymmetry. Asymmetry was an important aspect of the heroic era of early modernism in the 1920s and was found in the furniture of Breuer as well as in many modern architects.

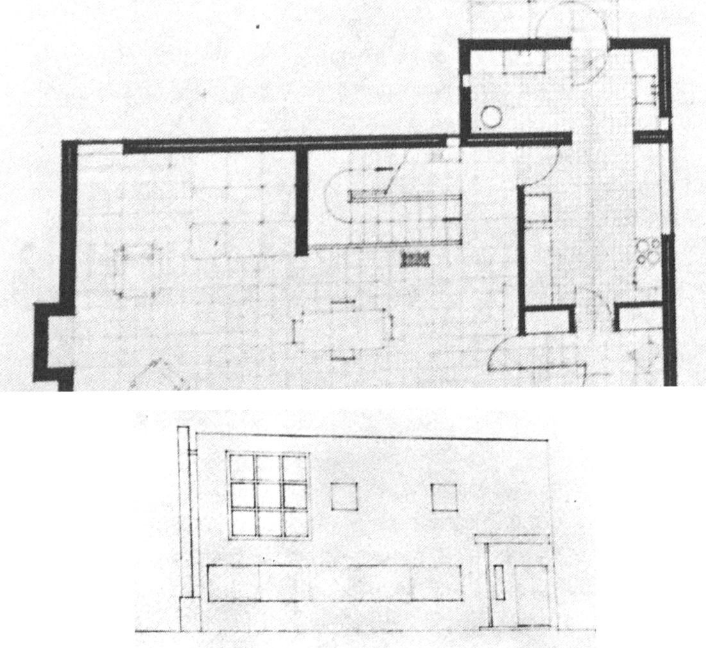

Martienssen "Greenside" ground-floor plan and facade.

Source: Gilbert Herbert, *Martienssen and the International Style: The Development of Modern Architecture in South Africa*, Cape Town and Rotterdam: Balkema (1975).

However, by 1929 and the culmination of Le Corbusier's "White Period" in the Villa Savoye, he had made a return to symmetry in the facade, a theme that Welz took both further and deeper in the Villa Darmstadter, via his own distinctive updating of Palladio. That could also be seen as pointing the way for modernism in the 1930s, another aspect of which Martienssen may have been unaware in his composition of the Greenside facade, which hearkens back to the fascination with asymmetry of the 1920s modernists.

Of the new elements Martienssen included, the frame is not central but around the whole facade and arguably quite different in its effect, and more radical in conception, because it signifies a projection of the center from the brick sides, rather than a "framing device."[5] The window framing is asymmetrical fenestration as though keen to differentiate itself from the confident symmetry of Darmstadter, which features full-height glazed sliding and/or opening doors rather than windows. The balcony projects, where in Darmstadter it is recessed and integrated into the whole, rather than sticking out literally as well as metaphorically.

The visual evidence of a substantial change in the facade is evident, but the fact and discussion of how that could have happened was commented upon, at length, at the time.

Martienssen wrote a long article on the "evolution of an architect's house," twenty-five pages, that discussed his influences at length, without a mention of Welz or Darmstadter.[6]

The article that followed it in the same issue, by another architect, Bernard Cooke, notes "the significant use of facebrick in the Greenside house as *a decisive step forward*, a broadening and maturing of the Modern Movement."[7] Herbert, in his book on Martienssen and the Modern Movement adds, "The use of the face brick panel is *another critical innovation* for Martienssen." [*My italics here and below.*]

Cooke suggested to Herbert,

> "The frame, as Martienssen conceived it, was a *picture frame*.... Indeed, there are in the Martienssen sketchbooks of 1938 a series of studies of projecting picture frames, which are strikingly similar ... to the Greenside frame ... the facade owes much [Martienssen] says, to the formal compositions of Léger and Hélion, and to the aesthetic theories of Kandinsky."

It doesn't appear he goes into detail on those debts, nor is it immediately obvious what the relevance of the extravagant name-dropping is. It is possible, of course, that Martienssen had seen the Darmstadter picture-frame in Welz's portfolio and had taken up the idea in his own way.

Herbert continues,

> "The classicism of the facade of the Greenside house is that of Italy.... In its emphasis on the facade it reflects one of the most enduring of Italian traditions; the frontality of its approach comes from Renaissance single-point perspective... it stems not from the Greek house, ... but from the monumentality of the *palazzo*."

The connection between Palladio and Darmstadter finds a notable echo in Herbert's astute observation. He continues, "Martienssen himself accounted for the decision to accentuate the principal facade, by attempting an equation between his suburban site and the European tradition of the town house. He was obviously sincere in his belief...."

Herbert adds,

> "The interior of the Greenside house is thoroughly convincing, both in its comfortable utility, and as an aesthetic experience of spatial flow. Here in the disposition and interrelationship of space, Martienssen is at his best... deliberately Corbusian in feeling, and indeed stem[ming]... from the initial project whose external form so closely related to Le Corbusier's work".

Yet, the Darmstadter Open Plan is a closer model than those of Le Corbusier, judging from the floor plan of Greenside, essentially a simple oblong on two floors, like Darmstadter, unlike the Villa Cook and Villa Stein-de-Monzi, which are both more complex and less open.

In decisive terms, Cooke explores the important contrasts between the initial project and the revised exterior. His mention of the picture-frame idea above notes Martienssen was working on it in his sketchbooks of 1938. We can be fairly precise about the window of time in which the meeting Martin Welz describes occurred, as Jean became seriously ill with tuberculosis during February 1939.

Further closing of the window is suggested, as Herbert noted, by Cooke in further comments made in the memorial issue to Martienssen a few months after his death: "In general," writes Cooke, "this building shows *a considerable change of direction from earlier work.* [*My italics here and below.*] Martienssen's absorption of various influences culminating in that of Le Corbusier is now complete, this building is one in which he expresses himself, *it is a Martienssen design, individual and mature."*[8]

However,

> "Martienssen *gives no outwards sign to indicate his own awareness that a radical change has taken place* … he *postulated* this house as the *inevitable outcome* of a decade-long architectural evolution … but *made no acknowledgment of a significant change of outlook*. The change, moreover, *had not been accomplished by an imperceptible, step-by-step evolution*: it was as *sudden* as it was *drastic*. As recently as … the end of 1938, Martienssen had been fully committed to the Corbusian idiom. But there is even more dramatic evidence than this, that the change occurred suddenly: for there is a *fully worked out scheme* for the Greenside house itself, *based on a (floor-)plan almost identical with that finally adopted, which is wholly within the International Style…* [That floor plan is the one featured on page 263, as is the facade.] … Martienssen, in his twenty-five-page account of the evolution of the Greenside house, *made no mention of this earlier scheme* … [a] *surprising omission….* Then — and there is *no hint of this crucial moment in Martienssen's own written account* — there comes a *critical change of mind*, or perhaps more correctly, *a change of heart*."[9]

This might suggest that if Martienssen was "fully committed to the Corbusian idiom … as recently as … the end of 1938," then the meeting with Welz occurred at some time between the "end" of 1938 and February 1939.

The combination of the visual evidence and Cooke spotting "a considerable change of direction" that is "radical," "sudden," "drastic," "dramatic," adding up to "a critical change of mind," "a change of heart" and that, in a "surprising omission," Martienssen makes "no admission of a significant change of outlook," "no hint of this crucial moment in Martienssen's own written account," which totals "twenty five pages," all adds up to an overwhelming suspicion that in those changes, Welz and his Villa Darmstadter were both decisive and wholly unacknowledged.

You might be tempted to ask, did Martienssen think he could get away with it, that no one would ever know of the Villa Darmstadter? One might also suspect that from such detailed comments that perhaps Cooke (and other colleagues who would read it) knew the truth, but in the circumstances felt unable to be explicit. Martienssen died in 1942, aged thirty-seven, of a heart attack, and it would appear that he took his secret to the grave. Until eighty years later, the gamble paid off — the Villa Darmstadter has remained almost completely unknown. That is perhaps the most mortifying aspect of the whole affair, not least as, to my eyes, the Welz design is so much more elegant, pure and rigorous.

If Martienssen was the "god" of modernism in South Africa, he looks from the evidence more like a fallen idol. And, yet again, Jean Welz does not exist.

NOTES

1 Gilbert Herbert's description of the pre-eminent status of Martienssen when he joined the architecture department as a student in Architecture, South Africa, 2011.

2 From Léger in the issue of the *South African Architectural Record*, November 1942, after Martienssen's death. It was Le Corbusier that introduced Martienssen to Léger in 1934, and they became friends.

3 Martin Welz, email to the author, October 2017.

4 The square windows could also be considered a Welz theme — going back to the Maison Dubin of 1928. The ramp is not unlike Welz's for the Pavillon d'Autriche, but was by no means an element unique to him.

5 This insight I owe to Tim Benton.

6 A further irony is that there is a photo of the Maison Cook, the house next to Welz's first Paris design, the Maison Dubin.

7 "Impressions of the Greenside House," in the *South African Architectural Record*, February 1942, by Bernard Cooke, pp. 45–49.

8 *South African Architectural Record*, November 1942 p. 327.

9 Cooke quoted in Herbert, pp. 220–21.

Gravestone for Karl Marx's daughter, Laura Lafargue. Photo from Welz's portfolio. Courtesy Welz family.

26

A TALE OF THREE MONUMENTS

IN 1930, JEAN DESIGNED A FUNERAL MONUMENT, a gravestone, for three leaders of the socialist party, including Marx's daughter, in the famous cemetery of Père Lachaise in Menilmontant. It was an early port of call for the Nazis following the occupation of Paris, destroying the monument. It is a favorite Welz design of mine, its apparent simplicity masks its nature as pure architecture. Loos's philosphy allowed monuments to be art and to my mind this one qualifies. There are three panels of concrete echoing the three name-panels in what appears to be a patinated bronze finish, perhaps an architectural expression of the idea of the three comrades united. The plaques are all of equal size and side-by-side, avoiding any sense of hierarchy that a vertical arrangement could suggest.

It is not an arrangement that everyone would propose, as it squeezes them into the width of a tall piece of stone (compare the much lower gravestone to the left in the photo) and leaves the rest of the stone completely bare.

The placing of the plaques is central with equal space above and below. If one assumes that such a choice would be no accident, we might see that as symbolizing the politics of equality. If he had put them in the top third, the kind of proportion often used in such a situation, with echoes of the golden section, it could be seen as raising their names aloft rather than in the middle of the people. The central placing is a choice that could perhaps have political echoes, but in artistic terms putting the plaques any lower would have spoiled the proportions as top heavy, so the middle is the better alternative also in those terms.

Above: Replacement gravestone for Marx's daughter, Laura Lafargue, and her husband Paul, documented April 11, 2022. Designer unknown. Photo courtesy of the author.

Below: Jean Welz's Union Festival Monument, Garden of Remembrance, Worcester Church Square, Western Cape, South Africa (1960). Note the use of plain brick here as in the 1930 gravestone pictured on page 268. Photo courtesy of the author.

The plinth at the bottom announces the three as the founders of the socialist party, and reminds one of the Villa Darmstadter plinth. In the foreground, the slope of the pathway is reflected in the symmetrical concrete surround and simple brick, another Darmstadter echo, and in contrast to the marble used either side. This is a modernist socialism in design, rather than the sentimental socialist realism that Stalin would demand in the Soviet Union.

The replacement gravestone lacks the simple elegance and proportion of Welz's original. The picture, seen opposite, is worth the fabled thousand words.

In the small garden to the rear of the Maison Dubin, Jean Welz designed an elegant water-feature with a shadow-gap around the basin edges, and consisting of four vertical pillars clad in mosaic.

That was in 1928. Over thirty years later, in 1960, he designed a monument of four vertical wood pillars to commemorate the Union of South Africa's centenary (see photo opposite). The wooden pillars were taken from a famous bridge recently demolished and protected in situ by a steel frame.

Returning to Welz's work at Wits University in 1938 (Chapter 24, "Corbusier's Note"), there is the further echo of the Dubin water-feature in the mosaic-clad pillars seen at the Hillman. The whole feature is clad with the small tiles, and it would be interesting to know if they were blue, suitable to a water feature, as the Hillman, ten years on, had striking blue mosaics to adorn its otherwise Corbusian pillars, an echo of that splendid sculptural water-feature.

Left: Pillar detail. Source: University of the Witwatersrand. Photographer unknown.
Right: Maison Dubin water feature. Source: *La Construction Moderne*, op. cit.

JEAN

PART VI

27

HOUSE ON THE LAKE

JEAN WELZ SPENT HIS TIME drawing during his eighteen months in the Springkell Sanatorium in Modderfontein. At the end of 1939, Inger was advised by his doctors that Jean's career as an architect was over.

His condition had only improved for the first months of treatment, and he was depressed and missed his family. Architect Fred Williamson of Emley and Williamson found them a golf-clubhouse to live in, which was where one day a big American car trundled up with the offer of the Tradouw Pass cottage.

By May 1940, Jean had nine works in the South African Academy show in Johannesburg, His 1942 show was reviewed by a fellow-architect: "His rich French background influences his work considerably. There are glimpses of Van Gogh in *The Dam Maker*, of the cubist in *Camp in Stones*, of Cezanne in his still-lifes, and of Matisse in his line drawings. But nowhere does he follow slavishly the form of expression of any particular artist, always he attempts to discover the 'origin of things'."[1] He was awarded the first ever South African Academy Silver Medal in 1947, and by 1950 had taken part in eight shows.

Although Jean was keen on abstraction, those paintings never sold too well in the conservative culture of South Africa, where still-lifes, landscapes, portraits and semi-abstract nudes were more acceptable. *House on the Lake* dates from 1964 and creates what could be called an "exploded" architecture (see Plates, Figure 9).

Welz's following statement about *House on the Lake* throws light on his aesthetics:

"Of course, I can only speak in metaphors, and these have only the relative value one is inclined to give them. I am here in search of a picturesque poetry. There is the motif of the foaming green water and the rock, then the house, which is built in straight lines and plates between the rocks. Vertically, top left, are a few windows. One of these small windows illuminates a chapel below, where a man sits at a table. All around, on and under the water are the bathers and the motif of the boats appears again. *The whole is, of course, not an illustration but a painterly equivalent of poetry and music. It is not by accident that this house, which is more or less spread over the whole picture and framed by nature in an abstract way, is the practically impossible dream of every good modern architect.*" [*My italics.*]
—Jean Welz, from the catalogue: Galerie Welz, Salzburg, 1965

There is a second text, perhaps by his younger brother Friedrich (there is no attribution in the catalog), that features an acute critical sense:

"This abstract composition of a house is interesting in that it is not illustrating a verbal conception but sets out to create a painterly equivalent of poetry and music — that is to say to use paint not in a literal manner but to show forces — nature and man — and to attempt to show "the practically impossible dream of every good modern architect" — by which we may sense Welz means a unity of nature and the man-made — they share the picture space but neither is reduced to the other and each has an independent existence while interwoven with the other. This is not Falling Water by Frank Lloyd Wright but is perhaps a poetic evocation of its aspiration to bring water and building together — but here in a much more dynamic relationship with nature dominant, more powerful, central to the picture frame, and providing itself a medium for man as bathers to be part of."

Jean's notion of his art as "a painterly equivalent of poetry and music" suggests the quality of his engagement with his adopted discipline which, in common with the best artists, is a reflection upon their medium and the search to discover its unique qualities — what art shares with and how it differs from music, for example. It also raises his thinking above the literal, as he himself declares. He is an artist of the caliber that sees in abstraction not merely an escape from the burden of representation, but the way art can transcend the literal, to access directly the metaphorical and the symbolic. In "exploding" representation he can bring to bear ideas that otherwise would be difficult or clumsy to fit in, could get in the way, or not be able to be fully explored. In picking what he wants to say with abstraction he can task the picture frame with a fluid accommodation of elements that might otherwise clash, and achieve a reverie that brings feeling to idea.

His commentary suggests the idea that by the time of this late painting, for Jean, nature was dominant. His architecture had featured a refined combination of the inside and the outside, the regular theme of modernist architecture. But with painting, as he perhaps conceived it, there was the possibility of the fusion of the inside and the outside, and a shift towards an outside that could afford a stronger union with a purer nature.

The second half of his life was given over to a passionate obsession with art, as the first half had been given over to an equally passionate commitment to the "man-made," that is, the built.

In his development as an artist, he arguably never left architecture behind (see Plates, Figure 11 for an earlier example of geometric abstraction), but perhaps increasingly saw it in the context of the power of nature. Maybe the compensation of art was through the task of observation, whether for a still life or a portrait or indeed with abstract forms, to bring him much closer to nature. The "practically impossible dream of the good modern architect" is perhaps to achieve not just a fusion with nature, but one that allows the forces of nature something of a dominant position, and to achieve that, the architecture has to some extent to give way, to fit in to nature's pattern rather than vice-versa — which is the impossible challenge — except in the space of a painting.

With the Atelier Kielberg (1929), Villa Darmstadter (1931) and Maison Zilveli (1933), Welz achieved a poetic combination of Loos-inspired ideas and a visual flair more reminiscent of Le Corbusier. What is also remarkable is how different those houses were, suggesting something of his versatility but also how far beyond those two "mentors" he had already gone, by the age of thirty-three, in etching a distinctive path that all his own, one that he did not have the opportunity to develop — except in the space of a painting.

NOTES

1 John Fassler, "The Jean Welz Exhibition — An Appreciation," *South African Architectural Record*, October 1942, pp. 284–26.

28

THE DIALOGUES OF JEAN WELZ

OVER THE NINE OR SO YEARS I learned about Welz's architecture, I increasingly came to feel that his development as a young architect in Paris took the form of dialogues with the work and ideas of two contemporaries, and on account of that, with the architect often acclaimed as the greatest of all time.

It is tempting to think of influences as academic, that is, a young architect might see a house in a magazine or read a book about someone's work, and take to it, so that s/he wants to capture what they admired, in their own thinking and designs. The other side of that coin, and probably the more common response, is to dislike the look of a design and react against it.

With Welz, we get both sides of the coin, except, and this is the big difference, he knew his two contemporaries personally, and well enough to be thought of as someone "special" by arguably the greatest architect of the twentieth-century, Le Corbusier, and to claim a close friendship with his lesser-known but increasingly well-thought-of Viennese equivalent, Adolf Loos.

The unknown Welz's first break was to design a house joined onto Le Corbusier's showpiece for The Five Points of Modern Architecture,[1] after a two-year friendship with Loos. In that remarkable, indeed unique, context, a trajectory in which Welz develops his ideas in practice, and inflected by Loos's thirty years of polemical Viennese thinking, it seems a perfectly natural development.

The "dialogues" that Jean conducts are, however, of an unusual kind. It is Welz reacting to Le Corbusier's manifesto, rather than a true dialogue of exchanges. It is entirely possible that Le Corbusier was not even aware of Welz's practical and philosophical critique, but it seems likely that there was some literal dialogue between them for Le Corbusier to form the view that Welz was special. That would suggest he noticed that Welz was an insightful thinker with distinctive views, rather than someone out for themselves, keen to impress to their own benefit. That sounds casual, but for someone like Le Corbusier, who never suffered fools, to form such an opinion was itself fairly unusual as such a person was rare, one that could hold their own from pure conviction rather than seeking advantage.

As for Welz having had any impact on Le Corbusier, the concept, let alone the timing is tricky.

One of the mysteries of modern architecture is that Le Corbusier abandoned his Five Points, never to return to them, and without ever mentioning, let alone explaining, the fact that he had done so.

One view has him disenchanted with his own manifesto by 1929, but the Pavillon Suisse of 1931 carries through an evolved version of the Five Points, as though they still carried force for him. If that was indeed the case, then it is just possible that the Villa Darmstadter of 1932, and also perhaps the Maison Zilveli of 1933, could possibly have made an impact on Le Corbusier.

Whether it could have gone as far as them being a catalyst in his abandoning the manifesto is a stretch of credulity as well as timing, and also involves several steps in Le Corbusier's reaction and thinking, from him spotting these were rather special, which was entirely possible, to the unspoken realization that they could embody a critique of ideas about which he had been himself having increasing doubts. In light of the depth I believe I see in Welz, I have no doubt that Le Corbusier's own depths would have made him instantly able to grasp the implicit critique — and at least some of its implications. It would however, even then require at least two more steps to agree with the implications and then adopt and adapt them to his thinking. Anyway, only Le Corbusier would know all that, and he never gave anything away that might have given comfort to his enemies, so all I am left with is a speculative string that it would be remarkable if it had existed and made such an impact. However, Le Corbusier's change of direction has never been quite satisfactorily explained, even today, so perhaps the intriguing possibility is not quite to be wholly discounted.

One area, for example, where there is an overlap, is that Welz, following Loos, rejected new materials as mere fashion until they had proved themselves. Concrete may have been permissible as the

Romans had their own version in the Pantheon of the second century, but Le Corbusier turning towards stone rather than concrete could potentially have been his version of a similar thought.

With Loos, Welz was almost certainly already very familiar with Loos's ideas through his tutors, Strnad and Frank (1919–21), and from Fellerer (1921–25), who were all active allies of Loos. Therefore, finally to meet the man himself, work for him, and develop a friendship over the crucial years in Paris, is likely to have been very important indeed for Welz.

Beyond that, though, I have a sense that Welz was far from passive with Loos's sophisticated critique, despite or perhaps because of its profundity which, for him, would have been a spur to independence rather than a bar to it. Martin Welz was very firm to me that his father was always his own man. He saw in his father that Jean might have taken on influences, but he was constitutionally unable to be under anyone's thumb, and would always have his own distinctive view on everything.

Could Welz have had an influence on Loos? The latter makes no mention of Welz in any writings we have; the standard book on Loos[2] says only that Welz worked with him "from time to time," and the only Welz family memory is that Claire Beck Loos described Welz as "a young man with blue eyes and very determined."[3]

Darko Kahle writes, "Loos once stated that after him only Zlatko Neumann (and one other student) was able to resolve the Raumplan in a satisfactory manner."[4] It would be another irony if Welz was that unnamed "student" — and from what we heard from Raymond Fischer on what the young Welz had taught him, it was perfectly possible.

There is no documentation of any influence going the other way, but Welz's friendship with Loos would suggest the relationship must have been, to some extent, mutual. If they were the close friends that Welz thought they were during that crucial six-year period in Paris (1926–31), given the disparity in status and age, it would seem likely that Loos respected Welz, his ideas and how he expressed them, over the expat-Viennese hours of discussion. I would also suggest that from what I see in his buildings, they would have both challenged and delighted Adolf Loos.

I certainly got the feeling that in relation to Palladio, Welz had gone a long way past Loos's fairly broad references to the Romans and Greeks, even if Vitruvius was Loos's bible, as Kokoschka claimed.

Unlike the relationship with his two contemporaries, Welz's

relation to Palladio must have been based on reading what others had written about his work and the *Four Books of Architecture*, regarded by some as the best book on architecture ever written. Loos may well have set him on the track, but it seems to me that Welz dug deeply on his own account, and in the direction of a pure architecture, of unity in the facade and beyond, and the first development of a modular approach.

That last element he may well have applied in South Africa at Witwatersrand, not inspired by Le Corbusier, as his colleagues thought, but perhaps by the High-Renaissance example of Palladio.

Loos focused on the interior, and the exterior was an outcome of that rather than a thing in itself.

Welz, on the other hand, followed Palladio in the value given to the external composition, while at the same time developing the Chemin Aérien to a degree of complexity that arguably surpassed Loos himself.

An interesting factor is that, around the same time that it appears Le Corbusier was reconsidering his manifesto of The Five Points, Loos was — as Christopher Long describes so well — reappraising the Raumplan in a late house such as the Villa Winternitz.[5] He was simplifying the route through the house and increasing the visibility of the route at the same time.

If Loos had seen the Villa Darmstadter, which achieves so much without a Chemin Aérien while remaining faithful to Palladio and radically bringing him up-to-date, it is conceivable that he saw what he was losing in devising a complex route through the house. It could be said that Welz was "building like the Romans," in a new way, and it is just possible that the clarity and simplicity of Darmstadter suggested the simpler route might be the better one.

The dates could possibly work as Darmstadter was completed in 1931 and the Winternitz contract only signed in the September of the same year.

There would also be a further irony that in 1933 Welz returned to the Chemin Aérien with a vengeance, but that was probably too late for the terminally-ill Loos to know much about it, and indeed it may have been something of a tribute to his friend and mentor as Loos lay ill.

For any architect, such dialogues would be impressive, but for the unknown Welz, it would be quite remarkable.

The sense that I have is that these dialogues, these relationships with the ideas of leading contemporaries, and then diving deeper into

Palladio, if that is indeed what he did, were all ways of seeking greater depth for his work. It was because Welz thought deeply about what architecture was, and had the strong intellectual, creative and character resources to find his own way, that these dialogues were in a sense merely grist to the mill, as with any good artist.

Welz's work reveals the mind of an architectural thinker at work — perhaps most clearly in his last two houses, but also for example in the Maison Dubin, the Villa Kolpa, Hôtel Godfray, the House for an Artist, the Rue Charonne flats, the Mont d'Or and Austrian Pavilion projects, and in the module he applied to the Central Building Foyer and the Hillman building at Witwatersrand. Although relatively few in number, this is a distinguished body of work for the unknown Jean Welz.

NOTES

1 Conversation with Tim Benton, October 11, 2021.

2 Rukschcio and Schachel, *Adolf Loos: Leben und Werk.*

3 This story comes from Inger Welz to her son Martin.

4 Darko Kahle, "Architect Zlatko Neumann: Buildings and Projects between the World Wars," *Prostor*, July 2015, p. 35.

5 Long, *Adolf Loos: The Last Houses.*

29

PAINS AND PLEASURES OF ANONYMITY

HOW DOES IT HAPPEN, that if Loos was a “close friend” and also Kertész, neither mention one word of Jean Welz? Corroboration is the insurance of scholarship, but here it is simply missing. There is a lot of backup to these friendships from family stories, for the most part via Inger, Jean’s wife. There is no reason to think they are not accurate in themselves and they are invaluable, but a lurking doubt remains without further sources to confirm them.

It is a reminder that we think in terms of witnesses as evidence, when in fact their evidence may be inconsistent, mis-remembered, concealed for a variety of reasons, or bilious. We are used to thinking that without multiple sources we cannot feel secure as to the truth, when it is quite possible that in fact multiple sources only overlap where they are in error.

Then there are the billions of scraps we never see, fragments that remain undiscovered or were destroyed. In numbers alone, is it not likely that what remains hidden outnumbers what is found? We would perhaps like to fondly imagine that what we find must be more important and has survived for that reason, but we can just as easily be mistaken about that from wishful thinking.

With Jean Welz, the little-known architect, he seems never to have striven for his moment of fame, and as luck would have it, nor did it fall in his lap, so that was enough to ensure his anonymity.

In one sense, anonymity was a welcome cloak for Welz. He could stay in the back room, keep his head in the design issues, and not be bothered too much with clients and cash-flow. But for me, trying to work out what he did and didn’t do, that was no help at all.

Fortunately, from his later life in South Africa, as a famous person, there was a lot of interest in him, ironically a journalist even came from Paris to interview Welz the painter.

Adolf Loos was already famous, knew everybody in Paris, a celebrity, a hero to the avant-garde before he even set foot in the city. So what if he meets a bright young architect, likes chatting with him, saves money, which is scarce, and still feels bohemian staying in his tiny flat? Loos had bigger fish to fry every moment of every day. But still, he did spend a lot of time with Welz, if the accounts are true. Why would he do that, and why did he never mention it?

Of course, Welz was still unknown when Loos died. If he had lived to see him a famous painter, things might have been different.

It's probably as simple as that with Loos, although one might have expected some kind words about Welz's work, some encouragement. That was probably given in private. And then there is the fact that it seems it was Loos that introduced Welz to Raymond Fischer, his self-proclaimed biggest fan in Paris. It would have been poor form to write about his "collaborator" and not about Fischer. I would guess that Loos very well knew the truth, that Jean was the designer and Fischer the money-man. But then he wouldn't want to embarrass Fischer in the public realm.

With Kertész it seems more difficult to explain. Both men were unknowns in 1925, of roughly equal status. They both changed their first names, perhaps at the same time, and both hung out in the Dôme Café.

For Welz, Kertész was a good friend. For Kertész's part, he said nothing, hitherto be discovered, about Jean.

There are quite a few memoirs from Kertész's Paris period, and in photos at the Dôme, for example, he pictures another, then unknown, architect, Ernö Goldfinger.

According to the Welz family, there are four photographs they have by Kertész. The first two are of Jerry as a baby, one apparently taken for a baby-milk advert (see next page).

The third is attributed to Kertész by Martin Welz, the fourth son (and confirmed by the state archive outside Paris that has a Kertész collection), a handsome three-quarter portrait of Jean (see Chapter 10, "The Third Man" and Plates). For the fourth, a sweet portrait of Jean, Inger and Jerry, now aged three or four, in the Maison Zilveli, presumably in 1933 or 1934 (see Chapter 20, "Maison Zilveli").

In 1927, there was the world's first one-man photographic

exhibition, at Sliwinski's Sacre du Printemps gallery, in 1927. That photographer was Kertész (see Chapter 10, "The Third Man"). Most of the photographs are portraits, but there seems to be no extant record of who the subjects were.

Kertész got a job to photograph the Tristan Tzara house, probably during the period Welz was working there. Whether it was through Welz, I do not know, but Kertész is said to have met Tzara in Switzerland earlier. Kertész also took photos of Loos in his apartment, with Zlatko Neumann, who had taken over from Welz in June 1926, only two months after the Guevrekian letter.

The photograph of Loos and Neumann together on the next page may have been taken on site at the Tristan Tzara build, but I can't say for sure.

It may be just circumstances, but there seem to be no Kertész photos of Welz with Loos, or with Neumann, or at the Tristan Tzara house. For some reason he was not in the pictures. That could be that Kertész came on the picture after he left, or that as the new boy, Loos would not have seen a reason for having his photo taken with Welz, at that point.

The contrast between the two sides of the story is striking — for Welz, a good friend in Paris is Kertész. For Kertész, Jean Welz, to coin a phrase, does not exist.

It is said of him that Kertész, in the Paris of the twenties, was not too attached to the truth and always felt under-recognized.[1] With Welz, he may not have felt inclined to mention a name nobody knew, preferring to recall his association with famous people — especially if he felt undervalued (as he apparently did all his life).

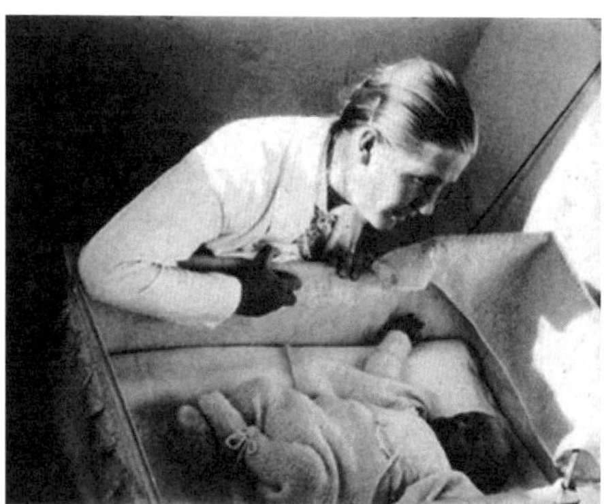

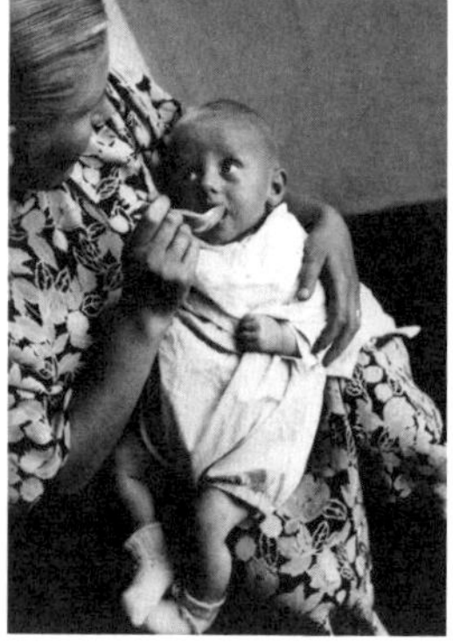

Inger and Jerry, 1930. Photos by André Kertész. Courtesy Welz family.

The Welz family story is that Jean met his wife (in 1928) through seeing two attractive blonds enter the Dôme and asking Kertész[2] to invite Inger and her friend to their table. The baby photo was only dated two years later.

Is it possible that Jean somehow imagined he was close to Loos and Kertész, and they didn't feel the same, that these relationships were much more important to Welz than to either of the famous men? Could he have been deluded about his social relationships, a fantasist?

From those who knew him in South Africa whom I met, he was seen as the opposite, a reserved and dignified figure to whom people looked up, and were very keen not to disappoint.

The most likely reason seems to be the imbalance of power between the two sides of the relationships. Both Loos and Kertész struggled for recognition in different ways, and perhaps could not spare any energy that was not employed in helping them to survive in a highly competitive world. In that context, Jean's invisibility makes perfect sense.

NOTES

1 I owe both these observations to Patricia Albers, who is writing a book on Kertész.

2 Another version has it as Peter Muller, Jean's Swiss poet friend who was a witness at the wedding.

Left: Jean Welz, passport photo from his Paris period, circa 1930s. Courtesy Welz family.

Right: Loos and Neumann, Paris, 1926. Photo André Kertész. Courtesy Ministry of Culture in France: Donation Kertész Collection at Médiathèque de l'architecture et du patrimoine.

Above: Jean Welz playing a practical joke, circa 1955–58. Photo: Jansje Wissema.

Below, left: Inger, Hannes and Jean on a seaside family holiday at St James on the southern end of the Cape Peninsula, probably 1963. Photographer unknown.

Below, right: Inger and Jean with four sons and Jerome's pet baboon, Rachel, on his lap, circa 1946–47. Left to right: Inger with Martin, born October 1945, the infant in her arms; Thomas; Stephan; Jean; Jerome with Rachel. (Hannes not yet born.) Photographer unknown.

All courtesy Welz family.

30

A SOLITARY ADVENTURE
THE CHARACTER OF JEAN WELZ

JEAN WELZ WAS A GIANT. At least, as a man of six-foot-five, he was exceedingly tall by the standards of his day. His combination of great height and serious demeanor was quite intimidating to those who knew him socially in South Africa. Jean was always the artist, whether architect or painter, always absorbed completely in the current aesthetic problem he was trying to solve in his head. That degree of concentration could make him seem a "formidable" character, to friends and family alike, creating a sense that here was a man whom you had to try to live up to, try to earn his good opinion, to be on your best behavior in his presence, so that he would not disapprove.

On the other hand, at home, he liked practical jokes to scare family and friends. One family friend recalled,

> "Many people found him scary, but why that should be is not, in retrospect, clear to me. He smiled beautifully and often, he made jokes such as bursting into a room — presumably to scare the assembled family or friends. I would say an 'innocent' (not to say, childlike) sense of humor.... He was obviously very intelligent, but in his daily dealings with other people and his family he seemed naive. I always got the idea that he was in awe of people with lots of money."[1]

On the surface, this comment contradicts the idea that Jean was not interested in money. In the light of what was perhaps Jean's own admission that he would have been unsuited to run a practice, with the financial responsibilities that would have been on his shoulders, it suggests that having made lots of money was something he could hardly imagine, and its magic would indeed be awe-inspiring, having had to struggle to survive for so long, between himself and the long-suffering Inger. The apparent ease with which some people acquire money is fascinating to those who struggle to acquire the bare necessities, and for Jean and Inger, that had been their life together for over twenty years. Jean eventually was able to make a living from painting, but not in the profusion that those dedicated to it sometimes manage.

The close descriptions of Jean Welz's work indirectly tell us a lot about the man behind them, but they are silent testimonies, however articulate as architecture. It is in the nature of things that the artist only fully expresses her- or himself in the work. The rest is noise, to a greater or lesser extent, and it would be a fatal error to mix up the man, bad or good, kind or cruel, too much with the silent witness afforded by the work.

However, it is only human nature to want to know about the man, if only for ourselves to consider what might be the relationship between our external access to his character and the similar access to the work.

Can we really get a sense of the man, or will that inevitably fall between the gaps, in the way his public profile failed to emerge and turn him into a sought-after architect?

It is only personal words that bring him alive for us. The closest we get to the man in Paris is perhaps the interpretation of Le Corbusier calling Welz "*drôle*," meaning that, to him, Jean was someone special. That minuscule fragment may mean Le Corbusier thought of Jean as both a special architect and a special person, but we don't know that. His effort in giving Jean a recommendation to take to South Africa does suggest that he held him in some regard.

From Jean's time in South Africa, there is the fact that a number of people who were his familiars, including at least two of his sons, described him as "formidable," and that echoes with the couple I met there who knew him well. The wife had been one of his models, and they bought Welz paintings. It was clear, listening to them, that they also thought Welz was indeed special, with an impressive presence, not just physically, but even more so psychologically. When he entered a room everyone fell quiet. People were in awe of his seriousness, and his charisma meant that they were careful not to say anything foolish or otherwise let themselves down — not a man for small-talk. On one occasion, the story goes, a well-known female photographer, and a friend, set out to provoke him with some risky comments, and he got so angry that he physically ejected her from the party. In some ways, Jean was forever the Viennese artist, for whom ideas could never to be taken lightly.

The strongest statement is, ironically, given his invisibility in Paris, from a French journalist who came from "the city of light" to interview him as the painter:

> "[Welz is]… classical, but always great…. Everything is controlled by the complexity of his thought and the elaboration of his ideas… The same intellect, sharp as a blade, raises fundamental questions and answers them with honesty without compromise…. He cannot stand stupidity or what he considers to be mental laziness…. In addition to his almost brutal, distant attitude, there is in him a tenderness, an understanding and a simplicity that make his person great…. He is subtle, deep, broad of ideas, unpredictable, prejudiced, impractical, adventurous, conservative — in a word: complex."[2]

Jean Welz, circa 1955–58. Photo: Jansje Wissema. Courtesy Welz family.

There is a great deal to unpack in these words, but note the appearance of "great" twice, a great man. Take some other words: classical, complexity of his thought, sharp as a blade, fundamental questions, brutal and distant but also a tenderness, an understanding and a simplicity.

Add to that the closing sentence: "subtle, deep, broad of ideas, unpredictable, prejudiced, impractical, adventurous, conservative — in a word: complex." These are qualities that, to me, appear in his architecture, the mind I felt I had discovered behind the Villa Darmstadter and Maison Zilveli.

"His intense concentration on artistic problems to the exclusion of everything else,"[3] was the view of most people who knew him. As a result, he often came across as a remote figure, including to his children. Even for the boys with whom he got on best, he could be a distant presence, a preoccupied one that they were wary of disturbing, that "formidable" figure described by Martin Welz. Inger, his "long-suffering" wife, went to enormous lengths in South Africa to create and protect Jean's *cordon sanitaire* within which he could work undisturbed. Inger's task was not an easy one. Jean was not an easy husband, in the sense that he was forever absent, not physically but mentally — that "exclusion of everything else," which was his usual state of mind. Inger was, in that sense, the classic artist's wife in putting enormous amounts of energy into protecting him from the world, the daily round, so that through her extraordinary efforts he could use all his energies on his art.

This image of the artist, working all hours, in his case often overnight by artificial light, within a protected zone that Inger had created for him, is not an unfamiliar one. He would drive her mad with his small anxieties, and it seems to have taken a lot out of her to create the appearance of calm within which he could create with the minimum of disturbance from the outside world.

Carmen, wife of the third son Stephan, has an interesting observation:

> "I often got the feeling that he was slightly unsure of himself — he was constantly quoted as saying that he came to art late and had to struggle to deal with the challenges. I had the idea that he kept over-painting and reworking paintings because of this feeling of uncertainty. Was it good enough or was it not? If someone, whose opinion he did not regard highly dared to express admiration or enthusiasm about a work in progress, it

happened very often that one would wake up in the morning to find the picture destroyed. And if Inger, or one of us, dared say anything, he was as likely as not to destroy a work out of sheer bloody mindedness!"

Esme Berman, doyenne of art criticism in South Africa, said of Jean Welz, "His career... had been a solitary adventure unrelated to surrounding trends or fashions."[4] As a self-taught artist of strong convictions, constitutionally able only to take his own path, and incapable of accepting anything less than the highest quality, his life was never going to be easy. It is not as though he was surrounded by artists of similar feelings, as he had been in Paris. He had only his own doubts and instincts to rely upon, and the former in particular were a relentless nag.

Picasso said of Cezanne that we loved him because of his doubts. That may be entirely functional for the art, but tough for the family trailing in the tortured wake.

Here was Jean, with his architectural past in which he had invested so much, forced by circumstance to set out on another path, one that was a constant struggle for him. He aimed at the highest standards, and would achieve at that level, but in "solitary," as it were, and beset by doubt.

As a person he could be kind,[5] but:[6] "He was mean about household spending, and negative about his grandchildren's abilities, to the extent that during one Christmas visit, we actually moved out."

On the other hand,

"He could be utterly charming in an unexpected way. On one occasion he announced at breakfast that he was going to buy me a present. He marched me off to the local shop and insisted on buying me a stainless-steel cooking pot (which I was at pains to say I did not need). I knew Jean for fifteen years, and in that time cannot remember him phoning Stephan (his third son) even once, in spite of the fact that Stephan was in hospital on a number of occasions during this time. I know of one occasion when he decided to go and visit one of his friends near Paarl — fifty km away. He took the car and just left, returning a day or two later. In the meantime, Inger was frantic with worry, and had no idea what had happened to him or who to phone — this at a time when there were of course no mobile phones. On his return, he could not understand what all the fuss was about!"

As a father, he was of his generation to some degree, and as an architect and as a painter he was self-obsessed, but he was also felt as lovable within his family and admired in his social set in South Africa.

Jean Welz was a man for whom his work was everything, it was not a job or even a vocation, but a passionate determination to accept nothing less than the best, whether we see that in the embers of paintings he destroyed after months of work, or in the purity of the Villa Darmstadter and the Maison Zilveli.

He was formidable enough, as a man and an architect, to count Le Corbusier as a friend, and Adolf Loos as a close friend. His achievements as a painter in South Africa, against the odds, are at one with the caliber of those friendships. If his struggle as a painter was solitary, it seems all the more heroic in the circumstances, however difficult it made life for his wife and five boys.

Many times he could be difficult, both working and also in company, where his somewhat martinet views tolerated no levity. It would not be true to say that he had no sense of humor, but it would be true to say that here was a very serious man, who took to heart the intellectual and artistic issues in which he had developed a

Jean Welz the Puppeteer, circa 1955–58. Photo: Jansje Wissema. Courtesy Welz family.

passionate interest in Vienna, as a student and a practicing architect in Josef Hoffmann's office. The abiding image, at least from the South African period, is of a man who brought an unusual tone of high seriousness to both his work and his life.

Those standards were perhaps inculcated in the intellectual hothouse of the Vienna he knew in the momentous years between 1918 and 1925. Both the shattering events of those times, and the fervent cultural atmosphere of Vienna could hardly fail to have a lasting impact on one of his intelligence and dedication.

His son, Martin, who traveled to Vienna and Paris in 1979 to meet some of his father's friends and acquaintances, has the clear view that, whatever the strength of those he met, and was perhaps influenced by, including a Le Corbusier or Adolf Loos, he was never one to fall under the influence of others to the exclusion of his own creative personality. He was his own man under all circumstances, which is how, as a young man of twenty-seven, he was more than able to take on the all-conquering ideas of Le Corbusier, and even the deepest thoughts of Adolf Loos, and emerge with a vision that was his own.

In Paris, he had almost ideal circumstances to develop his own ideas — working in the backroom — the front of house pressure taken by Raymond Fischer — and surrounded by the leading members of two avant-gardes, those of Paris and Vienna.

We should also not forget his formation under the auspices of the leading name of the first Viennese avant-garde, Josef Hoffmann. Welz may have reacted against Hoffmann as Loos did, but even in that case, he was reacting against the leading figure in Vienna as — I believe — he would later react against the architect widely regarded as the most influential of the twentieth century — Le Corbusier. In other words, Jean Welz was not one to be fazed by the fame of others.

His fearlessness in that sense, was quite possibly what brought him the good opinion of Le Corbusier and the close friendship of Adolf Loos. It is unlikely that without the strength of character he possessed that he would have survived and prospered in such company.

Domestically, Welz could be kind to his daughters-in-law and seems to have been a good teacher of art to children, but he could also be relentless and unforgiving, both to himself and others. But how else could he have achieved what I believe him to have achieved in those years in Paris?

His passion for music — the images of him almost fainting in a Busch concert, having to hold on tightly to his chair, and pasting a score on the walls of his small flat, walking around playing the violin after a long day at work in order to relax — gives a sense of what kind of man he was. Raymond Fischer learned the connection between architecture and music from Welz, and almost his first act on his first modern design — the small balcony on the front of the Maison Dubin — was to him the statement of a theme as in music, one to be developed throughout the intricate and demanding layout of that house.

It is something difficult to understand in today's febrile climate of celebrity culture that an artist — an architect who achieved what he did — could possibly remain so deeply in the shadows, that he is unknown to virtually every architect today. The fact of his seriousness, his dedication, one might say his uncompromising passion, might have only succeeded artistically to the degree that it did precisely because he was a back-room boy, a "nègre," an unknown.

If he had started his own practice, spending time searching for clients and paying his staff, he would not have been able to focus exclusively on the art of architecture. The shadows were his protection. He would have been a quite different kind of character if he had been preoccupied more with fame and fortune, reputation and celebrity. The other side of the coin of anonymity was a certain freedom.

Even as a painter, Jean Welz perhaps did not have the freedom he had in Paris as an architect. Although paid little, he had a flat and a wife and one child, and could manage, even if his relations were shocked by his poverty. In South Africa, he eventually had five children, was forced by ill-health to give up architecture, and literally had the future of his family in his hands. He had to earn a living through his art. South Africa was not Paris. His first writing in South Africa was on the abstract in art, but his abstract paintings were always difficult to sell, where landscapes, still lifes and nudes were not.

So, even as an artist, he had more constraints on his creativity in South Africa than he did in Paris. However, he made the most of it and had real success as an artist — but South Africa was not where he could expect to push the boundaries as a painter, as I believe he had as an architect in Paris.

Nice to women and children, formidable to men and his own boys. Naive and unworldly but also fierce and unforgiving. A man of principle, who felt South Africans should walk down the street with their heads bowed in shame, yet one who went out of his way to learn Afrikaans. A man who gave his architectural skills to the local Black-African school, but was disgusted when the students smashed things up.

Welz was no saint, he could be mean, angry, uncaring, dismissive, impatient, and pig-headed to the extent of cutting off his nose to spite his face.[7] He was not a man to seek a reputation for himself, whether as an architect or later as a painter. A solitary adventure indeed.

NOTES

1 Via a family friend in South Africa, 2014.

2 Miles, *The World of Jean Welz.*

3 Carmen Welz, wife of Stephan Welz, the third son of Jean. An eminent auctioneer, ex-head of Sotheby's South Africa, he died Christmas Eve, 2015. Cora Welz, wife of Jerome Welz, first son, made similar comments. Jerome, "Jerry," Welz, born in Paris in 1930 died in 2017; Cora said Jean was her image of the artist, both lovable and fierce, kind and short-fused, and always intensely focused on artistic concerns.

4 Esme Berman, *Art and Artists of South Africa*, Cape Town: A. A. Balkema, 1970.

5 As Cora, the wife of his first son, told me, during my trip to South Africa

6' To Carmen, wife of Stephan, the third son.

7 Carmen Welz, in relation to his constant changes to paintings, email May 14, 2018.

31

CHRISTENSEN GALLERY
INGER WELZ

JEAN MET INGER CHRISTENSEN IN PARIS in 1928, persuading his friend André Kertész to invite her and her blonde Swedish friend to join them at their table at the Dôme Café. From that moment on, Jean and Inger's lives were enmeshed. When twelve years later, in 1940, Jean and Inger moved to an isolated house on the Tradouw Pass in an arid region of South Africa known as the Little Karoo, their story, as told together by daughter-in-law Carmen Welz (widow of son Stephan) and son Martin Welz,[1] proceeded thus:

> "The climate and situation was ideal for a tuberculosis sufferer in recovery, but it was up to Inger to find food and other necessities. She sometimes walked the fifteen kilometers to the nearest village... if she was lucky, she would get a lift from a passing car or donkey cart. Inger had a whole bartering system going — she would exchange Jean's small ink drawings for honey, eggs or whatever she could get from local farmers and shopkeepers. Their ten-year-old son Jerome attended the school 'for poor whites' established in the village with funding from the Carnegie Foundation.
>
> "The desperation Inger must have felt influenced her forever. For a start, she could never let any possibility of a lift, going in any direction go by. (Inger never learned to drive; Jean only learned to drive at the age of forty-six, and remained a frighteningly bad driver for the rest of his life.) Some of the traveling salesmen who stopped by once a month on their country rounds became lifelong friends.

“Inger did all in her power to keep Jean working, healthy and stress-free.

“Her taste was impeccable and timeless, from an appreciation of antique Chinese porcelain, antique English silverware and Persian carpets on one end of the scale, to modern Finnish fabrics and German stainless steel cutlery on the other. She sold both — and much more — in her shop, Christensen Gallery in Worcester, which over the years became a cultural hub in this somewhat larger country town one hundred and twenty-odd kilometers from Cape Town to which they moved in 1943. Widely read and an inveterate newspaper reader — two a day on weekdays, three on Sundays — Inger's dream had been to start a bookshop, but these country people were not book buyers. So she moved on and, supported by a sympathetic bank manager, started importing containers full of quality Scandinavian silver, fabrics, crockery etc. while also scouring antique shops and auction rooms in Cape Town for antique porcelain and silverware to her taste. Her bartering abilities stood her in good stead because many of the farmers' wives who admired and bought

Inger in her Christensen Gallery, circa early 1960s. Courtesy Welz family. Photographer unknown.

her stock spent the money behind their husband's backs, and she was happy to exchange antiques or crockery for a monthly supply of eggs, or rusks or whatever fruit and vegetables were in season.

> "Not enough has been said about Inger's role in Jean's life. She was an extremely capable, highly intelligent and also totally unpretentious woman. While he was going on trips of the imagination and feeding the soul, she walked an hour a day, six days a week along a rough and rising road in freezing rain and hellishly hot sun to work at her shop — so that she could make ends meet. Despite the necessity, she sold only things that she herself loved and admired. While focused all the while on paying the bills and feeding the family, her shop also gave her a status and identity in her own right. Jean accepted that, never interfered and frequently expressed his appreciation for her taste and enterprise. Each understood and admired the other."

Inger was, by all accounts, a remarkable and formidable woman.

As a painter, Jean was far from easy. He could be depressed, irritable, irascible, and Inger took it upon herself to keep the world away from him, so that he could devote all his energies to his art. In 1940, his energies were much depleted by tuberculosis, but after he recovered, the matter of his mind, his psychology, took over.

Welz destroyed over half his paintings and carried on painting and repainting many others, driving Inger, his clients, and himself mad in doing so. As his family said, he never knew when to stop. According to them,

> "Without her strength and perseverance, he would never have finished anything. Besides keeping the family more or less fed over the years from the modest income she made from her little shop in Worcester, she kept him sheltered from financial worries and unwelcome people — no one could see Jean without Inger's mediation and arrangement — so that he could focus on his art."[2]

Inger had much to put up with. No money and five boys ranked high in the early years, and Jean remained a tortured artist to the end. After his death, she traveled to Paris in 1985, taking the photos of his architectural work from his portfolio with her and meeting up with Jean-Louis Avril, who was to write the first article about Jean, having discovered the decaying Maison Zilveli. She also met Raymond Fischer, then in his eighties, and he wrote her an appreciative letter following her visit.

Even in her eighties, and in a wheelchair, she traveled the world — Hong Kong, Europe and America — nominally to find stock, recruiting young people in need of money to push her wheelchair.

> "At eighty, she flew to New York to nurse her youngest son, Hannes, who was dying of AIDS, until he breathed his last and then stayed on to pack up his things and arrange for transport back to South Africa.
>
> "She had come to Paris in 1927 as a nineteen-year-old determined to 'see the world,' working as an au pair and learning French. The eldest of seven children, she fled the restraints imposed by years of having to care for half a dozen younger siblings, a depressive father and small-town rural Denmark."[4]

Inger secured the job of au pair to the four children of the Comte and Comtesse du Mesnil du Buisson. Part of her remuneration was to be weekly French lessons from the Comte himself. Upon her arrival at the Gare du Nord, a pre-arranged taxi was waiting to take her directly to 63 rue de Varenne.

She was well-equipped to appreciate all the cultural benefits that Paris had to offer. Both her parents were teachers at the small school in Ringe, the Danish village where she grew up; both came from well-established farming families and were well-read.

The house in Ringe, now a museum, where Inger grew up, and where her father was a teacher. Courtesy Welz family. Photographer unknown.

Her mother was an accomplished classical pianist. Her maternal grandfather, who was very influential in her life, was a particularly successful farmer, unusually widely read and a collector of art.

As an au pair in Paris, her greatest joy was to take the Count's children to the gardens of the Rodin Museum at no 77. Soon after her arrival in Paris she became a trusted and supportive friend to Astrid Noack, twenty years her senior, then the proverbial desperately poor artist living in a garret in Montmartre. Noack would later be recognized as one of Denmark's most celebrated sculptors.[4]

Inger easily fitted in with Jean's circle of friends who, besides Swiss poet Pierre Muller, included Le Corbusier and the latter's brother and sister-in-law as well as Adolf Loos, who would regularly seek refuge from the demands of his French clients and sympathy for his declining health, as syphilis took its toll, by spending a night or two with Jean and Inger in their small apartment. Hungarian-born photographer André Kertész, of course, took several photographs of Jean and Inger at home with their infant son, Jerome Pierre (named after Muller).

Inger provided stability for an often unpredictable, mood-driven star. Jean was extremely gifted and worked extremely hard — when it suited him. All those hours spent drinking coffee and debating architecture, art and philosophy with Muller and other friends — feeding the soul — were noticed by his absence from the otherwise more conventional and commercially-oriented Fischer office. His already menial salary was docked for the hours of his absence. This did not seem to overly concern Jean, but for obviously good reasons, Inger was not amused and called Pierre Muller to account for what she regarded as selfish irresponsibility.

In an effort to earn extra money, Inger took to submitting short news reports and essays to *Fyns Tidende*, the Danish provincial newspaper her parents had subscribed to throughout her childhood. And she accepted occasional catwalk modeling gigs for Paris fashion houses keen to have a Scandinavian blond in the line-up. A perk of the job, for someone who was otherwise totally unconcerned with fashion, was that the models got to keep some of the clothes in which they paraded on the runway.

Forty years later, in 1971, Inger visited Paris again with her youngest son, Hannes, and wrote a charming story in South Africa's most widely read Afrikaans newspaper about those early years. On her trip down memory lane, she actually went back to no. 63 after taking Hannes on a tour of the Rodin Museum and discovered that the Comte was still alive and still living in the same house, although the Comtesse Inger knew had died and he had remarried.

Late in 1936, Jean's position as an Austrian working illegally in Paris was increasingly precarious. A return to Austria, by then in the early thralls of nationalist fascism, was no option, according to Martin Welz — "Jean said, 'There was a loudspeaker shouting at you from every street corner.'" Always practical, Inger started visiting embassies to find out where jobs could be had and which country would welcome immigrants. There were a few options, but South Africa was the cheapest to get to, and there were architectural jobs advertised in *The Star*, a major Johannesburg newspaper. As Jean traveled there, Inger stayed behind in Paris, writing articles for the Danish newspaper to earn her and Jerome's passage to Africa, once they were sure Jean had secured a job as an architect. In the meantime, the child had been taken to stay with Inger's parents in Denmark.[5]

Carmen told me, "I admired her very much and for good reason, but she was not an easy person — at least not to my mind. The hard life probably took its toll."[6]

Inger Welz, at the time she and Jean lived in Paris. Source: Miles, *The World of Jean Welz*. Courtesy Welz Family.

Inger was what might be called a "natural socialist" in her ideas, more of a humanist, admiring committed idealists, as she probably saw Jean, and "had read all the progressive socialist and feminist writers of the twenties and thirties, including Colette, Simone de Beauvoir, and the more earnest Beatrice Webb, as well as the Scandinavian classics from Ibsen to Kierkegaard, and in practical terms she was unusually generous in her will to her employees. Life had taught her empathy for the poor."[7]

According to members of her family with whom I spoke, Inger found people interesting regardless of race, age or social standing and was a very enthusiastic hostess and very good cook, having learned from her time in Paris.

Although empathetic to people, she could be competitive, occasionally to the point of nastiness[8] — but with Jean a particularly strong, formidable character himself, who could easily dominate a conversation and in so doing earn respect and admiration — she needed to be able to keep her end up.

She was never one to have a huff, but when Jean absented himself for two days and returned without any recognition of the worry he had caused, Inger walked out of the house herself, without a word, only the action.

"Inger had perfect taste, as she showed endlessly in her gallery, especially in matters of color, and had many artist friends in South Africa who held her in high regard."[9] In that way, she was an artist manqué, and in that perhaps was the source of her patience and sympathy with Jean's tortured soul as an artist.

Inger was never the shrinking violet. "Jean having his meager salary docked by the long-suffering Raymond Fischer exasperated Inger, who was struggling with a small child in a basement flat."[10] Raymond Fischer had a certain sympathy for Inger, and bullied Jean into finally getting his divorce sorted in Vienna, when Inger had a son of five, and had lost a daughter, born prematurely after a dreadful coughing-fit had brought on labor.

In the early South African days, when Jean was incapacitated, Inger had to live very much by her wits and wrote secret letters for help when times were at their hardest. The difficulties of those days eventually took their toll. In old age she was hunched and half-blind, although her brain was as sharp as ever. If she was not tough to start with, she either would not have been able to be the support to Jean that she always was, or she had to learn in a hard school and pretty fast. "She was a survivor who never gave up on life."[11]

If Jean was the classic case of "behind every great artist is a strong woman," then Inger fulfilled that brief far beyond the average.

"Inger clearly loved Jean and he loved her — they were very, very fond of each other mutually. His last words to her, as his adored Mozart played in the background, were: 'You made me very happy.'"[12]

NOTES

1 Carmen Welz, FaceTime conversation, February 6, 2021, supplemented by details via email from Martin Welz, February 5–6, 2021 and April 19, 2022.

2 Carmen Welz, by email, January 13, 2021.

3 Martin Welz, February 6, 2021.

4 Martin Welz, February 6, 2021.

5 Carmen Welz, Martin Welz, February 5–6, 2021., supplemented by Martin Welz, April 19, 2022.

6 Carmen Welz, February 6, 2021.

7 Martin Welz, February 6, 2021 and April 19, 2022.

8 Carmen Welz and Martin Welz, February 6, 2021, supplemented by this comment from Martin, April 19, 2022: "Her shop's role in maintaining her status and self-esteem played out somewhat differently in her relationship with her children. Three of her sons followed careers that directly derived from her interests and influence: Thomas started a similar business to hers that eventually evolved into a successful second-hand bookshop — her dream. Stephan became South Africa's most respected and successful-by-far art and antiques auctioneer and agent for Sothebys. Martin became a featured journalist on national newspapers. Instead of pride, she seemed to have experienced this as diminishing of her own hard-earned achievements and status, which she would on occasion re-assert by making demeaning critical comments, rather than complimenting her children on their achievements.

9 Carmen Welz, February 6, 2021.

10 Carmen Welz, February 6, 2021.

11 Martin Welz, April 19, 2022.

12 Carmen Welz, February 6, 2021. Born March 4, 1900, Jean Welz died at age seventy-five, December 24, 1975.

32

ZILVELI DESTROYED

THE LOSS OF THE MAISON ZILVELI comes not as a surprise but, nevertheless, as a huge blow. As I write, it still stands, but demolition is imminent. The sad saga is, in a way, just another chapter in the price of anonymity for Jean Welz's legacy.

There is a certain irony, in fact, a full set of ironies about its *disparition*, in that Zilveli was bought by a very famous and successful commercial artist who had protested long and hard about his dream of saving the house, only to wage a relentless campaign to ensure its destruction.

The one aspect of the saga I want to focus on drew my attention as part of that campaign.

The eminent new owner is a master of media manipulation in his work, and also proved to be so with the French press in what appeared to be a very painstaking management of *his own* legacy (at the age of eighty-three). With extensive access to press coverage of the purchase and his plans, he went to great pains to convince all and sundry that Zilveli simply had to be demolished, that regretfully he had no alternative, but that he would demonstrate his fealty by constructing a replica, a copy of the house, on the site. The key, which leaked out in an interview he conducted, was the intention to create a "shoe-box" beneath the facsimile to hold the archive of his life's work.

I confess I was amazed that the French press and public appeared to swallow the story and the idea of a copy, hook, line and sinker, despite its absurdity in every conceivable way. The fact was that he is a very popular figure, and both press and public were quite prepared to give him the benefit of the doubt. Added to that, the Minister of Culture supported the idea of a copy based on Welz's plans, something of a suicide note in a country where *droits d'auteur* ("author's rights") are sacred and their infringement could hasten the tumbrils beneath the guillotine.

I had met the new owner, who lives next door but one to Zilveli, two or three years ago, around the time he had won it at auction. He had paid over two million euros and proposed to spend more again on the project. It appeared to me that he had zero interest in the house or the architect and was set upon demolition on the nominal grounds that his architect had declared it the only option.

It only became crystal clear to me in the course of this year, 2022, and through his media campaign, that this had possibly been his intention all along. The archive for his work was the goal, Zilveli was merely the hurdle.

Part of his campaign was to prove Zilveli could not be saved, and his architect as well as an *architecte du patrimoine* (conservation architect) he had employed had both condemned the design as "very bad" in structural terms, adding that Welz was very inexperienced, had little background managing projects, and gave the impression Welz had been brave, indeed reckless, but out of his depth with Zilveli.[1]

That did not go down well with me.

What it did do was to send me back to look at the structural aspect of the Zilveli design.

In the slightly magical way that this project had thrown up connections throughout, often unexpected but always relevant, another such moment occurred just as I was checking the bibliographic details for this book.

20

Le Journal des Arts

PATRIMOINE & MUSÉES

PATRIMOINE DU XXe SIÈCLE

VILLA ZILVELI : PROTÉGER OU RECONSTRUIRE ?

Surplombant la butte Bergeyre à Paris, la villa moderniste devrait être démontée puis reconstruite selon le dessin originel par son propriétaire, Jean-Paul Goude. Tout autre est le choix des défenseurs du patrimoine du XXe siècle, qui plaident en faveur de la préservation de l'édifice

« Je veux faire avec cette villa ce que j'ai fait dans la réclame : la sublimer »

Problème de structure

Une « déconstruction » plutôt qu'une destruction

I had missed an article by a South African architect and one-time head of the University of Witwatersrand School of Architecture, written about one of the first Jean Welz exhibitions as an artist, dated October 1942. In it, the architect, John Fassler, mentioned his first meetings with Welz, when he was working on the design for the Central Building foyer that was to arouse much interest among the "modernists" at the University:

> "In the somewhat torrid atmosphere of a wood and iron hut that served as an office for the architectural staff, we discussed painting, sculpture and architecture whenever we met. It was apparent then from what passed that Mr. Welz had enjoyed an extensive contact in Paris with contemporary French artists, architects and structural engineers. Picasso, Le Corbusier and Fressinet were more than mere names to him. He knew them personally, and from a contact extending over a period of twelve years could follow with understanding what each was striving to achieve in his particular sphere. It is one thing to know artists through the medium of their work alone, but quite another to know them personally."[2]

I was puzzled by the name "Fressinet" and by the reference to "structural engineers," but then I was able to put two and two together. In fact, the name was a misspelling for Freyssinet. There was a French architect of the period called Fressinet, but the key was the term "structural engineers."

Freyssinet (1879–1962) was as eminent as a structural engineer as Le Corbusier was as an architect. He was the doyen of his field, but more than that, he was known for a creative and imaginative approach to engineering, a pioneer in reinforced concrete, "thin-shell" roofs, and had invented a process for "pre-stressed" concrete that permitted slimmer structures than would otherwise be possible.

Tim Benton told me that Freyssinet was unusually open to the new generation of modern architects, perhaps because of their interest in new materials and methods, and he would often show up at events where the younger generation figured. Le Corbusier had written to him praising his extraordinary work on large hangar-structures, and the "Freyssinet Hall" had been constructed in Paris between 1927 and 1929, then ironically saved from destruction by a listing as a *Monument Historique* as late as 2012.

Welz began work in 1937 on the Central Hall, and it would have been then he had the discussions with Fassler, only four years after Zilveli.

My thinking was that for Welz to have mentioned Freyssinet in such a way that Fassler remembered it so clearly suggests potentially rather more than dropping a name, which was not the sort of thing Welz would do anyway, but a strong connection. If Welz did actually know Freyssinet personally, as Fassler suggested, that might well indicate it was more than a nodding acquaintance, and the connection between the structure of Zilveli and the kind of experimental work Freyssinet undertook — for example, the pre-stressed process he invented in 1929 — might have not have been incidental.

The two key structural elements of Zilveli were both thinner than appears they might need to be. The extraordinary balcony support was only six-centimeters thick,[3] and the cruciform pillars likewise appear potentially slimmer than what might pass as comfortable and secure for a conventional structural engineer.[4]

Let us turn back for a moment to Welz's skills in the matter of structure.

Welz completed his architecture degree in Vienna in June 1921. Technical training there at that time was arguably the most rigorous and sophisticated in the world. As we have seen, his final report was written by one of his professors, Oskar Strnad, a considerable architect, a leading light of the Second Wave of Viennese modernism, and a colleague of both Josef Hoffmann (head of the course) and Adolf Loos.

> "Technically talented, skilled at drawing, very conscientious, has a masterly knowledge of the practical aspects of building, and very good taste."[5]
>
> "A very conscientious skilled draftsman with much technical understanding, very [the very was added later] capable on all kinds of building work."

In France, Welz had gone on from the Tzara House (1925–26) to build his first design alongside Le Corbusier's Villa Cook, the Maison Dubin (1927–28); the 'house for an artist' studio for Sir FMK Kielberg (1929); the Villa Kolpa (1929); the Rue de Charonne block of flats (1930–31); and the Villa Darmstadter (1932), before building the Maison Zilveli the following year (1933), besides his involvement in Villa Dury (1928), Hôtel Godfray (1929), Maison St. Leger (1929), and the houses at Montauban (1931), all for Raymond Fischer, and in addition, his independent commission, the Maison Landau (1931).

Herr Hans Welz besitzt technische Begabung, zeichnerisches Geschick, sehr guten Geschmack, beherrscht das Bauhandwerk, war sehr gewissenhaft, strebsam und ernst.

Herr Hans Welz ist ernst, technisch begabt, zeichnerisch geschickt sehr gewissenhaft und beherrscht das Bauhandwerk. Er hat sehr guten Geschmack

WIEN · AM · 30. Juni · 1921.

Prof. Dr. Strnad: technisch begabt, zeichnerisch geschickt sehr gewissenhaft beherrscht das Bauhandwerk und hat sehr guten Geschmack

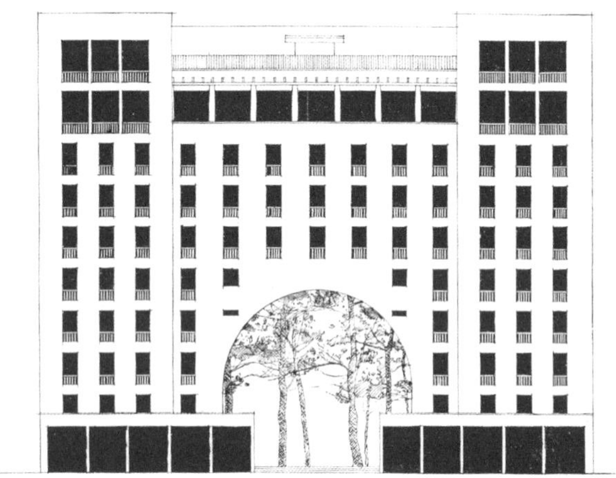

Above: Welz's final report by Oskar Strnad. Courtesy Vienna Technical University.

Below: Loos's hotel for Juan-les-Pins features a drawing with trees that, to my eye, are clearly by the hand of Jean Welz, who helped to publish Loos's project in *L'Architecture d'Aujourd'hui* via Fischer, according to Martin Welz. Martin related to me the story of Loos telling Jean to go to Kniže haberdashery on the Champs Élysées where his payment for this drawing would be waiting. He did, it wasn't.
"Project to rescue a pine wood. By Adolf Loos." Source: *L'Architecture d'Aujourd'hui*, October 7, 1931, p. 67, via via portaildocumentaire.citedelarchitecture.fr.

If we add in the idea that from the Maison Dubin of 1927–28 onwards he was developing the ideas of Adolf Loos's version of modernism — against the Five Points of Le Corbusier — then Welz's skills and experience appear very substantial indeed.

Painting Welz as a neophyte served the new owner's campaign, but rendered an enormous disservice to the reputation and legacy, since legacies are at stake, of Jean Welz.

The overlap between Freyssinet's famed creative exploration of reinforced-concrete and the structural innovations of the Maison Zilveli appear more than coincidental. As Jean-Louis Cohen put it to me, "structural invention… should be underlined as one of the strong points of the Zilveli house."[6]

There is no straight line between Freyssinet's pre-stressed techniques and the Zilveli supports, not least as the former involve complex technical apparatus far beyond the low-budget Zilveli project. However, it is conceivable that Welz both discussed the Zilveli structural issues with Freyssinet and came up with his own economical solutions to creating thin-walled structures to support the Zilveli aerial floor. Welz may have even adapted Freyssinet's pre-stressed techniques. With the balcony support, imagine the wooden boxing, into which the concrete would be poured, with the metal rods attached to a steel beam at one end, and a similar metal bar at the other end. With some kind of archimedes screw that would allow the bars to be tightened, this would create an element of pre-stressing of the six-centimeter support, with the pillars being made in a similar way. I have to admit this is only my speculation, but what it does suggest is that a proper expert analysis of Zilveli, along the lines of the *comité scientifique* that was appointed for the restoration of the Eileen Gray house, E1027, could yield insights into exactly what Welz innovated for Zilveli.

The Minister of Culture declined to intervene, despite a late-November 2021 letter signed by around a dozen of the world's leading experts, but did note that a detailed analysis of the house prior to demolition should be carried out. However, that was proposed by the owner, involving his architect, who may not have the expert knowledge and experience required to carry that out satisfactorily.

Let us turn to the condition of Zilveli. In 2012, it looked ready to collapse. In 2022, it looks worse. It still has the incongruous wooden supports the family managed to have installed without cost by the *Compagnons*,[7] more used to medieval structures than modernism.

The owner is far from alone in declaring the house cannot be saved; in fact, the whole French establishment shares that view. Monument Historiques, Architectes du Batiment de France, DRAC,[8] and the local Town Hall are unanimous.

One might reasonably assume that these august bodies are peopled with experts in reinforced-concrete, twentieth-century architecture and conservation of modernist buildings.

The rather shocking fact is that is not the case. So far, those who have made the weighty declaration appear wholly untroubled by expertise and experience in the salient matters. There are those who would characterize the French bureaucracy as Bourboniste, but I am no expert in that matter.

The brief description is that the balcony was demolished in 1986 as a public-safety threat, and the rest is threatened likewise, with the main floor having descended by over sixty centimeters due to the loss of the structural integrity of the pillars.

The main floor has a broken back, twisted, and the cracks in the kitchen (party) wall are big enough to put your fist in, as well as the fact that the front street elevation is leaning to one side.

To the untutored eye, Zilveli looks ready only to fall down.

The big question is whether the 'authorities' could be wrong? There are two basic issues — the sub-soil and the structure. The local area is infamous for subsidence. Many of the neighboring houses have had periods of being propped up, and the assumption has been that the Zilveli site is similarly vulnerable — as one of the reasons the house has moved around.

However, I recall seeing a geo-phys (like an X-ray image) produced by the local school of architecture at Belleville, and from what I could see, in fact, there were no "caves" beneath Zilveli.

Various structural engineers have proposed the conventional solution, which is to create a reinforced concrete raft below the

A tell-tale, fixed across a crack in a twelfth-century castle in rural France (author photo).

house with pillars going down from that to solid ground perhaps thirty meters below. That would be an expensive solution, but more than that, if there are not actually "caves" under Zilveli, it is possibly unnecessary. My own feeling is that if there really is substantial movement under the site, there is no guarantee that a raft and pillars would not be susceptible to further movement and cracking. Clearly, that pairing would offer a rigid platform, but I would want to know, if it were my money, that it was necessary beyond doubt.

The simple way of testing for movement is to put "tell-tales" across existing cracks and check them for any movement at intervals.

The main issue in terms of Welz's design is the condition of the structure itself. Compare these three photos: first, Zilveli in 1933, second, the black and white photograph taken forty years later, around 1973.

While the 1973 building looks uncared for, it still has the balcony, without much deterioration of the structure (a crack is visible on the side and what looks like a steel bar has lost its concrete covering on the front), and the end pillars of the house appear still functional. There is no apparent collapse visible of the main features.

Now look at the 2013 photo, a further forty years on.

Counter-clockwise: Zilveli, 1933 (above left), photographer unconfirmed, possibly André Kertész; Zilveli, 1973 (below left) and Zilveli, 2013 (right), both courtesy of Jean-Louis Avril.

The point here is that after the first forty years, there appears to be no deterioration in the structural integrity of Zilveli. A further forty years on and the building has to be propped — the question is why?

The problems of reinforced concrete have been known for at least fifty or sixty years. The way Zilveli was built would have been, as suggested, to create wooden formers for the balcony support and the pillars. Steel reinforcement rods would have been inserted in the void and liquid concrete poured around them.

What was not realized at the time Zilveli was built in 1933 was that although the concrete eventually dried, it retained moisture and that moisture corroded the steel reinforcement bars, which expanded from the rust, in turn cracking or "blowing" the concrete around them. That would be enough to compromise the structural integrity of the pillars, leading to the sort of collapse visible in the 2013 photo but not apparent on the surface in the photo from 1973.

Today there is worldwide experience in effecting repairs in that situation — the corroded metal is removed and where necessary replaced with galvanized, and the concrete is repaired with modern resins.

It is possible, and I can say no more than this, that if that treatment were to be used at Zilveli, the main problem would be solved. It would involve potentially jacking up the aerial floor to its original height while the repairs dry, but then — if the subsoil is not such a problem — structural integrity may be returned.

As far as the broken back, cracks in the kitchen wall, and lean on the front elevation, again it is possible that those are all the result of the pillars collapsing, perhaps differentially, and the main floor twisting as a result.

I must be clear that this is all my guesswork, but it is based on the kind of 'best practice' seen in both archaeology and architecture, whereby minimal intrusion is made into the existing fabric, not least so that future generations may clearly see the history of a building, rather than have it lost or covered by later work.

The origins of this approach go back to William Morris and the Society for the Preservation of Ancient Buildings, whose minimal approach ("just clean the gutters") was in contrast to Viollet Le Duc and his "imaginative reconstruction" of Carcassonne, which horrified Morris.

At the least, such an approach is relatively inexpensive, proceeds slowly, and destroys little.

Were a *comité scientifique* to be appointed, it could carry out an assessment using such methods and, if at worse it turns out much more intrusive techniques would be necessary, little is lost.

If, on the other hand, it were to be discovered that the problems were solvable, and perhaps that Jean Welz had taken an experimental but sensible approach to the innovative structure of Zilveli, there would be much to gain, and much to discover.

In 1964, the then Minister of Culture, André Malraux, saved the Villa Savoye from demolition. Zilveli is the Savoye of 2022, but there appears to be no such savior in the wings.

The Lost Architecture of Jean Welz was not intended to be a literal title, but as I write these last words, it is in danger of becoming so — and with Welz's last house — the truly remarkable Maison Zilveli.

Jean Welz was, to my mind, unlikely to have taken untoward risks with the Zilveli structure. A proper analysis of his decisions may yet have revealed further confirmation of his genius as an architect.

NOTES

1 The Conservation architect parted company with the new owner when she could not support the idea of a copy.

2 Fassler, "The Jean Welz Exhibition."

3 See Chapter 20, "Maison Zilveli" for the close-up photo of the balcony.

4 I had a construction company in London 2012–19, often working on "listed" buildings, and worked with a number of structural engineers; there is a big difference between the conventional "over specified" approach and the much-rarer creative approach that reduces weight and cost, but without endangering structural integrity.

5 Translation by Christopher Long.

6 Email. November 18, 2021.

7 *Compagnons du Devoir*, a French organization of craftsmen and artisans dating from the Middle Ages.

8 Direction Régionale des Arts et Culture (Regional Direction for Art and Culture), founded by André Malraux in 1964.

Le Corbusier's Villa Savoye as a ruin, used to store hay. Sources: e-architect.com/paris/villa-savoye, photo: Victor Gubbins (left) and archiwik.org, photographer unknown (right).

APPENDICES

Above: Welz family house, Worcester, Western Cape, South Africa (1950).
Courtesy Welz family.

Center: Jean Welz, The Little Theatre at Worcester, Little Karoo (1960).
Photo courtesy of the author, July 2014.

Below: Union Monument plaque (1960), Worcester.
Photo courtesy of the author, July 2014.

AFTER ARCHITECTURE
SOUTH AFRICA ADDENDUM

THE WITWATERSRAND BUILDINGS WERE NOT the only designs by Jean Welz in South Africa. In 1950, he designed a simple family house on a very limited budget; in 1960, a small theatre next to the art-gallery he ran for a few years; and a Union memorial, also in 1960 (see Chapter 26, "A Tale of Three Monuments").

Although these were modest projects, the family house included a double-height space under the pitched roof crest, the angled window-ledges and long horizontal niche he had put into Montauban in 1931, and the memorial of four wood pillars in steel frames was reminiscent of his garden water-feature in his first Paris design, the Maison Dubin, in 1928. (See Plates for color images of these.)

Jean was also keen on conserving the traditional Cape cottages that were increasingly being demolished, seeing them as worthwhile examples of vernacular architecture. He made friends with a leading modernist architect, Revel Fox, (practicing in Worcester and later in Cape Town) and the story goes that he would arrive at the practice virtually every day to inspect the work on the drawing-boards in order to see that standards were being kept up. That rather belies the idea that he had completely given up his interest in architecture. Old colleagues like Professor Pearse and Fassler, who reviewed one of his first shows as a painter, kept in touch, and critics noticed certain architectural qualities in some of his paintings, although — as in the case of *The Architect's House* or *The House on the Lake* (see Plates, Figure 9) — they tended to the opaque.

The Maison Zilveli of 1933 was his last house before the family house of 1950, so naturally it begs the question of what we might expect of this return to architecture. I learned from the family[1] that a key factor in the design was the use of an A-frame for reasons of economy. It allowed the main bedroom to be in the roof without increasing the footprint of the house, and Welz added a balcony to it, doubling as protection for a terrace below and for the front door entrance, adding an overhang to the roof, partly sheltering the bedroom terrace and the part of the terrace below that was not under the balcony.

"The roof was highly unusual and probably cut out some cost in respect to walls."[2] Every penny counted at this point, but the front facade shows ingenuity and concision: the overhang is functional for both the bedroom terrace and the lower "pergola" to the right. The terrace doubles as protection for entering the front door, the side wall to the right is extended to contribute to the "pergola" section of the terrace. From the photo, one can see that these were later additions.

Internally, the layout was not conventional, the lounge and dining room were combined and what otherwise might have been the dining area was set up as a studio for Jean's painting (the double-height area which uses the pitch of the roof to add a sense of space overhead at little or no cost).

Welz family house, garden side. View of balcony and pergola. Worcester, Western Cape, South Africa. Photo courtesy of the author, July 2014.

The pillars support the bedroom above, but are free-standing to make the most of the space around them. A Viennese/Loos influence is visible in the exotic wood veneers, still in situ sixty-odd years on.

The contrast between the bare painted brick and simple floor tiles and the "luxury" of the beauty of the veneered wood demonstrates that Jean Welz had never lost his faith in the Loosian lessons.

The 1950 house is unconventional in a South African context for the time, but I see the design as another example of how versatile in his thinking Welz was — always able to propose a unique solution adapted to each project, including site, budget and client.

Two views of the Lounge/Dining Room with main bedroom above it; exotic wood veneers add a Loosian touch. Photos courtesy of the author, July 2014.

By 1950, Welz had given up architecture for over a decade, but in his return, perforce, to architecture with the family house, there are elements of his thoughts about the symbolic relayed first in his 1937 article "Abstraction," translated from French for his South African audience.

> "...In this life of platitude, let us greet the artist who humbly undertakes to get hold with his camera of that magic, white, and sparkling form—the foam of water! Look at that image of whiteness, hear the word: foam! Then that 'name' will instantly reveal an unexpected power, filling you with joy. It is the abstraction which has created an evocative sign: a symbol."

The name's constant use erases the sense of the thing. Water is so familiar that it takes a symbol — foam produced by fast-flowing water — to reawaken us to its qualities. Welz contrasts the routine of "platitude" with the cleansing by "fasting" that effects a return to essence. Welz has developed the Loosian removal of decoration to a positive return to the essential. Refreshed by turning away from unnecessary decorative additions, one can grasp the original value of things. Abstraction as purification.

Both the Villa Darmstadter and the Maison Zilveli bear out this purity, differently, but in every regard. His family house of 1950, with its pitched roof, was closer to a child's symbolic drawing of a house.

In a talk Welz gives that year at Johannesburg Art Gallery, "Symbolic and Intimate Knowledge," he discusses the architect's experience of the symbol, describing a symbolic room of white marble squares with the room proportions according to the Golden Rule, and with a window made by cutting a wall off short in one corner so the two walls do not meet, as "we must not make holes in our walls."

He returns to the theme of abstraction, invoking a Klee drawing and a Mozart sonata, but admits he cannot feel for the South African veldt as for the French Gothic hillside town of Vezelay, for example, as he needs "something of man in order to make my symbols."[3]

The most teasing part of the talk is where he shows a portrait of "one of the greatest architects of our time" who knew better than anyone that the house is a symbol, building houses that were "symbolic in expression, strange and new in conception, and never at any time lost sight of the fundamental symbolic factor." We may never know: was that Adolf Loos or Le Corbusier, perhaps? "Strange and new"

A B S T R A C T I O N

I have followed with great interest the preparation for the exhibition of "Abstract Art," and I would like to give my small contribution to this manifestation which is of the greatest value for the young architects in this country.

In Paris I have been able to follow, for many years, that movement of radical purification at its very source; that is to say the movement of liberation from the maze of the so-called "decorative" arts.

Abstract thinking will redirect the artists towards the "things."

Abstraction cannot be an end in itself, but it can be the miraculous medium for bringing about a conception of things perfect, and a crystallisation of their pure forms.

The attempt to realise the work of man in images and in abstract forms forces the artist into a great effort towards concentration and wholesome meditation. Wholesome in the sense that it obliges him to shun all routine and that in the end it inevitably leads him towards the origin of things: the word.

It is, in fact, of great importance to respect and realise the "name" appertaining to a thing before undertaking the realisation of any of its forms or manifestations, or even showing some correlation between these things.

Every object has a "name" belonging to it, and whoever uses the "name" carelessly effaces its contour day by day and loses the sense of its quality.

The name "blood," so frequently misused and blasphemed, embraces in itself a whole universe.

And it is evident, for example, that it would be necessary to have grasped and experienced the name "water" before attempting to make its abstract image.

I am prepared to show you that the ancient Greeks knew better how to respect the element "water" than we do nowadays, although we can give its chemical formula.

To-day we generally know hardly more than that one fills the bath with it and that one washes one's stockings in it, that is all.

As for the "lyrics" of water, we have reason to be sceptical. I believe that the resonance evoked in the heart of men and women by the name "water," as a rule goes hardly beyond a vague conception of some small sails floating on a big blue splash of colour. Sentimental.

The dynamic force of water, on the other hand, we just leave to the engineer.

We are still far, it appears, from being able to grasp, even to touch at the limpid and mysterious secret of the element "water."

In this general confusion, in this life of platitude, let us greet the artist who humbly undertakes to get hold with his camera of that magic, white, and sparkling form—the foam of water!

Look at that image of whiteness, hear the word: foam! Then that "name" will instantly reveal an unexpected power, filling you with joy.

It is the abstraction which has created an evocative sign: a symbol.

There have been favoured epochs when the artist was able to make a true "creation" out of his image, showing a multitude of different visual and moral qualities.

Compared with the work of Michel Angelo our abstraction must be poor, because it can give only relatively few elements and a restricted number of correlations in the visual or plastic field.

Abstraction by necessity turns away from plenitude. But our plenitude has been lost in routine; it has become obscure, and therefore it has become difficult to make use of it in the intellectual realm.

These are times of fasting and it is good to make a clean sweep, so that it becomes possible again to conceive and to construct as a free man and master.

The beginning: to re-establish the values in abstraction.

JEAN WELZ.

(Translated from the French original.)

Jean Welz, "Abstraction" (translated from French), *South African Architectural Index*, July 1937, n.p.

SYMBOLIC AND INTIMATE KNOWLEDGE

Extracts from a lecture delivered during the Academy at the Municipal Art Gallery, Johannesburg, on Wednesday, 18th October, 1950.

BY JEAN WELZ

Mr. Welz began his lecture by describing "intimate knowledge" as that which is acquired by all human beings throughout life from birth to death, knowledge which, however, cannot be communicated to others except through the use of sounds, words, gestures, objects made by man or creations such as works of art. All such means of communication he described as symbols, and familiarity with such symbols as have been used throughout human civilisation, plus the ability to evolve symbols, as "symbolic knowledge."

The artist is a person who has the ability to use symbols to express adequately his intimate knowledge for the benefit, enlightenment, (and delight), of others. The first requirements for an artist are that he must be able to love and be prepared to suffer.

He then has before him a choice of materials out of which to make his symbols. The artist can work in the usual two or three dimensions, but he has at his disposal a number of others which he can feel in himself, but which are perhaps too personal, too difficult, to describe in words. The feeling of space, the essence of colour, the texture of the medium, of the ground,—all these might be described as extra dimensions.

The artist has far more in common with the scientist than is generally understood, and often scientific discovery is anticipated by the artist. An instance was the revolution in the art world caused by the Impressionist painters, who departed from the symbols generally in use for the representation of the human being and replaced them by a concentration of dots of colour. Surely this was an anticipation of the scientific recognition of the human being as composed of a multitude of minute atoms!

Representational painting is no less symbolic than purely abstract painting, but the tendency nowadays is for the artist to make more use of abstract symbols.

"The artist often sees analogies which are not obvious to the scientist. Once I experimented with four German words: Lieben — to love; Leben — to live; Laben — to revive, to succour; Loben — to praise. In the German words one letter only changes each time,—but how the meaning of each is linked up with the previous one and how much life there is in each! There is no man who isn't capable of praising something, or at least if such a one lives, I should not like to see his face!

"Let us consider the architect and his experience of the symbol. The symbol he uses most commonly is the house, but it is difficult for him to bring to realisation his symbolic idea of the house because he is tied down by consideration of expense, by the necessity to use stock elements, and so on. Nevertheless it might be interesting for me to work out a symbolic room which would suit me, just to give you an idea of what I mean. I should like the floor, walls and ceiling to be made of squares of white marble with length and width of the room proportioned according to the Golden Rule. Then we must have a door or entrance! We might remove two marble blocks from the floor and cause a staircase to descend to a lower level and other parts of the house, or we might hinge a marble slab invisibly so that nothing should interfere with the purity of the wall. And then a window! We must not make holes in our walls. We will cut our walls off short at one corner so that the two shall not meet and the space left between shall be our window. There is my symbolic room!

"The architects of Gothic and Renaissance times knew that the house was a symbol. There is a town in France—Vezeloy—which has managed to keep itself unspoiled since Gothic times. The Gothic houses cluster on a hill, surrounded by a wall. You see a long white road leading to the town. It is all symbolic of the life of the people living within it. The landscape, the cloudy sky, are infused by the symbolism of man exemplified, in his houses, his roads, his wall—in fact by his town.

"I cannot feel for the wild South African landscape as I do for this scene. The veld is still raw, untouched and uninfluenced by the symbolism of man; it still has not become part of our civilisation. In order to paint a landscape I need something of man in order to make my symbols.

"Here is a drawing by Paul Klee. It is made up of lines without any attempt at 'representation,' without shade or light or perspective or colour. And yet how magnificent it is. Just as Mozart wrote sonatas telling no story, with just a beautiful arrangement of sounds woven together into pattern, so Klee's lines weave into a pattern which is joy to the eye as the music is to the ear.

"This is a portrait of one of the greatest architects of our time. None knew better than he that the house is a symbol. He designed houses which were symbolic in expression, strange and new in conception, and never at any time lost sight of the fundamental symbolic factor.

"I have always liked this picture of a cock by Picasso because he is so 'cocky.' You will see that he isn't only one cock, but three, and we can imagine him jerking his head back and forth and crowing as he walks."

Mr. Welz used his own painting, "Veiled Woman," from the Academy exhibition, to illustrate his incorporation of symbolic ideas.

In reply to a question regarding the symbolic town, he referred to the use of the word "Jerusalem" in the Bible—that "Jerusalem," which is the golden city, the ideal town and home, the dream and goal of any good Jew. "Jerusalem" symbolises the perfect town.

10

Jean Welz, "Symbolic and Intimate Knowledge: Extracts from a lecture delivered during the Academy at the Municipal Art Gallery, Johannesburg, Wednesday, 18th October 1950." *South African Architectural Index*, January 1951, p. 10.

could suggest Le Corbusier, but the emphasis on the symbolic might point to Adolf Loos.

It would be more interesting, in a way, if it was Le Corbusier, as Welz's work in Paris was, if my surmise is true, devoted to overturning his Five Points of Modern Architecture and, although the Chapel at Ronchamp was begun in 1950, and would fit the description rather well, it would be a surprise if Welz was aware of that design.

Either way, the family house and the lecture both confirm the consistency of Welz's commitment to the symbolic. Starting with the 1937 article on Abstraction, the year he arrived in South Africa, to both house and article thirteen years on, they reaffirm and enlarge upon the consistency his architecture showed in Paris from the first to the last, from the modest symbolic cubic balcony on the Maison Dubin facade (1928) to the exuberance of the Maison Zilveli (1933) balcony, the climax of his most imaginative "Chemin Aérien."

NOTES

1 Information from Carmen Welz, widow of Stephan Welz, email August 27–28, 2018.

2 Carmen Welz, August 27–28, 2018.

3 Eileen Gray's partner, Jean Badovici, restored a number of old houses in Vezelay, becoming a modernist magnet.

Le Corbusier, Notre-Dame du Haut, Ronchamp, France (1955), a UNESCO World Heritage Site. Photo Marcel Lombard. © Fondation Le Corbusier.

BIBLIOGRAPHY

Ackerman, James S. *Palladio*. London: Penguin, 1966.

Antoniades, Anthony C. "Masterpieces/ Meritpieces," *Mag11/ Hydra*, Nov. 2005.

L'Architecture d'Aujourd'hui (various).

Artefacts. Entries on Pearse, GE and Welz, Johann Max Friedrich (Jean).

Avril, Jean-Louis. "Jean Welz (1900–75)," *Le Moniteur Architecture — AMC*, no. 38, February 1993.

Ayers, Andrew. *The Architecture of Paris*. Paris: Edition Axel Menges, 2003.

Berman, Esme. *Art and Artists of South Africa*. Cape Town: A. A. Balkema, 1970.

Bollerey, Franziska. Case Study 7, in *Restaurants and Dining Rooms*, edited by Franziska Bollerey and Christoph Grafe. London: Routledge, 2019.

Brest, Pierre-Yves. "Raymond Fischer (1898–1988), Architekt," in *Allgemeines Künstlerlexikon (Thieme & Becker)*. Leipzig: Saur, 2004.

Cladel, Gerard and Bodenan, Philippe. "Raymond Fischer (1898–1988)," Rapport de recherche 574/89. *Inventaires*. Versailles: Secrétariat de la recherche architecturale (SRA); Ecole nationale supérieure d'architecture de Versailles. 1989. hal-01905395.

Cobos, LR. *The Concept of the Raumplan and the Architecture of Raymond Fischer*. Dissertation. Paris: Ecole d'Architecture de Paris Belleville, June 1998.

La Construction Moderne (various).

Cooke, Bernard. "Impressions of the Greenside House." *South African Architectural Record*, February 1942.

Fassler, John. "The Jean Welz Exhibition — An Appreciation." *South African Architectural Record*, October 1942.

Field, Frank. *The Last Days of Mankind: Karl Kraus and His Vienna*. London: Macmillan,1967.

Fischer, Raymond with Philippe Dehan. *Entretiens*. Paris: Connivences, 1988.

Fischer, Raymond. *Villas et Petits Hôtels*. Paris: Charles Massin, 1930.

Giedion, Siegfried. *Space, Time and Architecture*. 2nd Edition. Cambridge, Mass: Harvard, 1949.

Gravagnuolo, Benedetto. *Adolf Loos: Theory and Works*. Milan: Idea Books, 1982/1995.

Haerdtl, Carmela. "Una Nuova Casa di Josef Frank." *Domus* 4, August 1931.

Heikinheimo, Marianna. *Architecture and Technology, Alvar Aalto's Paimio Sanatorium*. Dissertation. Espoo: Aalto University, 2016.

Herbert, Gilbert. *Martienssen and the International Style: The Development of Modern Architecture in South Africa*. Cape Town and Rotterdam: Balkema, 1975.

———. *Recollections of the School of Architecture, Wits University — in 'the Golden Age,' in Architecture South*

Africa. Johannesburg: *South African Institute of Architects*, 2011.

Herbert, Gilbert and Donchin, Mark. *The Collaborators: Interactions in the Architectural Design Process.* Ashgate Studies in Architecture. London: Routledge, 2016.

Janik, Allan and Toulmin, Stephen Edelston. *Wittgenstein's Vienna.* Chicago: Ivan R. Dee. 1996.

Johnston, William M. *The Austrian Mind.* Los Angeles: UCLA Press, 1972.

Kahle, Darko. "Architect Zlatko Neumann: Buildings and Projects between the World Wars." *Prostor*, July 2015.

Kerschbaumer, Gert. *Meister des Verwirrens: Die Geschäfte des Kunsthändlers Friedrich Welz (Master of Intrigues: The Dealings of the Art Dealer Friedrich Welz).* Vienna: Czernin Verlag, 2000.

Langseth-Christensen, Lilian. *A Design for Living.* New York: Viking, 1987.

Léger, Fernand. "RD Martienssen: Tribute after his death in 1942." *South African Architectural Record*, January 1943.

Lhota, Karel. "Architekt A. Loos." *Architekt SIA* 32, 1933.

Long, Christopher. *Adolf Loos, The Last Houses.* Prague: Kant, 2020.

———. *The New Space: Movement and Experience in Viennese Modern Architecture.* New Haven: Yale, 2016.

Loos, Adolf. *Adolf Loos, On Architecture*, edited by Opel, Adolf and Opel, Daniel. Riverside, Calif.: Ariadne Press, 2002.

Loos, Claire Beck. *The Private Adolf Loos.* Los Angeles: DoppelHouse Press, 2020.

MacMillan, Andrew. "Houses for Art Lovers and the Modern Movement," in *House for an Art Lover*, 2nd Edition, edited by Billcliffe, Roger. Glasgow: House for an Art Lover, 2004.

Maschek, Joseph. *Adolf Loos: The Art of Architecture.* London: Bloomsbury, 2013.

Meder, Iris. "Fragmente zu Leben und Werk des Architekten Otto Bauer: 'Ihr Platz ist in der Welt.'" *DAVID: Jüdische Kulturzeitschrift*, no date.

Miles, Elza. *The World of Jean Welz.* Vlaeberg, South Africa: Fernwood Press/ Rembrandt Van Rijn Art Foundation, 1997.

Moretti, Bruno. *Ville.* Milano: Hoepli, 1952.

Munro, Katherine. "The Hillman Building." *Wits Quarterly*, Autumn 2010.

Münz, Ludwig and Künstler, Gustav. *Adolf Loos, Pioneer of Modern Architecture.* London: Thames & Hudson, 1966.

Palladio, Andrea. *The Four Books of Architecture, Book Four.* London: John Watts, 1715. Smithsonian Library.

Poulain, Roger. *Villas Modernes.* Paris: Vincent, Fréal et Cie, 1931.

Rukschcio, Burkhardt and Schachel, Roland. *Adolf Loos: Leben und Werk.* Vienna: Residenz Verlag, 1982.

Stiller, Adolf / Architekturzentrum Wien. *Oswald Haerdtl, Architekt und Designer.* Salzburg: Anton Pustet, 2000.

South African Architectural Record (various).

South African Architectural Index (various).

Welz, Jean. "Pour Vivre Heureux" (To Live Happily). *La Libérté*, Dec. 4, 1929.

Wyeth, Peter. "A Factory for Working In." *The Modernist*, no. 17, 2016.

Zeller, Pascal. *Raymond Fischer 1898–1988 Le Chemin Aérien.* Dissertation. Lyon: Ecole d'Architecture de Lyon, July 2, 1992.

INDEX

Z

ACKNOWLEDGMENTS

Without the assistance of the Welz family, this book would not have been possible. Thank you to all who provided photographs; to Cora and the late Jerome Welz for showing me the Tradouw Pass and Worcester; to Martin Welz for driving me around on my South Africa visit and for answering a host of questions both then and ever since; and most of all, to the late Stephan Welz and his wife Carmen, stalwart supporters from first to last, a very special debt of thanks.

My gratitude to the constantly generous Jean-Louis Avril, to Loos-expert Christopher Long for his many acts of kindness, and to Tim Benton, expert on Le Corbusier, for many valuable suggestions. Pascal Zeller welcomed me to Lyon and shared his key dissertation on Raymond Fischer. Publisher Carrie Paterson has gone well above and beyond to prepare this book for publication.

Cecile Poulot generously shared her research on Loos in Paris, PY Brest looked back to his very thorough research on Raymond Fischer, and the late Dr. Peter Prokop very kindly volunteered his time in the Vienna archives.

Michael Corbe was there from the start and kindly translated my first article on Zilveli into French and placed it with an architecture website where it had the most hits in their history.

Laurence Nguyen (née Zilveli) first showed me her grandmother's house and hoped she could somehow find a way to save her childhood home, and Frederic Botte introduced me to her and has maintained a constant enthusiasm for saving Zilveli since years before I first saw the house.

Thanks to Madame Tzara, Madame de la Croix and photographer Fabrice Fouillet for their kind permission to use photographs as well as the numerous archives who permitted use of their photographs or illustrations, in particular the Fondation Le Corbusier.

Thanks always to my wife Kate and to my elder son Hugh, and finally, to the international galaxy of eminent experts who appealed to the Minister of Culture to save Zilveli for lending their support to the cause, and to this effort's facilitator, Richard Klein of Docomomo France. (As of this publication, the Minister has failed to acknowledge or respond to the letter.)

PLATES

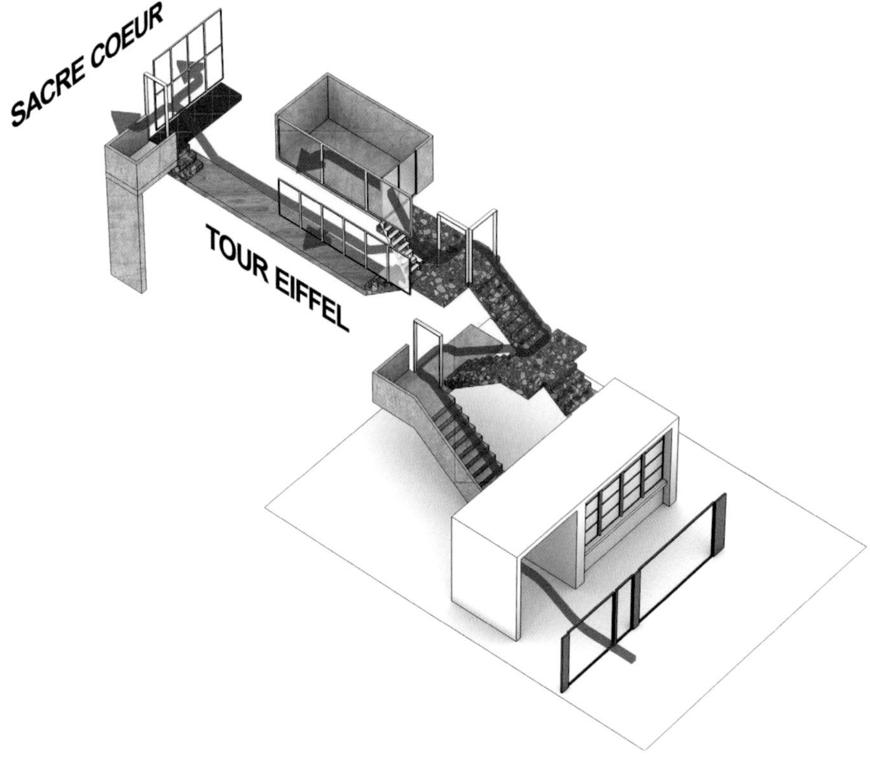

Figure 1. Le Chemin Aérien / The Aerial Way at the Maison Zilveli.
3-D render by Hugh Wyeth.

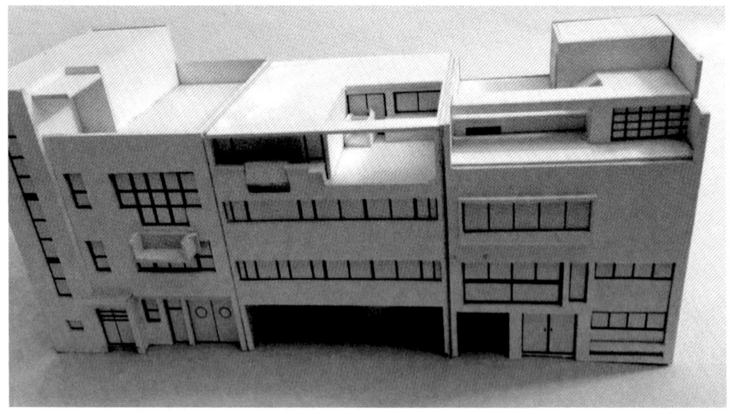

Figure 2: Model of the terrace featuring houses designed by Mallet-Stevens, Le Corbusier and Welz. Courtesy of architect Pascal Zeller. The same arrangement of houses is shown in the photos below.

Figures 3, 4, and 5, left to right: Mallet-Stevens, Villa Collinet (1925–26); Le Corbusier, Maison Cook (1926); Jean Welz for Raymond Fischer, Maison Dubin (1927–28). (There may be references to the Mallet-Stevens house as 1924, but the official listing gives 1926.) Photos: M. Gravot. Source: Fischer, *Villas et Petits Hôtels.*

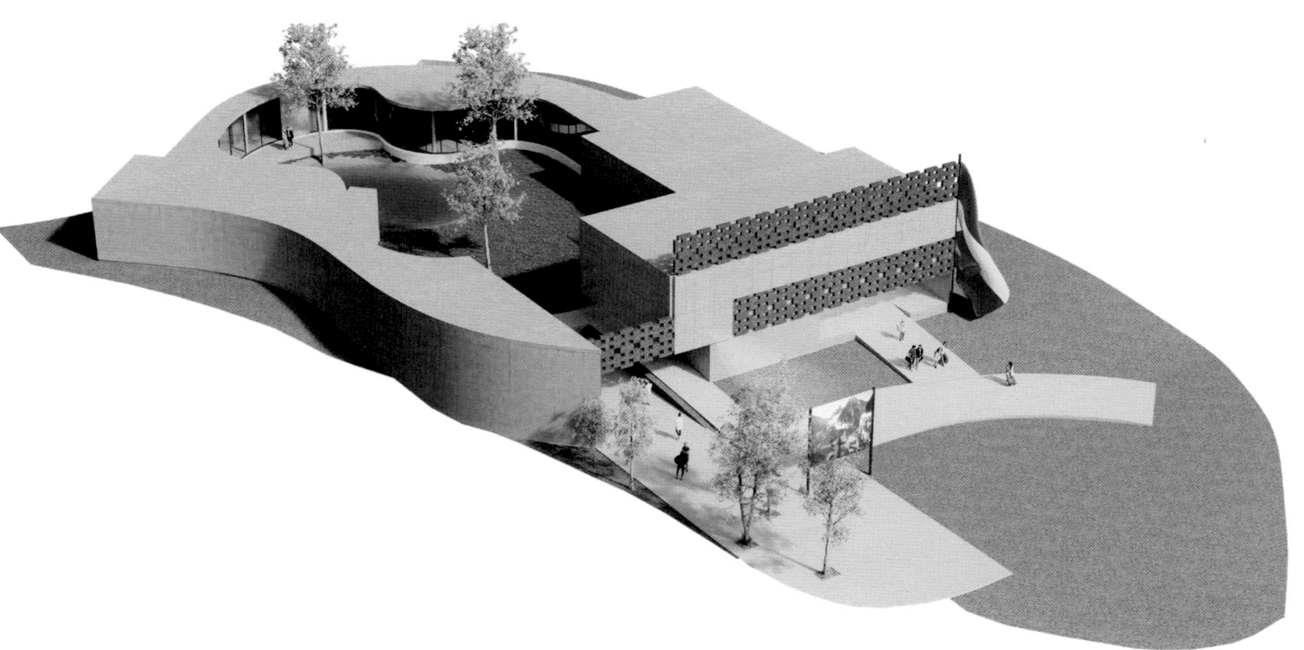

Figure 6. Jean Welz's entry for the 1937 Paris Exhibition, the Austrian Pavilion. 3-D render by Hugh Wyeth.

Figure 7. Jean Welz by André Kertész (date unknown, possibly 1927 and featured in the Kertész one-man show at the Sacre du Printemps gallery in Paris).

Figure 8. Jean Ginsberg & Berthold Lubetkin, 25 Avenue des Versailles (1931). Jean Welz was pictured standing on this roof (see page 16). Note the Eiffel Tower view in the background and the projecting balcony, both taken up in Welz's own way two years later at the Maison Zilveli. Courtesy RIBA Collections.

Figure 9. Jean Welz, *The House on the Lake*, oil on canvas, 89.5 x 64 cms, 1964. Courtesy Welz family.

Welz family house, Worcester, Western Cape, South Africa (1950).
Above: Colored panes and garden view from the steel window in the double-height drawing-room.
Below, left: double-height space using the pitched roof to gain height.
Below, right, top and bottom: views of the niche between rooms — as in the Montauban small block of flats of 1931.
All photos courtesy of the author, July 2014.

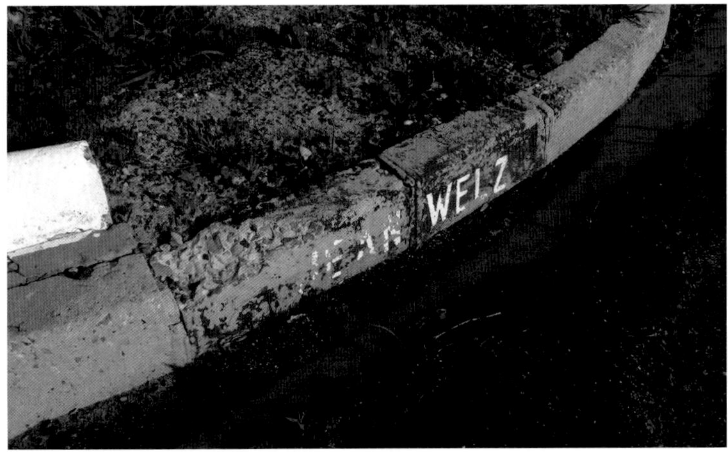

Above: Union Festival Monument, Garden of Remembrance, Worcester Church Square, Western Cape, South Africa (1960).
Center: Monument Plaque: "Memorial designed by Jean Welz."
Below: Street name lettering, Worcester, Western Cape, South Africa.

All photos courtesy of the author, July 2014.

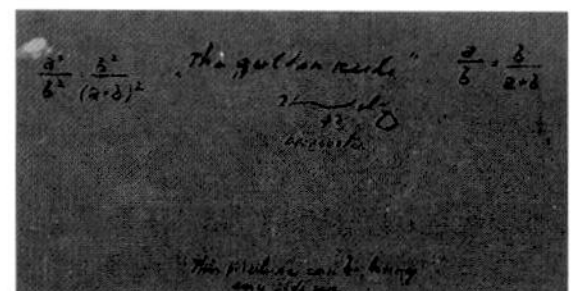

Figure 10. Jean Welz, self-portrait, oil on plywood, 43 x 31 cms, 1944.

Figure 11. Jean Welz, *The Golden Rule*, oil on board, 39 x 39 cms, 1943. Equations quoted on the back. "This picture can be hung any side up."

Source for both: Miles, *The World of Jean Welz*. Courtesy Welz family.